Textbook Outlines, Highlights, and Practice Quizzes

Organic Chemistry

by Marc Loudon, 5th Edition

All "Just the Facts101" Material Written or Prepared by Cram101 Publishing

Title Page

"Just the Facts101" is a Cram101 publication and tool designed to give you all the facts from your textbooks. Visit Cram101.com for the full practice test for each of your chapters for virtually any of your textbooks.

Cram101 has built custom study tools specific to your textbook. We provide all of the factual testable information and unlike traditional study guides, we will never send you back to your textbook for more information.

YOU WILL NEVER HAVE TO HIGHLIGHT A BOOK AGAIN!

Cram101 StudyGuides
All of the information in this StudyGuide is written specifically for your textbook. We include the key terms, places, people, and concepts... the information you can expect on your next exam!

Want to take a practice test?
Throughout each chapter of this StudyGuide you will find links to cram101.com where you can select specific chapters to take a complete test on, or you can subscribe and get practice tests for up to 12 of your textbooks, along with other exclusive cram101.com tools like problem solving labs and reference libraries.

Cram101.com
Only cram101.com gives you the outlines, highlights, and PRACTICE TESTS specific to your textbook. Cram101.com is an online application where you'll discover study tools designed to make the most of your limited study time.

By purchasing this book, you get 50% off the normal subscription free!. Just enter the promotional code **'DK73DW20423'** on the Cram101.com registration screen.

www.Cram101.com

ISBN(s): 9781478418603. PUBI-6.201299

Learning System

Organic Chemistry
Marc Loudon, 5th

CONTENTS

Chapter 1. CHEMICAL BONDING AND CHEMICAL STRUCTURE

CHAPTER OUTLINE: KEY TERMS, PEOPLE, PLACES, CONCEPTS

______ Lauric acid

______ Molecular orbital

______ Gabriel synthesis

______ Hydrogen bromide

______ Malonic ester synthesis

______ Ionic compound

______ Octet rule

______ Sigmatropic reaction

______ Valence electron

______ Methyl iodide

______ Ionic bond

______ Hydrogen

______ Covalent bond

______ Lewis structure

______ Formal charge

______ Double bond

______ Carbonium ion

______ Hofmann rearrangement

______ Molecular geometry

Chapter 1. CHEMICAL BONDING AND CHEMICAL STRUCTURE

CHAPTER OUTLINE: KEY TERMS, PEOPLE, PLACES, CONCEPTS

______ Propiophenone

______ Bond length

______ Bond order

______ VSEPR theory

______ Mass spectrum

______ Molecular model

______ Boron trifluoride

______ Dihedral angle

______ Hydrogen atom

______ Pyruvic acid

______ Atomic orbital

______ Aufbau principle

______ Pauli exclusion principle

______ Sigma bond

______ Methane

______ Ammonia

Lauric acid	Lauric acid the saturated fatty acid with a 12-carbon atom chain, thus falling into the medium chain fatty acids, is a white, powdery solid with a faint odor of bay oil or soap. Lauric acid, as a component of triglycerides, comprises about half of the fatty acid content in coconut oil, laurel oil, and in palm kernel oil (not to be confused with palm oil), Otherwise it is relatively uncommon. It is also found in human breast milk (6.2% of total fat), cow's milk (2.9%), and goat's milk (3.1%).
Molecular orbital	In chemistry, a molecular orbital is a mathematical function describing the wave-like behavior of an electron in a molecule. This function can be used to calculate chemical and physical properties such as the probability of finding an electron in any specific region. The term 'orbital' was first used in English by Robert S. Mulliken as the English translation of Schrödinger's 'Eigenfunktion'.
Gabriel synthesis	The Gabriel synthesis is named for the German chemist Siegmund Gabriel. Traditionally, it is a chemical reaction that transforms primary alkyl halides into primary amines using potassium phthalimide. The Gabriel reaction has since been generalized to include the alkylation of sulfonamides and imides, followed by deprotection, to obtain amines .
Hydrogen bromide	Hydrogen bromide is the diatomic molecule HBr. HBr is a gas at standard conditions. Hydrobromic acid forms upon dissolving HBr in water.
Malonic ester synthesis	The malonic ester synthesis is a chemical reaction where diethyl malonate or another ester of malonic acid is alkylated at the carbon alpha (directly adjacent) to both carbonyl groups, and then converted to a substituted acetic acid. The major drawback of malonic ester synthesis is that the alkylation stage can also produce dialkylated structures. This makes separation of products difficult and yields lower.
Ionic compound	In chemistry, an ionic compound is a chemical compound in which ions are held together in a lattice structure by ionic bonds. Usually, the positively charged portion consists of metal cations and the negatively charged portion is an anion or polyatomic ion. Ions in ionic compounds are held together by the electrostatic forces between oppositely charged bodies.
Octet rule	The octet rule is a chemical rule of thumb that states that atoms tend to combine in such a way that they each have eight electrons in their valence shells, giving them the same electronic configuration as a noble gas. The rule is applicable to the main-group elements, especially carbon, nitrogen, oxygen, and the halogens, but also to metals such as sodium or magnesium.

Chapter 1. CHEMICAL BONDING AND CHEMICAL STRUCTURE

CHAPTER HIGHLIGHTS & NOTES: KEY TERMS, PEOPLE, PLACES, CONCEPTS

Sigmatropic reaction

A sigmatropic reaction in organic chemistry is a Pericyclic reaction wherein the net result is one σ-bond is changed to another σ-bond in an uncatalyzed intramolecular process. The name sigmatropic is the result of a compounding of the long-established sigma designation from single carbon-carbon bonds and the Greek word tropos, meaning turn. In this type of rearrangement reaction, a substituent moves from one part of a π-bonded system to another part in an intramolecular reaction with simultaneous rearrangement of the π system.

Valence electron

In chemistry, valence electrons are the electrons of an atom that can participate in the formation of chemical bonds with other atoms. Valence electrons are the 'own' electrons, present in the free neutral atom, that combine with valence electrons of other atoms to form chemical bonds. In a single covalent bond both atoms contribute one valence electron to form a shared pair.

Methyl iodide

Methyl iodide, and commonly abbreviated 'MeI', is the chemical compound with the formula CH_3I. It is a dense, colorless, volatile liquid. In terms of chemical structure, it is related to methane by replacement of one hydrogen atom by an atom of iodine. It is naturally emitted by rice plantations in small amounts.

Ionic bond

An ionic bond is a type of chemical bond formed through an electrostatic attraction between two oppositely charged ions. Ionic bonds are formed between a cation, which is usually a metal, and an anion, which is usually a nonmetal. Pure ionic bonding cannot exist: all ionic compounds have some degree of covalent bonding.

Hydrogen

Hydrogen is the chemical element with atomic number 1. It is represented by the symbol H. With an average atomic weight of 1.00794 u (1.007825 u for hydrogen-1), hydrogen is the lightest element and its monatomic form (H_1) is the most abundant chemical substance, constituting roughly 75% of the Universe's baryonic mass. Non-remnant stars are mainly composed of hydrogen in its plasma state.

At standard temperature and pressure, hydrogen is a colorless, odorless, tasteless, non-toxic, nonmetallic, highly combustible diatomic gas with the molecular formula H_2.

Covalent bond

A covalent bond is a form of chemical bonding that is characterized by the sharing of pairs of electrons between atoms, and other covalent bonds. In short, the stable balance of attractive and repulsive forces between atoms when they share electrons is known as covalent bonding.

Covalent bonding includes many kinds of interaction, including σ-bonding, π-bonding, metal to metal bonding, agostic interactions, and three-center two-electron bonds.

Formal charge

In chemistry, a formal charge is the charge assigned to an atom in a molecule, assuming that electrons in a chemical bond are shared equally between atoms, regardless of relative electronegativity.

The formal charge of any atom in a molecule can be calculated by the following equation:

$$FC = V - N - \frac{B}{2}$$

Where V is the number of valence electrons of the atom in isolation (atom in ground state); N is the number of non-bonding valence electrons on this atom in the molecule; and B is the total number of electrons shared in covalent bonds with other atoms in the molecule.

When determining the correct Lewis structure (or predominant resonance structure) for a molecule, the structure is chosen such that the formal charge on each of the atoms is minimized.

Double bond

A double bond in chemistry is a chemical bond between two chemical elements involving four bonding electrons instead of the usual two. The most common double bond, that between two carbon atoms, can be found in alkenes. Many types of double bonds between two different elements exist, for example in a carbonyl group with a carbon atom and an oxygen atom.

Carbonium ion

A carbonium ion is a carbocation of the penta- or tetracoordinated nonclassical type such as an ion of the type R_5C^+.

Methanium

The parent compound methanium or CH_5^+ is protonated methane and a superacid. This ion exists as a reactive intermediate in the interstellar medium and can be produced in the laboratory in low concentrations in the gas phase at low temperatures.

Hofmann rearrangement

The Hofmann rearrangement is the organic reaction of a primary amide to a primary amine with one fewer carbon atom.

This reaction is also sometimes called the Hofmann degradation or the Harmon Process, and should not be confused with the Hofmann elimination. Mechanism

The reaction of bromine with sodium hydroxide forms sodium hypobromite in situ, which transforms the primary amide into an intermediate isocyanate.

Molecular geometry

Molecular geometry is the three-dimensional arrangement of the atoms that constitute a molecule.

It determines several properties of a substance including its reactivity, polarity, phase of matter, color, magnetism, and biological activity.

The molecular geometry can be determined by various spectroscopic methods and diffraction methods.

Propiophenone

Propiophenone is an aryl ketone. It is a clear liquid that is insoluble in water, but miscible with methanol, ethanol, diethyl ether, benzene and toluene.

Propiophenone is used in the synthesis of ephedrine and propiophenone derivatives such as cathinone, and methcathinone.

Bond length

In molecular geometry, bond length is the average distance between nuclei of two bonded atoms in a molecule.

Bond length is related to bond order, when more electrons participate in bond formation the bond will get shorter. Bond length is also inversely related to bond strength and the bond dissociation energy, as (all other things being equal) a stronger bond will be shorter.

Bond order

Bond order is the number of chemical bonds between a pair of atoms. For example, in diatomic nitrogen N≡N the bond order is 3, while in acetylene H−C≡C−H the bond order between the two carbon atoms is also 3, and the C−H bond order is 1. Bond order gives an indication to the stability of a bond. In a more advanced context, bond order need not be an integer.

VSEPR theory

Valence shell electron pair repulsion (VSEPR) rules are a model in chemistry used to predict the shape of individual molecules based upon the extent of electron-pair electrostatic repulsion. It is also named Gillespie-Nyholm theory after its two main developers.

The premise of VSEPR is that the valence electron pairs surrounding an atom mutually repel each other, and will therefore adopt an arrangement that minimizes this repulsion, thus determining the molecular geometry. The number of electron pairs surrounding an atom, both bonding and nonbonding, is called its steric number.

VSEPR theory is usually compared and contrasted with valence bond theory, which addresses molecular shape through orbitals that are energetically accessible for bonding.

Mass spectrum

A mass spectrum is an intensity vs. m/z (mass-to-charge ratio) plot representing a chemical analysis. Hence, the mass spectrum of a sample is a pattern representing the distribution of ions by mass (more correctly: mass-to-charge ratio) in a sample. It is a histogram usually acquired using an instrument called a mass spectrometer.

Molecular model

A molecular model, in this article, is a physical model that represents molecules and their processes. The creation of mathematical models of molecular properties and behaviour is molecular modelling, and their graphical depiction is molecular graphics, but these topics are closely linked and each uses techniques from the others. In this article, 'molecular model' will primarily refer to systems containing more than one atom and where nuclear structure is neglected.

Boron trifluoride

Boron trifluoride is the chemical compound with the formula BF_3. This pungent colourless toxic gas forms white fumes in moist air. It is a useful Lewis acid and a versatile building block for other boron compounds.

Dihedral angle

In geometry, a dihedral angle or torsion angle is the angle between two planes.

The dihedral angle of two planes can be seen by looking at the planes 'edge on', i.e., along their line of intersection. The dihedral angle φ_{AB} between two planes denoted A and B is the angle between their two normal unit vectors $\mathbf{n}_A$ and $\mathbf{n}_B : \cos\varphi_{AB} = \mathbf{n}_A \cdot \mathbf{n}_B$.

A dihedral angle can be signed; for example, the dihedral angle φ_{AB} can be defined as the angle through which plane A must be rotated (about their common line of intersection) to align it with plane B. Thus, $\varphi_{AB} = -\varphi_{BA}$.

Hydrogen atom

A hydrogen atom is an atom of the chemical element hydrogen. The electrically neutral atom contains a single positively-charged proton and a single negatively-charged electron bound to the nucleus by the Coulomb force. Atomic hydrogen comprises about 75% of the elemental mass of the universe.

Pyruvic acid

Pyruvic acid is an organic acid, a ketone, as well as the simplest of the alpha-keto acids. The carboxylate (COO^-) anion of pyruvic acid, its Brønsted-Lowry conjugate base, CH_3COCOO^-, is known as pyruvate, and is a key intersection in several metabolic pathways.

Pyruvate can be made from glucose through glycolysis, converted back to carbohydrates (such as glucose) via gluconeogenesis, or to fatty acids through acetyl-CoA. It can also be used to construct the amino acid alanine and be converted into ethanol.

Atomic orbital

An atomic orbital is a mathematical function that describes the wave-like behavior of either one electron or a pair of electrons in an atom. This function can be used to calculate the probability of finding any electron of an atom in any specific region around the atom's nucleus.

Chapter 1. CHEMICAL BONDING AND CHEMICAL STRUCTURE

CHAPTER HIGHLIGHTS & NOTES: KEY TERMS, PEOPLE, PLACES, CONCEPTS

Aufbau principle	The Aufbau principle is used to determine the electron configuration of an atom, molecule or ion. The principle postulates a hypothetical process in which an atom is 'built up' by progressively adding electrons. As they are added, they assume their most stable conditions (electron orbitals) with respect to the nucleus and those electrons already there.
Pauli exclusion principle	The Pauli exclusion principle is the quantum mechanical principle that no two identical fermions (particles with half-integer spin) may occupy the same quantum state simultaneously. A more rigorous statement is that the total wave function for two identical fermions is anti-symmetric. The principle was formulated by Austrian physicist Wolfgang Pauli in 1925.
Sigma bond	In chemistry, sigma bonds (σ bonds) are the strongest type of covalent chemical bond. Sigma bonding is most clearly defined for diatomic molecules using the language and tools of symmetry groups. In this formal approach, a σ-bond is symmetrical with respect to rotation about the bond axis.
Methane	Appendix: extraterrestrial methane Methane has been detected or is believed to exist in several locations of the solar system. In most cases, it is believed to have been created by abiotic processes. Possible exceptions are Mars and Titan.
Ammonia	Ammonia is a compound of nitrogen and hydrogen with the formula NH_3. It is a colourless gas with a characteristic pungent smell. Ammonia contributes significantly to the nutritional needs of terrestrial organisms by serving as a precursor to food and fertilizers.

Chapter 1. CHEMICAL BONDING AND CHEMICAL STRUCTURE

1. The _________ is a chemical reaction where diethyl malonate or another ester of malonic acid is alkylated at the carbon alpha (directly adjacent) to both carbonyl groups, and then converted to a substituted acetic acid. The major drawback of _________ is that the alkylation stage can also produce dialkylated structures. This makes separation of products difficult and yields lower.

   a. Solvolysis
   b. Malonic ester synthesis
   c. Thiolysis
   d. Weinreb ketone synthesis

2. A _________ in chemistry is a chemical bond between two chemical elements involving four bonding electrons instead of the usual two. The most common _________, that between two carbon atoms, can be found in alkenes. Many types of _________s between two different elements exist, for example in a carbonyl group with a carbon atom and an oxygen atom.

   a. Double bond
   b. pi bond
   c. sigma bond
   d. triple bond

3. _________ the saturated fatty acid with a 12-carbon atom chain, thus falling into the medium chain fatty acids, is a white, powdery solid with a faint odor of bay oil or soap.

   _________, as a component of triglycerides, comprises about half of the fatty acid content in coconut oil, laurel oil, and in palm kernel oil (not to be confused with palm oil), Otherwise it is relatively uncommon. It is also found in human breast milk (6.2% of total fat), cow's milk (2.9%), and goat's milk (3.1%).

   a. Lauric acid
   b. Lignoceric acid
   c. Linoelaidic acid
   d. Linoleic acid

4. The _________ is the quantum mechanical principle that no two identical fermions (particles with half-integer spin) may occupy the same quantum state simultaneously. A more rigorous statement is that the total wave function for two identical fermions is anti-symmetric. The principle was formulated by Austrian physicist Wolfgang Pauli in 1925.

   a. Bent bond
   b. Pauli exclusion principle
   c. Covalent bond
   d. double bond

5. . A _________ in organic chemistry is a Pericyclic reaction wherein the net result is one σ-bond is changed to another σ-bond in an uncatalyzed intramolecular process. The name sigmatropic is the result of a compounding of the long-established sigma designation from single carbon-carbon bonds and the Greek word tropos, meaning turn.

In this type of rearrangement reaction, a substituent moves from one part of a π-bonded system to another part in an intramolecular reaction with simultaneous rearrangement of the π system.

a. Smiles rearrangement
b. Stevens rearrangement
c. Stieglitz rearrangement
d. Sigmatropic reaction

ANSWER KEY
Chapter 1. CHEMICAL BONDING AND CHEMICAL STRUCTURE

1. b
2. a
3. a
4. b
5. d

Chapter 2. ALKANES

CHAPTER OUTLINE: KEY TERMS, PEOPLE, PLACES, CONCEPTS

_______________ Hydrogen bromide

_______________ Ethyl group

_______________ Homologous series

_______________ Structural formula

_______________ Alkane

_______________ Ethane

_______________ Dihedral angle

_______________ Eclipsed conformation

_______________ Staggered conformation

_______________ Butane

_______________ Van der Waals radius

_______________ Mass spectrometry

_______________ Methyl group

_______________ Substituent

_______________ Hydrogen

_______________ Molecular orbital

_______________ Melting point

_______________ Clemmensen reduction

_______________ Grignard reagents

Chapter 2. ALKANES

CHAPTER OUTLINE: KEY TERMS, PEOPLE, PLACES, CONCEPTS

______________ Elemental analysis

______________ Haloform reaction

______________ Natural gas

______________ Functional group

______________ Phenyl group

CHAPTER HIGHLIGHTS & NOTES: KEY TERMS, PEOPLE, PLACES, CONCEPTS

Hydrogen bromide

Hydrogen bromide is the diatomic molecule HBr. HBr is a gas at standard conditions. Hydrobromic acid forms upon dissolving HBr in water.

Ethyl group

In chemistry, an ethyl group is an alkyl substituent derived from ethane (C_2H_6). It has the formula -C_2H_5 and is very often abbreviated -Et. Ethyl is the IUPAC nomenclature of organic chemistry term for an alkane (or alkyl) molecule, using the prefix 'eth-' to indicate the presence of two carbon atoms in the molecule.

Homologous series

In chemistry, a homologous series is a series of compounds with a similar general formula, possessing similar chemical properties due to the presence of the same functional group, and showing a gradation in physical properties as a result of increase in molecular size and mass . For example, ethane has a higher boiling point than methane since it has more Van der Waals forces (intermolecular forces) with neighbouring molecules. This is due to the increase in the number of atoms making up the molecule.

Structural formula

The structural formula of a chemical compound is a graphical representation of the molecular structure, showing how the atoms are arranged. The chemical bonding within the molecule is also shown, either explicitly or implicitly. There are several common representations used in publications.

Alkane

Alkanes (also known as paraffins or saturated hydrocarbons) are chemical compounds that consist only of hydrogen and carbon atoms and are bonded exclusively by single bonds (i.e., they are saturated compounds) without any cycles (or loops; i.e., cyclic structure). Alkanes belong to a homologous series of organic compounds in which the members differ by a constant relative molecular mass of 14. They have 2 main commercial sources, crude oil and natural gas.

Each carbon atom has 4 bonds (either C-H or C-C bonds), and each hydrogen atom is joined to a carbon atom (H-C bonds).

Ethane

Ethane is a chemical compound with chemical formula C_2H_6. It is the only two-carbon alkane that is an aliphatic hydrocarbon. At standard temperature and pressure, ethane is a colorless, odorless gas.

Dihedral angle

In geometry, a dihedral angle or torsion angle is the angle between two planes.

The dihedral angle of two planes can be seen by looking at the planes 'edge on', i.e., along their line of intersection. The dihedral angle φ_{AB} between two planes denoted A and B is the angle between their two normal unit vectors $\mathbf{n}_A$ and $\mathbf{n}_B$: $\cos\varphi_{AB} = \mathbf{n}_A \cdot \mathbf{n}_B$.

A dihedral angle can be signed; for example, the dihedral angle φ_{AB} can be defined as the angle through which plane A must be rotated (about their common line of intersection) to align it with plane B. Thus, $\varphi_{AB} = -\varphi_{BA}$.

Eclipsed conformation

In chemistry an eclipsed conformation is a conformation in which two substituents X and Y on adjacent atoms A, B are in closest proximity, implying that the torsion angle X-A-B-Y is 0°. Such a conformation exists in any open chain single chemical bond connecting two sp^3 hybridised atoms, and is normally a conformational energy maximum. This maximum is often explained by steric hindrance, but its origins sometimes actually lie in hyperconjugation (as when the eclipsing interaction is of two hydrogen atoms).

Staggered conformation

In organic chemistry, a staggered conformation is a chemical conformation of an ethane-like moiety abcX-Ydef in which the substituents a,b,and c are at the maximum distance from d,e,and f. This requires the torsion angles to be 60°.

Such a conformation exists in any open chain single chemical bond connecting two sp^3 hybridised atoms, and is normally a conformational energy minimum.For some molecules such as those of n-butane, there can be special versions of staggered conformations called gauche and anti.

Butane

Butane is a gas with the formula C_4H_{10} that is an alkane with four carbon atoms.

The term may refer to either of two structural isomers, n-butane or isobutane or to a mixture of these isomers. In the IUPAC nomenclature, however, 'butane' refers only to the n-butane isomer (which is the isomer with the unbranched structure).

Van der Waals radius

Van der Waals radii

The van der Waals radius, r_w, of an atom is the radius of an imaginary hard sphere which can be used to model the atom for many purposes. It is named after Johannes Diderik van der Waals, winner of the 1910 Nobel Prize in Physics, as he was the first to recognise that atoms had a finite size (i.e., that atoms were not simply points) and to demonstrate the physical consequences of their size through the van der Waals equation of state. Van der Waals volume

The van der Waals volume, V_w, also called the atomic volume or molecular volume, is the atomic property most directly related to the van der Waals radius.

Mass spectrometry

Mass spectrometry is an analytical technique that measures the mass-to-charge ratio of charged particles. It is used for determining masses of particles, for determining the elemental composition of a sample or molecule, and for elucidating the chemical structures of molecules, such as peptides and other chemical compounds. MS works by ionizing chemical compounds to generate charged molecules or molecule fragments and measuring their mass-to-charge ratios.

Methyl group

Methyl group is an alkyl derived from methane, containing one carbon atom bonded to three hydrogen atoms --CH_3. The group is often abbreviated Me. Such hydrocarbon groups occur in many organic compounds.

Substituent

In organic chemistry and biochemistry, a substituent is an atom or group of atoms substituted in place of a hydrogen atom on the parent chain of a hydrocarbon. The terms substituent, side-chain, group, branch, or pendant group are used almost interchangeably to describe branches from a parent structure, though certain distinctions are made in the context of polymer chemistry. In polymers, side chains extend from a backbone structure.

Hydrogen

Hydrogen is the chemical element with atomic number 1. It is represented by the symbol H. With an average atomic weight of 1.00794 u (1.007825 u for hydrogen-1), hydrogen is the lightest element and its monatomic form (H_1) is the most abundant chemical substance, constituting roughly 75% of the Universe's baryonic mass. Non-remnant stars are mainly composed of hydrogen in its plasma state.

Molecular orbital

In chemistry, a molecular orbital is a mathematical function describing the wave-like behavior of an electron in a molecule. This function can be used to calculate chemical and physical properties such as the probability of finding an electron in any specific region. The term 'orbital' was first used in English by Robert S. Mulliken as the English translation of Schrödinger's 'Eigenfunktion'.

Melting point

The melting point of a solid is the temperature at which it changes state from solid to liquid. At the melting point the solid and liquid phase exist in equilibrium. The melting point of a substance depends (usually slightly) on pressure and is usually specified at standard pressure.

Clemmensen reduction

Clemmensen reduction is a chemical reaction described as a reduction of ketones (or aldehydes) to alkanes using zinc amalgam and hydrochloric acid. This reaction is named after Erik Christian Clemmensen, a Danish chemist.

The Clemmensen reduction is particularly effective at reducing aryl-alkyl ketones.

Grignard reagents

The Grignard reaction is an organometallic chemical reaction in which alkyl- or aryl-magnesium halides (Grignard reagents) add to a carbonyl group in an aldehyde or ketone. This reaction is an important tool for the formation of carbon-carbon bonds. The reaction of an organic halide with magnesium is not a Grignard reaction, but provides a Grignard reagent.

Elemental analysis

Elemental analysis is a process where a sample of some material (e.g., soil, waste or drinking water, bodily fluids, minerals, chemical compounds) is analyzed for its elemental and sometimes isotopic composition. Elemental analysis can be qualitative (determining what elements are present), and it can be quantitative (determining how much of each are present). Elemental analysis falls within the ambit of analytical chemistry, the set of instruments involved in deciphering the chemical nature of our world.

Haloform reaction

The haloform reaction is a chemical reaction where a haloform (CHX_3, where X is a halogen) is produced by the exhaustive halogenation of a methyl ketone (a molecule containing the R-CO-CH_3 group) in the presence of a base. R may be H, alkyl or aryl. The reaction can be used to produce chloroform ($CHCl_3$), bromoform ($CHBr_3$), or iodoform (CHI_3).

Natural gas

Natural gas is a naturally occurring hydrocarbon gas mixture consisting primarily of methane, with up to 20 % of other hydrocarbons as well as impurities in varying amounts such as carbon dioxide. Natural gas is widely used as an important energy source in many applications including heating buildings, generating electricity, providing heat and power to industry, as fuel for vehicles and as a chemical feedstock in the manufacture of products such as plastics and other commercially important organic chemicals.

Chapter 2. ALKANES

CHAPTER HIGHLIGHTS & NOTES: KEY TERMS, PEOPLE, PLACES, CONCEPTS

Functional group

In organic chemistry, functional groups are lexicon specific groups of atoms or bonds within molecules that are responsible for the characteristic chemical reactions of those molecules. The same functional group will undergo the same or similar chemical reaction(s) regardless of the size of the molecule it is a part of. However, its relative reactivity can be modified by nearby functional groups.

Phenyl group

In organic chemistry, the phenyl group is a cyclic group of atoms with the formula C_6H_5. Phenyl groups are closely related to benzene. Phenyl groups have six carbon atoms bonded together in a hexagonal planar ring, five of which are bonded to individual hydrogen atoms, with the remaining carbon bonded to a substituent.

CHAPTER QUIZ: KEY TERMS, PEOPLE, PLACES, CONCEPTS

1. _________ is the diatomic molecule HBr. HBr is a gas at standard conditions. Hydrobromic acid forms upon dissolving HBr in water.

a. Hydrogen bromide
b. Lanthanum oxide
c. Lead azide
d. Lithium hypochlorite

2. _________ is a gas with the formula C_4H_{10} that is an alkane with four carbon atoms. The term may refer to either of two structural isomers, n-_________ or isobutane or to a mixture of these isomers. In the IUPAC nomenclature, however, '_________' refers only to the n-_________ isomer (which is the isomer with the unbranched structure).

a. Carbon dioxide
b. Carbon tetrachloride
c. Butane
d. 1-Chloro-1,2,2,2-tetrafluoroethane

3. _________ is an analytical technique that measures the mass-to-charge ratio of charged particles. It is used for determining masses of particles, for determining the elemental composition of a sample or molecule, and for elucidating the chemical structures of molecules, such as peptides and other chemical compounds. MS works by ionizing chemical compounds to generate charged molecules or molecule fragments and measuring their mass-to-charge ratios.

a. Mass spectrometry
b. Nucleotidase
c. Polyol pathway
d. Pro-oxidant

4. In chemistry, an _________ is an alkyl substituent derived from ethane (C_2H_6).

It has the formula -C_2H_5 and is very often abbreviated -Et. Ethyl is the IUPAC nomenclature of organic chemistry term for an alkane (or alkyl) molecule, using the prefix 'eth-' to indicate the presence of two carbon atoms in the molecule.

a. Isopropyl
b. Lanthanum oxide
c. Lead azide
d. Ethyl group

5. The _________ of a chemical compound is a graphical representation of the molecular structure, showing how the atoms are arranged. The chemical bonding within the molecule is also shown, either explicitly or implicitly. There are several common representations used in publications.

a. 1,2-Dioxetanedione
b. Lanthanum oxide
c. Lead azide
d. Structural formula

ANSWER KEY
Chapter 2. ALKANES

1. a
2. c
3. a
4. d
5. d

Chapter 3. ACIDS AND BASES. THE CURVED-ARROW NOTATION

CHAPTER OUTLINE: KEY TERMS, PEOPLE, PLACES, CONCEPTS

______ Octet rule

______ Mass spectrum

______ Conjugate acid

______ Electrophile

______ Nucleophile

______ Dissociation constant

______ Pivalic acid

______ Solvent effects

______ Equilibrium constant

______ Addition reaction

______ Carboxylic acid

______ Electron affinity

______ Periodic trends

______ Diethylene glycol

______ Fluoroacetic acid

______ Polar effect

______ Trifluoroacetic acid

______ Dimethyl ether

______ Protecting group

CHAPTER OUTLINE: KEY TERMS, PEOPLE, PLACES, CONCEPTS

______ Chloroacetic acid

______ Phenyl group

CHAPTER HIGHLIGHTS & NOTES: KEY TERMS, PEOPLE, PLACES, CONCEPTS

Octet rule

The octet rule is a chemical rule of thumb that states that atoms tend to combine in such a way that they each have eight electrons in their valence shells, giving them the same electronic configuration as a noble gas. The rule is applicable to the main-group elements, especially carbon, nitrogen, oxygen, and the halogens, but also to metals such as sodium or magnesium. In simple terms, molecules or ions tend to be most stable when the outermost electron shells of their constituent atoms contain eight electrons.

Mass spectrum

A mass spectrum is an intensity vs. m/z (mass-to-charge ratio) plot representing a chemical analysis. Hence, the mass spectrum of a sample is a pattern representing the distribution of ions by mass (more correctly: mass-to-charge ratio) in a sample. It is a histogram usually acquired using an instrument called a mass spectrometer.

Conjugate acid

Within the Brønsted-Lowry acid-base theory (protonic), a conjugate acid is the acid member, HX, of a pair of two compounds that transform into each other by gain or loss of a proton (hydrogen ion). A conjugate acid can also be seen as the chemical substance that releases, or donates, a proton (hydrogen ion) in the forward chemical reaction, hence, the term acid. The base produced, X^-, is called the conjugate base, and it absorbs, or gains, a proton in the backward chemical reaction.

Electrophile

In general, electrophiles are positively charged species that are attracted to an electron rich centre; but they can also be uncharged species such as a Lewis acid. In chemistry, an electrophile is a reagent attracted to electrons that participates in a chemical reaction by accepting an electron pair in order to bond to a nucleophile. Because electrophiles accept electrons, they are Lewis acids .

Nucleophile

A nucleophile is a species that donates an electron-pair to an electrophile to form a chemical bond in a reaction. All molecules or ions with a free pair of electrons or at least one pi bond can act as nucleophiles. Because nucleophiles donate electrons, they are by definition Lewis bases.

Dissociation constant

In chemistry, biochemistry, and pharmacology, a dissociation constant is a specific type of equilibrium constant that measures the propensity of a larger object to separate (dissociate) reversibly into smaller components, as when a complex falls apart into its component molecules, or when a salt splits up into its component ions. The dissociation constant is usually denoted K_d and is the inverse of the association constant. In the special case of salts, the dissociation constant can also be called an ionization constant.

Pivalic acid

Pivalic acid is a carboxylic acid with a molecular formula of $(CH_3)_3CCO_2H$. This colourless, odiferous organic compound is solid at room temperature. Industrial route

Pivalic acid is prepared by 'hydrocarboxylation' of isobutene via the Koch reaction:$(CH_3)_2C{=}CH_2 + CO + H_2O \rightarrow (CH_3)_3CCO_2H$

Such reactions require an acid catalyst such as hydrogen fluoride. tert-Butyl alcohol and isobutyl alcohol can also be used in place of isobutene.

Solvent effects

In chemistry, solvent effects is the group of effects that a solvent has on chemical reactivity. Solvents can have an effect on solubility, stability and reaction rates and choosing the appropriate solvent allows for thermodynamic and kinetic control over a chemical reaction.

A solute dissolves in a solvent when it forms favorable interactions with the solvent.

Equilibrium constant

For a general chemical equilibrium $\alpha A + \beta B ... \rightleftharpoons \sigma S + \tau T ...$

the equilibrium constant can be defined by

$$K = \frac{\{S\}^{\sigma}\{T\}^{\tau} ...}{\{A\}^{\alpha}\{B\}^{\beta} ...}$$

where {A} is the activity of the chemical species A, etc. (activity is a dimensionless quantity). It is conventional to put the activities of the products in the numerator and those of the reactants in the denominator.

Addition reaction

An addition reaction, in organic chemistry, is in its simplest terms an organic reaction where two or more molecules combine to form a larger one.

Addition reactions are limited to chemical compounds that have multiple bonds, such as molecules with carbon-carbon double bonds (alkenes), or with triple bonds (alkynes). Molecules containing carbon--hetero double bonds like carbonyl (C=O) groups, or imine (C=N) groups, can undergo addition as they too have double bond character.

Carboxylic acid

Carboxylic acids (

) are organic acids characterized by the presence of at least one carboxyl group. The general formula of a carboxylic acid is R-COOH, where R is some monovalent functional group. A carboxyl group (or carboxy) is a functional group consisting of a carbonyl (RR'C=O) and a hydroxyl (R-O-H), which has the formula -C(=O)OH, usually written as -COOH or $-CO_2H$.

Carboxylic acids are Brønsted-Lowry acids because they are proton (H^+) donors.

Electron affinity

The electron affinity of an atom or molecule is defined as the amount of energy released when an electron is added to a neutral atom or molecule to form a negative ion. $X + e^- \rightarrow X^-$

This property is measured for atoms and molecules in the gaseous state only, since in the solid or liquid states their energy levels would be changed by contact with other atoms or molecules. A list of the electron affinities was used by Robert S. Mulliken to develop an electronegativity scale for atoms, equal to the average of the electron affinity and ionization potential.

Periodic trends

In chemistry, periodic trends are the tendencies of certain elemental characteristics to increase or decrease as one progresses along a row or column of the periodic table of elements.

The atomic radius is the distance from the atomic nucleus to the outermost stable electron orbital in an atom that is at equilibrium. The atomic radius tends to decrease as one progresses across a period from left to right because the effective nuclear charge increases, thereby attracting the orbiting electrons and lessening the radius.

Diethylene glycol

Diethylene glycol is an organic compound with the formula $(HOCH_2CH_2)_2O$. It is a colorless, practically odorless, poisonous, and hygroscopic liquid with a sweetish taste. It is miscible in water, alcohol, ether, acetone and ethylene glycol. DEG is a widely used solvent.

Fluoroacetic acid

Fluoroacetic acid is a chemical compound with formula CH_2FCOOH. The sodium salt, sodium fluoroacetate is used as a pesticide.

Polar effect

The Polar effect is the effect exerted by a substituent on modifying electrostatic forces operating on a nearby reaction center. The main contributors to the polar effect are the inductive effect, mesomeric effect and the through-space electronic field effect.

An electron withdrawing group or EWG draws electrons away from a reaction center.

Trifluoroacetic acid

Trifluoroacetic acid is the simplest stable perfluorinated carboxylic acid chemical compound, with the formula CF_3CO_2H. It is a strong carboxylic acid due to the influence of the electronegative trifluoromethyl group. TFA is almost 100,000-fold more acidic than acetic acid. TFA is widely used in organic chemistry.

CHAPTER HIGHLIGHTS & NOTES: KEY TERMS, PEOPLE, PLACES, CONCEPTS

Dimethyl ether	Dimethyl ether also known as methoxymethane, is the organic compound with the formula CH_3OCH_3. The simplest ether, it is a colourless gas that is a useful precursor to other organic compounds and an aerosol propellant. Today, DME is primarily produced by converting hydrocarbons sourced from natural gas or coal via gasification to synthesis gas (syngas).
Protecting group	A protecting group is introduced into a molecule by chemical modification of a functional group in order to obtain chemoselectivity in a subsequent chemical reaction. It plays an important role in multistep organic synthesis. In many preparations of delicate organic compounds, some specific parts of their molecules cannot survive the required reagents or chemical environments.
Chloroacetic acid	Chloroacetic acid, industrially known as monochloroacetic acid is the organochlorine compound with the formula $ClCH_2CO_2H$. This carboxylic acid is a useful building-block in organic synthesis. The production of chloroacetic acid was 706,000 tonnes/year in 2010, of which over half is produced in China. Other countries with significant production capacity are Germany (105,000), the Netherlands (100,000), India (>65,000), and the United States (55,000).
Phenyl group	In organic chemistry, the phenyl group is a cyclic group of atoms with the formula C_6H_5. Phenyl groups are closely related to benzene. Phenyl groups have six carbon atoms bonded together in a hexagonal planar ring, five of which are bonded to individual hydrogen atoms, with the remaining carbon bonded to a substituent.

CHAPTER QUIZ: KEY TERMS, PEOPLE, PLACES, CONCEPTS

1. The _________ is a chemical rule of thumb that states that atoms tend to combine in such a way that they each have eight electrons in their valence shells, giving them the same electronic configuration as a noble gas. The rule is applicable to the main-group elements, especially carbon, nitrogen, oxygen, and the halogens, but also to metals such as sodium or magnesium. In simple terms, molecules or ions tend to be most stable when the outermost electron shells of their constituent atoms contain eight electrons.

   a. Allixin
   b. Ethyl maltol
   c. Aceglutamide
   d. Octet rule

2. A _________ is a species that donates an electron-pair to an electrophile to form a chemical bond in a reaction. All molecules or ions with a free pair of electrons or at least one pi bond can act as _________s. Because _________s donate electrons, they are by definition Lewis bases.

   a. Passive binding
   b. Polar effect
   c. Nucleophile
   d. Taft equation

3. In chemistry, _________ is the group of effects that a solvent has on chemical reactivity. Solvents can have an effect on solubility, stability and reaction rates and choosing the appropriate solvent allows for thermodynamic and kinetic control over a chemical reaction.

   A solute dissolves in a solvent when it forms favorable interactions with the solvent.

   a. 1,2-Dioxetanedione
   b. Solvent effects
   c. Potassium hydrogen phthalate
   d. Pravastatin

4. In chemistry, biochemistry, and pharmacology, a _________ is a specific type of equilibrium constant that measures the propensity of a larger object to separate (dissociate) reversibly into smaller components, as when a complex falls apart into its component molecules, or when a salt splits up into its component ions. The _________ is usually denoted K_d and is the inverse of the association constant. In the special case of salts, the _________ can also be called an ionization constant.

   a. 1,2-Dioxetanedione
   b. Dissociation constant
   c. Ring strain
   d. Taft equation

5. . A _________ is an intensity vs. m/z (mass-to-charge ratio) plot representing a chemical analysis. Hence, the _________ of a sample is a pattern representing the distribution of ions by mass (more correctly: mass-to-charge ratio) in a sample. It is a histogram usually acquired using an instrument called a mass spectrometer.

a. Tandem mass spectrometry
b. 1,2-Dioxetanedione
c. Fluorinert
d. Mass spectrum

ANSWER KEY
Chapter 3. ACIDS AND BASES. THE CURVED-ARROW NOTATION

1. d
2. c
3. b
4. b
5. d

Chapter 4. INTRODUCTION TO ALKENES STRUCTURE AND REACTIVITY

CHAPTER OUTLINE: KEY TERMS, PEOPLE, PLACES, CONCEPTS

______ Unsaturated hydrocarbon

______ Ethylene

______ Molecular orbital

______ Stereocenter

______ Allyl group

______ Degree of unsaturation

______ Alkene

______ Polar effect

______ Double bond

______ Exothermic reaction

______ Methyl radical

______ Methyl salicylate

______ Bond strength

______ Hydrogen bromide

______ Hydrogen halide

______ Addition reaction

______ Hydrogenation

______ Regioselectivity

______ Reaction mechanism

Chapter 4. INTRODUCTION TO ALKENES STRUCTURE AND REACTIVITY

CHAPTER OUTLINE: KEY TERMS, PEOPLE, PLACES, CONCEPTS

- Reactive intermediate
- Methyl group
- Carbocation
- Weerman degradation
- Reaction rate
- Transition state
- Rate-determining step
- Catalysis
- Catalyst
- Catalytic converter
- Heck reaction
- Microscopic reversibility
- Nucleophilic substitution
- Substitution reaction
- Enzyme
- Fumarase
- Active site

Unsaturated hydrocarbon

Unsaturated hydrocarbons are hydrocarbons that have double or triple covalent bonds between adjacent carbon atoms. Those with at least one double bond are called alkenes and those with at least one triple bond are called alkynes. Each double bond is represented by a number preceding the name of the base chain, representing on which hydrocarbon in the chain the double or triple bond can be found.

Ethylene

Ethylene is an organic compound, a hydrocarbon with the formula C_2H_4 or $H_2C{=}CH_2$. It is a colorless flammable gas with a faint 'sweet and musky' odor when pure. It is the simplest alkene (a hydrocarbon with carbon-carbon double bonds), and the simplest unsaturated hydrocarbon after acetylene (C_2H_2).

Molecular orbital

In chemistry, a molecular orbital is a mathematical function describing the wave-like behavior of an electron in a molecule. This function can be used to calculate chemical and physical properties such as the probability of finding an electron in any specific region. The term 'orbital' was first used in English by Robert S. Mulliken as the English translation of Schrödinger's 'Eigenfunktion'.

Stereocenter

A stereocenter is an atom, bearing groups such that an interchanging of any two groups leads to a stereoisomer.

A chirality center is a stereocenter consisting of an atom holding a set of ligands (atoms or groups of atoms) in a spatial arrangement which is not superposable on its mirror image. A chiral center is a generalized extension of an asymmetric carbon atom, which is a carbon atom bonded to four different entities, such that an interchanging of any two groups gives rise to an enantiomer.

Allyl group

An allyl group is a substituent with the structural formula $H_2C{=}CH{-}CH_2R$, where R is the connection to the rest of the molecule. It is made up of a methylene ($-CH_2-$), attached to a vinyl group ($-CH{=}CH_2$). The name is derived from the Latin word for garlic, Allium sativum.

Degree of unsaturation

The degree of unsaturation (also known as the index of hydrogen deficiency (IHD) or rings plus double bonds) formula is used in organic chemistry to help draw chemical structures. The formula lets the user determine how many rings, double bonds, and triple bonds are present in the compound to be drawn. It does not give the exact number of rings or double or triple bonds, but rather the sum of the number of rings and double bonds plus twice the number of triple bonds.

Alkene

In organic chemistry, an alkene, olefin, or olefine is an unsaturated chemical compound containing at least one carbon-to-carbon double bond. The simplest acyclic alkenes, with only one double bond and no other functional groups, form an homologous series of hydrocarbons with the general formula C_nH_{2n}.

Chapter 4. INTRODUCTION TO ALKENES STRUCTURE AND REACTIVITY

CHAPTER HIGHLIGHTS & NOTES: KEY TERMS, PEOPLE, PLACES, CONCEPTS

Polar effect

The Polar effect is the effect exerted by a substituent on modifying electrostatic forces operating on a nearby reaction center. The main contributors to the polar effect are the inductive effect, mesomeric effect and the through-space electronic field effect.

An electron withdrawing group or EWG draws electrons away from a reaction center.

Double bond

A double bond in chemistry is a chemical bond between two chemical elements involving four bonding electrons instead of the usual two. The most common double bond, that between two carbon atoms, can be found in alkenes. Many types of double bonds between two different elements exist, for example in a carbonyl group with a carbon atom and an oxygen atom.

Exothermic reaction

An exothermic reaction is a chemical reaction that releases energy in the form of light or heat. It is the opposite of an endothermic reaction.

Expressed in a chemical equation: reactants → products + energyOverview

An exothermic reaction is a chemical reaction that is accompanied by the release of heat.

Methyl radical

Methyl radical is a trivalent radical derived from methane, produced by the ultraviolet disassociation of halomethanes.

Methyl salicylate

Methyl salicylate is an organic ester that is naturally produced by many species of plants. Some of the plants which produce it are called wintergreens, hence the common name.

Plants containing methyl salicylate produce this organic ester (a combination of an organic acid with an alcohol) most likely as an anti-herbivore defense.

Bond strength

In chemistry, bond strength is measured between two atoms joined in a chemical bond. It is the degree to which each atom linked to another atom contributes to the valency of this other atom. Bond strength is intimately linked to bond order.

Hydrogen bromide

Hydrogen bromide is the diatomic molecule HBr. HBr is a gas at standard conditions. Hydrobromic acid forms upon dissolving HBr in water.

Hydrogen halide

Hydrogen halides (or hydrohalic acids) are inorganic compounds with the formula HX where X is one of the halogens: fluorine, chlorine, bromine, iodine, and astatine. Hydrogen halides are gases that dissolve in water to give acids.

The hydrogen halides are diatomic molecules with no tendency to ionize in the gas phase.

Addition reaction	An addition reaction, in organic chemistry, is in its simplest terms an organic reaction where two or more molecules combine to form a larger one. Addition reactions are limited to chemical compounds that have multiple bonds, such as molecules with carbon-carbon double bonds (alkenes), or with triple bonds (alkynes). Molecules containing carbon--hetero double bonds like carbonyl (C=O) groups, or imine (C=N) groups, can undergo addition as they too have double bond character.
Hydrogenation	Hydrogenation, to treat with hydrogen, also a form of chemical reduction, is a chemical reaction between molecular hydrogen (H_2) and another compound or element, usually in the presence of a catalyst. The process is commonly employed to reduce or saturate organic compounds. Hydrogenation typically constitutes the addition of pairs of hydrogen atoms to a molecule, generally an alkene.
Regioselectivity	In chemistry, regioselectivity is the preference of one direction of chemical bond making or breaking over all other possible directions. It can often apply to which of many possible positions a reagent will affect, such as which proton a strong base will abstract from an organic molecule, or where on a substituted benzene ring a further substituent will add. A specific example is a halohydrin formation reaction with 2-propenylbenzene: Because of the preference for the formation of one product over another, the reaction is selective.
Reaction mechanism	In chemistry, a reaction mechanism is the step by step sequence of elementary reactions by which overall chemical change occurs. Although only the net chemical change is directly observable for most chemical reactions, experiments can often be designed that suggest the possible sequence of steps in a reaction mechanism. Recently, electrospray ionization mass spectrometry has been used to corroborate the mechanism of several organic reaction proposals.
Reactive intermediate	In chemistry a reactive intermediate is a short-lived, high energy, highly reactive molecule. When generated in a chemical reaction it will quickly convert into a more stable molecule. Only in exceptional cases can these compounds be isolated and stored, e.g. low temperatures, matrix isolation.
Methyl group	Methyl group is an alkyl derived from methane, containing one carbon atom bonded to three hydrogen atoms --CH_3. The group is often abbreviated Me. Such hydrocarbon groups occur in many organic compounds.
Carbocation	A carbocation is an ion with a positively-charged carbon atom.

The charged carbon atom in a carbocation is a 'sextet', i.e. it has only six electrons in its outer valence shell instead of the eight valence electrons that ensures maximum stability (octet rule). Therefore carbocations are often reactive, seeking to fill the octet of valence electrons as well as regain a neutral charge.

Weerman degradation

The Weerman degradation is an organic reaction in carbohydrate chemistry in which an aldonamide (derived from an aldonic acid) is degraded by sodium hypochlorite, forming a new sugar with one less carbon. The reaction is named after R.A. Weerman

The reaction mechanism is that of the related Hofmann degradation. One study demonstrated the direct oxidation of glucose to arabinose by the same sodium hypochlorite, skipping the aldonic acid and aldoamide steps.

Reaction rate

The reaction rate or speed of reaction for a reactant or product in a particular reaction is intuitively defined as how fast or slow a reaction takes place. For example, the oxidation of iron under the atmosphere is a slow reaction which can take many years, but the combustion of butane in a fire is a reaction that takes place in fractions of a second.

Chemical kinetics is the part of physical chemistry that studies reaction rates.

Transition state

The transition state of a chemical reaction is a particular configuration along the reaction coordinate. It is defined as the state corresponding to the highest energy along this reaction coordinate. At this point, assuming a perfectly irreversible reaction, colliding reactant molecules will always go on to form products.

Rate-determining step

The rate-determining step is a chemistry term for the slowest step in a chemical reaction. The rate-determining step is often compared to the neck of a funnel; the rate at which water flows through the funnel is determined by the width of the neck, not by the speed at which water is poured in. In similar manner, the rate of reaction depends on the rate of the slowest step.

Catalysis

Catalysis is the change in rate of a chemical reaction due to the participation of a substance called a catalyst. Unlike other reagents that participate in the chemical reaction, a catalyst is not consumed by the reaction itself. A catalyst may participate in multiple chemical transformations.

Catalyst

Catalysis is the change in rate of a chemical reaction due to the participation of a substance called a catalyst. Unlike other reagents that participate in the chemical reaction, a catalyst is not consumed by the reaction itself. A catalyst may participate in multiple chemical transformations.

Catalytic converter

A catalytic converter is an exhaust emission control device which converts toxic chemicals in the exhaust of an internal combustion engine into less toxic substances.

Inside a catalytic converter, a catalyst stimulates a chemical reaction in which noxious byproducts of combustion are converted to less toxic substances by way of catalysed chemical reactions. The specific reactions vary with the type of catalyst installed.

Heck reaction

The Heck reaction is the chemical reaction of an unsaturated halide (or triflate) with an alkene and a base and palladium catalyst or palladium nanomaterial-based catalyst to form a substituted alkene. Together with the other palladium-catalyzed cross-coupling reactions, this reaction is of great importance, as it allows one to do substitution reactions on planar centers. It is named after Tsutomu Mizoroki and Richard F. Heck.

Microscopic reversibility

The principle of Microscopic reversibility in physics and chemistry is twofold:•First, it states that the microscopic detailed dynamics of particles and fields is time-reversible because the microscopic equations of motion are symmetric with respect to inversion in time (T-symmetry);•Second, it relates to the statistical description of the kinetics of macroscopic or mesoscopic systems as an ensemble of elementary processes: collisions, elementary transitions or reactions. For these processes, the consequence of the microscopic T-symmetry is: '

Corresponding to every individual process there is a reverse process, and in a state of equilibrium the average rate of every process is equal to the average rate of its reverse process. 'History of Microscopic reversibility

The idea of microscopic reversibility was born together with physical kinetics.

Nucleophilic substitution

In organic and inorganic chemistry, nucleophilic substitution is a fundamental class of reactions in which an electron nucleophile selectively bonds with or attacks the positive or partially positive charge of an atom or a group of atoms called the leaving group; the positive or partially positive atom is referred to as an electrophile.

The most general form for the reaction may be given asNuc: + R-LG → R-Nuc + LG:

The electron pair (:) from the nucleophile (Nuc) attacks the substrate (R-LG) forming a new bond, while the leaving group (LG) departs with an electron pair. The principal product in this case is R-Nuc.

Substitution reaction

In a substitution reaction, a functional group in a particular chemical compound is replaced by another group. In organic chemistry, the electrophilic and nucleophilic substitution reactions are of prime importance.

Chapter 4. INTRODUCTION TO ALKENES STRUCTURE AND REACTIVITY

CHAPTER HIGHLIGHTS & NOTES: KEY TERMS, PEOPLE, PLACES, CONCEPTS

Enzyme	Enzymes ( ) are biological molecules that catalyze (i.e., increase the rates of) chemical reactions. In enzymatic reactions, the molecules at the beginning of the process, called substrates, are converted into different molecules, called products. Almost all chemical reactions in a biological cell need enzymes in order to occur at rates sufficient for life.
Fumarase	Fumarase is an enzyme that catalyzes the reversible hydration/dehydration of Fumarate to S-malate. Fumarase comes in two forms: mitochondrial and cytosolic. The mitochondrial isoenzyme is involved in the Krebs Cycle (also known as the Citric Acid Cycle), and the cytosolic isoenzyme is involved in the metabolism of amino acids and fumarate.
Active site	In biology the active site is part of an enzyme where substrates bind and undergo a chemical reaction. The majority of enzymes are proteins but RNA enzymes called ribozymes also exist. The active site of an enzyme is usually found in a cleft or pocket that is lined by amino acid residues (or nucleotides in ribozymes) that participate in recognition of the substrate.

CHAPTER QUIZ: KEY TERMS, PEOPLE, PLACES, CONCEPTS

1. _________s ( ) are biological molecules that catalyze (i.e., increase the rates of) chemical reactions. In enzymatic reactions, the molecules at the beginning of the process, called substrates, are converted into different molecules, called products. Almost all chemical reactions in a biological cell need _________s in order to occur at rates sufficient for life.

   a. Enzyme
   b. TaqMan
   c. Telomerization
   d. Thermal decomposition

2. _________ is an organic ester that is naturally produced by many species of plants. Some of the plants which produce it are called wintergreens, hence the common name.

   Plants containing _________ produce this organic ester (a combination of an organic acid with an alcohol) most likely as an anti-herbivore defense.

   a. Phenyl salicylate
   b. Potassium salicylate
   c. Methyl salicylate
   d. Salsalate

3. . The _________ is the effect exerted by a substituent on modifying electrostatic forces operating on a nearby reaction center. The main contributors to the _________ are the inductive effect, mesomeric effect and the through-space electronic field effect.

An electron withdrawing group or EWG draws electrons away from a reaction center.

a. Ring strain
b. Polar effect
c. Walsh diagram
d. In-Methylcyclophane

4. _________ is the diatomic molecule HBr. HBr is a gas at standard conditions. Hydrobromic acid forms upon dissolving HBr in water.

a. Hydrogen cyanide
b. Hydrogen bromide
c. Lead azide
d. Lithium hypochlorite

5. An _________ is a substituent with the structural formula $H_2C{=}CH{-}CH_2R$, where R is the connection to the rest of the molecule. It is made up of a methylene ($-CH_2-$), attached to a vinyl group ($-CH{=}CH_2$). The name is derived from the Latin word for garlic, Allium sativum.

a. Allyl group
b. Allixin
c. Ethyl maltol
d. Strain

ANSWER KEY
Chapter 4. INTRODUCTION TO ALKENES STRUCTURE AND REACTIVITY

---

1. a
2. c
3. b
4. b
5. a

Chapter 5. ADDITION REACTIONS OF ALKENES

CHAPTER OUTLINE: KEY TERMS, PEOPLE, PLACES, CONCEPTS

- Addition reaction
- Heck reaction
- Hydroboration
- Mass spectrum
- Crown ether
- Grignard reaction
- Sodium borohydride
- Alkyne
- Material safety data sheet
- Alkene
- Claisen rearrangement
- Diglyme
- Molozonide
- Ozone
- Ozonide
- Ozonolysis
- Dimethyl sulfide
- Hydrogen bromide
- Hydrogen halide

Chapter 5. ADDITION REACTIONS OF ALKENES

CHAPTER OUTLINE: KEY TERMS, PEOPLE, PLACES, CONCEPTS

_______________ Free-radical addition

_______________ Heterolysis

_______________ Homolysis

_______________ Radical initiator

_______________ Free-radical reaction

_______________ Steric effects

_______________ Electrophilic substitution

_______________ Bond strength

_______________ Addition polymer

_______________ Polyethylene

_______________ Polymer

_______________ Low-density polyethylene

_______________ Polymerization

_______________ High-density polyethylene

_______________ Ethyl group

Chapter 5. ADDITION REACTIONS OF ALKENES

CHAPTER HIGHLIGHTS & NOTES: KEY TERMS, PEOPLE, PLACES, CONCEPTS

Addition reaction

An addition reaction, in organic chemistry, is in its simplest terms an organic reaction where two or more molecules combine to form a larger one.

Addition reactions are limited to chemical compounds that have multiple bonds, such as molecules with carbon-carbon double bonds (alkenes), or with triple bonds (alkynes). Molecules containing carbon--hetero double bonds like carbonyl (C=O) groups, or imine (C=N) groups, can undergo addition as they too have double bond character.

Heck reaction

The Heck reaction is the chemical reaction of an unsaturated halide (or triflate) with an alkene and a base and palladium catalyst or palladium nanomaterial-based catalyst to form a substituted alkene. Together with the other palladium-catalyzed cross-coupling reactions, this reaction is of great importance, as it allows one to do substitution reactions on planar centers. It is named after Tsutomu Mizoroki and Richard F. Heck.

Hydroboration

In chemistry, hydroboration refers to the addition of a hydrogen-boron bond to C-C, C-N, and C-O double bonds, as well as C-C triple bonds. This chemical reaction is useful in the organic synthesis of organic compounds. The development of this technology and the underlying concepts was recognized by the Nobel Prize in Chemistry to Herbert C. Brown.

Mass spectrum

A mass spectrum is an intensity vs. m/z (mass-to-charge ratio) plot representing a chemical analysis. Hence, the mass spectrum of a sample is a pattern representing the distribution of ions by mass (more correctly: mass-to-charge ratio) in a sample. It is a histogram usually acquired using an instrument called a mass spectrometer.

Crown ether

Crown ethers are cyclic chemical compounds that consist of a ring containing several ether groups. The most common crown ethers are oligomers of ethylene oxide, the repeating unit being ethyleneoxy, i.e., $-CH_2CH_2O-$. Important members of this series are the tetramer (n = 4), the pentamer (n = 5), and the hexamer (n = 6).

Grignard reaction

The Grignard reaction is an organometallic chemical reaction in which alkyl- or aryl-magnesium halides (Grignard reagents) add to a carbonyl group in an aldehyde or ketone. This reaction is an important tool for the formation of carbon-carbon bonds. The reaction of an organic halide with magnesium is not a Grignard reaction, but provides a Grignard reagent.

Sodium borohydride

Sodium borohydride, is an inorganic compound with the formula $NaBH_4$. This white solid, usually encountered as a powder, is a versatile reducing agent that finds wide application in chemistry, both in the laboratory and on a technical scale. Large amounts are used for bleaching wood pulp.

Alkyne

Alkynes are hydrocarbons that have a triple bond between two carbon atoms, with the formula C_nH_{2n-2}.

Alkynes are traditionally known as acetylenes, although the name acetylene also refers specifically to C_2H_2, known formally as ethyne using IUPAC nomenclature. Like other hydrocarbons, alkynes are generally hydrophobic but tend to be more reactive.

Material safety data sheet

A Material Safety Data Sheet Safety Data Sheet (SDS), or Product Safety Data Sheet (PSDS) is an important component of product stewardship and workplace safety. It is intended to provide workers and emergency personnel with procedures for handling or working with that substance in a safe manner, and includes information such as physical data (melting point, boiling point, flash point, etc)., toxicity, health effects, first aid, reactivity, storage, disposal, protective equipment, and spill-handling procedures. MSDS formats can vary from source to source within a country depending on national requirements.

Alkene

In organic chemistry, an alkene, olefin, or olefine is an unsaturated chemical compound containing at least one carbon-to-carbon double bond. The simplest acyclic alkenes, with only one double bond and no other functional groups, form an homologous series of hydrocarbons with the general formula C_nH_{2n}.

The simplest alkene is ethylene (C_2H_4), which has the International Union of Pure and Applied Chemistry (IUPAC) name ethene.

Claisen rearrangement

The Claisen rearrangement is a powerful carbon-carbon bond-forming chemical reaction discovered by Rainer Ludwig Claisen. The heating of an allyl vinyl ether will initiate a [3,3]-sigmatropic rearrangement to give a γ,δ-unsaturated carbonyl.

Discovered in 1912, the Claisen rearrangement is the first recorded example of a [3,3]-sigmatropic rearrangement.

Diglyme

Diglyme, is a solvent with a high boiling point. It is an organic compound which is the dimethyl ether of diethylene glycol. (The name 'diglyme' is a portmanteau of 'diglycol methyl ether.') It is a clear, colorless liquid with a slight ether-like odor.

Molozonide

A molozonide is a term for a 1,2,3-trioxolane. It is a class of unstable cyclic organic compounds, which includes three oxygen atoms and two sp^3-hybridized carbon atoms. A molozonide is an intermediate formed during ozonolysis as a precursor of the ozonide complex formed during cleavage.

Ozone

Ozone or trioxygen, is a triatomic molecule, consisting of three oxygen atoms. It is an allotrope of oxygen that is much less stable than the diatomic allotrope (O_2), breaking down with a half life of about half an hour in the lower atmosphere, to normal dioxygen.

Chapter 5. ADDITION REACTIONS OF ALKENES

CHAPTER HIGHLIGHTS & NOTES: KEY TERMS, PEOPLE, PLACES, CONCEPTS

Ozonide

Ozonide is an unstable, reactive polyatomic anion O_3^-, derived from ozone, or an organic compound similar to organic peroxide formed by a reaction of ozone with an unsaturated compound.

Inorganic ozonides are dark red ionic compounds containing the reactive O_3^- anion. The anion has the V shape of the ozone molecule.

Ozonolysis

Ozonolysis is the cleavage of an alkene or alkyne with ozone to form organic compounds in which the multiple carbon-carbon bond has been replaced by a double bond to oxygen. The outcome of the reaction depends on the type of multiple bond being oxidized and the workup conditions.

Alkenes can be oxidized with ozone to form alcohols, aldehydes or ketones, or carboxylic acids.

Dimethyl sulfide

Dimethyl sulfide or methylthiomethane is an organosulfur compound with the formula $(CH_3)_2S$. Dimethyl sulfide is a water-insoluble flammable liquid that boils at 37 °C (99 °F) and has a characteristic disagreeable odor. It is a component of the smell produced from cooking of certain vegetables, notably maize, cabbage, beetroot and seafoods. It is also an indication of bacterial infection in malt production and brewing.

Hydrogen bromide

Hydrogen bromide is the diatomic molecule HBr. HBr is a gas at standard conditions. Hydrobromic acid forms upon dissolving HBr in water.

Hydrogen halide

Hydrogen halides (or hydrohalic acids) are inorganic compounds with the formula HX where X is one of the halogens: fluorine, chlorine, bromine, iodine, and astatine. Hydrogen halides are gases that dissolve in water to give acids.

The hydrogen halides are diatomic molecules with no tendency to ionize in the gas phase.

Free-radical addition

Free-radical addition is an addition reaction in organic chemistry involving free radicals. The addition may occur between a radical and a non-radical, or between two radicals.

The basic steps with examples of the free radical addition (also known as radical chain mechanism) are:•Initiation by a radical initiator: A radical is created from a non-radical precursor.•Chain propagation: A radical reacts with a non-radical to produce a new radical species•Chain termination: Two radicals react with each other to create a non-radical species

Free radical reactions depend on a reagent having a (relatively) weak bond, allowing it to homolyse to form radicals (often with heat or light).

Heterolysis	In chemistry, heterolysis is chemical bond cleavage of a neutral molecule generating a cation and an anion. In this process the two electrons that make up the bond are assigned to the same fragment. The more electronegative fragment receives both electrons.
Homolysis	The term homolysis generally means breakdown (lysis) to equal pieces (homo = same). There are separate meanings for the word in chemistry and biology. In chemistry, homolysis or homolytic fission is chemical bond dissociation of a neutral molecule generating two free radicals.
Radical initiator	In chemistry, radical initiators are substances that can produce radical species under mild conditions and promote radical reactions . These substances generally possess weak bonds--bonds that have small bond dissociation energies. Radical initiators are utilized in industrial processes such as polymer synthesis.
Free-radical reaction	A free-radical reaction is any chemical reaction involving free radicals. This reaction type is abundant in organic reactions. Two pioneering studies into free radical reactions have been the discovery of the triphenylmethyl radical by Moses Gomberg (1900) and the lead-mirror experiment described by Friedrich Paneth in 1927. In this last experiment tetramethyllead is decomposed at elevated temperatures to methyl radicals and elemental lead in a quartz tube.
Steric effects	Steric effects arise from the fact that each atom within a molecule occupies a certain amount of space. If atoms are brought too close together, there is an associated cost in energy due to overlapping electron clouds , and this may affect the molecule's preferred shape (conformation) and reactivity. Steric hindrance Steric hindrance occurs when the large size of groups within a molecule prevents chemical reactions that are observed in related molecules with smaller groups.
Electrophilic substitution	Electrophilic substitution reactions are chemical reactions in which an electrophile displaces a group in a compound, typically but not always hydrogen. Electrophilic aromatic substitution is characteristic of aromatic compounds and is an important way of introducing functional groups onto benzene rings. The other main reaction type is electrophilic aliphatic substitution.
Bond strength	In chemistry, bond strength is measured between two atoms joined in a chemical bond. It is the degree to which each atom linked to another atom contributes to the valency of this other atom. Bond strength is intimately linked to bond order.

Chapter 5. ADDITION REACTIONS OF ALKENES

CHAPTER HIGHLIGHTS & NOTES: KEY TERMS, PEOPLE, PLACES, CONCEPTS

Addition polymer	An addition polymer is a polymer which is formed by an addition reaction, where many monomers bond together via rearrangement of bonds without the loss of any atom or molecule. This is in contrast to a condensation polymer which is formed by a condensation reaction where a molecule, usually water, is lost during the formation. With exception of combustion, the backbone of addition polymers are generally chemically inert.
Polyethylene	Polyethylene or polythene (IUPAC name polyethene or poly(methylene)) is the most common plastic. The annual production is approximately 80 million metric tons. Its primary use is within packaging (plastic bag, plastic films, geomembranes, etc)..
Polymer	A polymer is a large molecule (macromolecule) composed of repeating structural units. These sub-units are typically connected by covalent chemical bonds. Although the term polymer is sometimes taken to refer to plastics, it actually encompasses a large class of compounds comprising both natural and synthetic materials with a wide variety of properties.
Low-density polyethylene	Low-density polyethylene is a thermoplastic made from petroleum. It was the first grade of polyethylene, produced in 1933 by Imperial Chemical Industries (ICI) using a high pressure process via free radical polymerization. Its manufacture employs the same method today.
Polymerization	In polymer chemistry, polymerization is a process of reacting monomer molecules together in a chemical reaction to form polymer chains or three-dimensional networks. There are many forms of polymerization and different systems exist to categorize them. In chemical compounds, polymerization occurs via a variety of reaction mechanisms that vary in complexity due to functional groups present in reacting compounds and their inherent steric effects explained by VSEPR Theory.
High-density polyethylene	High-density polyethylene or polyethylene high-density (PEHD) is a polyethylene thermoplastic made from petroleum. It takes 1.75 kilograms of petroleum (in terms of energy and raw materials) to make one kilogram of HDPE. HDPE is commonly recycled, and has the number '2' as its recycling symbol. In 2007, the global HDPE market reached a volume of more than 30 million tons.
Ethyl group	In chemistry, an ethyl group is an alkyl substituent derived from ethane (C_2H_6). It has the formula -C_2H_5 and is very often abbreviated -Et. Ethyl is the IUPAC nomenclature of organic chemistry term for an alkane (or alkyl) molecule, using the prefix 'eth-' to indicate the presence of two carbon atoms in the molecule.

1. _________ reactions are chemical reactions in which an electrophile displaces a group in a compound, typically but not always hydrogen. Electrophilic aromatic substitution is characteristic of aromatic compounds and is an important way of introducing functional groups onto benzene rings. The other main reaction type is electrophilic aliphatic substitution.

   a. Oxidative decarboxylation
   b. Electrophilic substitution
   c. Glycopolymer
   d. Glycorandomization

2. The _________ is the chemical reaction of an unsaturated halide (or triflate) with an alkene and a base and palladium catalyst or palladium nanomaterial-based catalyst to form a substituted alkene. Together with the other palladium-catalyzed cross-coupling reactions, this reaction is of great importance, as it allows one to do substitution reactions on planar centers. It is named after Tsutomu Mizoroki and Richard F. Heck.

   a. Hoesch reaction
   b. Hydrazone iodination
   c. Heck reaction
   d. Krapcho decarboxylation

3. An _________, in organic chemistry, is in its simplest terms an organic reaction where two or more molecules combine to form a larger one.

   _________s are limited to chemical compounds that have multiple bonds, such as molecules with carbon-carbon double bonds (alkenes), or with triple bonds (alkynes). Molecules containing carbon--hetero double bonds like carbonyl (C=O) groups, or imine (C=N) groups, can undergo addition as they too have double bond character.

   a. Adduct purification
   b. Ammoxidation
   c. Addition reaction
   d. Arrow pushing

4. . _________ is an addition reaction in organic chemistry involving free radicals. The addition may occur between a radical and a non-radical, or between two radicals.

   The basic steps with examples of the free radical addition (also known as radical chain mechanism) are:•Initiation by a radical initiator: A radical is created from a non-radical precursor.•Chain propagation: A radical reacts with a non-radical to produce a new radical species•Chain termination: Two radicals react with each other to create a non-radical species

   Free radical reactions depend on a reagent having a (relatively) weak bond, allowing it to homolyse to form radicals (often with heat or light).

   a. Leaving group
   b. Lindemann mechanism
   c. Free-radical addition

5. In chemistry, _________ refers to the addition of a hydrogen-boron bond to C-C, C-N, and C-O double bonds, as well as C-C triple bonds. This chemical reaction is useful in the organic synthesis of organic compounds. The development of this technology and the underlying concepts was recognized by the Nobel Prize in Chemistry to Herbert C. Brown.

   a. Keto-enol tautomerism
   b. Hydroboration
   c. Kharasch addition
   d. Kochi reaction

ANSWER KEY
Chapter 5. ADDITION REACTIONS OF ALKENES

1. b

2. c

3. c

4. c

5. b

Chapter 6. PRINCIPLES OF STEREOCHEMISTRY

CHAPTER OUTLINE: KEY TERMS, PEOPLE, PLACES, CONCEPTS

Stereochemistry

Enantiomer

Stereocenter

Absolute configuration

Polarimeter

Glucuronic acid

Glutamic acid

Specific rotation

Racemic mixture

Racemization

Thalidomide

Meso compound

Electrocyclic reaction

Sigmatropic reaction

Tartaric acid

Steric effects

Pseudoephedrine

Chapter 6. PRINCIPLES OF STEREOCHEMISTRY

CHAPTER HIGHLIGHTS & NOTES: KEY TERMS, PEOPLE, PLACES, CONCEPTS

Stereochemistry

Stereochemistry, a subdiscipline of chemistry, involves the study of the relative spatial arrangement of atoms within molecules. An important branch of stereochemistry is the study of chiral molecules.

Stereochemistry is also known as 3D chemistry because the prefix 'stereo-' means 'three-dimensionality'.

Enantiomer

In chemistry, an enantiomer is one of two stereoisomers that are mirror images of each other that are non-superposable (not identical), much as one's left and right hands are the same except for opposite orientation.

Organic compounds that contain an asymmetric (chiral) Carbon usually have two non-superimposable structures. These two structures are mirror images of each other and are, thus, commonly called enantiomorphs (enantio = opposite ; morph = form) Hence, optical isomerism (which occurs due to these same mirror-image properties) is now commonly referred to as enantiomerism

Enantiopure compounds refer to samples having, within the limits of detection, molecules of only one chirality.

Stereocenter

A stereocenter is an atom, bearing groups such that an interchanging of any two groups leads to a stereoisomer.

A chirality center is a stereocenter consisting of an atom holding a set of ligands (atoms or groups of atoms) in a spatial arrangement which is not superposable on its mirror image. A chiral center is a generalized extension of an asymmetric carbon atom, which is a carbon atom bonded to four different entities, such that an interchanging of any two groups gives rise to an enantiomer.

Absolute configuration

An absolute configuration in stereochemistry is the spatial arrangement of the atoms of a chiral molecular entity and its stereochemical description e.g. R or S.

Absolute configurations for a chiral molecule (in pure form) are most often obtained by X-ray crystallography. All enantiomerically pure chiral molecules crystallise in one of the 65 Sohncke Groups (Chiral Space Groups).

Alternative techniques are Optical rotatory dispersion, vibrational circular dichroism and the use of chiral shift reagents in proton NMR.

Polarimeter

A polarimeter is a scientific instrument used to measure the angle of rotation caused by passing polarized light through an optically active substance.

Some chemical substances are optically active, and polarized (aka unidirectional) light will rotate either to the left (counter-clockwise) or right (clockwise) when passed through these substances. The amount by which the light is rotated is known as the angle of rotation.

Glucuronic acid

Glucuronic acid is a carboxylic acid. Its structure is similar to that of glucose. However, glucuronic acid's sixth carbon is oxidized to a carboxylic acid.

Glucuronic acid is common in carbohydrate chains of proteoglycans. It is part of mucous animal secretions (such as saliva), cell glycocalyx and intercellular matrix (for instance hyaluronan).

Glutamic acid

Glutamic acid is one of the 20-22 proteinogenic amino acids, and its codons are GAA and GAG. It is a non-essential amino acid. The carboxylate anions and salts of glutamic acid are known as glutamates. In neuroscience, glutamate is an important neurotransmitter that plays a key role in long-term potentiation and is important for learning and memory.

Specific rotation

In stereochemistry, the specific rotation of a chemical compound $[\alpha]$ is defined as the observed angle of optical rotation α when plane-polarized light is passed through a sample with a path length of 1 decimeter and a sample concentration of 1 gram per 1 millilitre. It is the main property used to quantify the chirality of a molecular species or a mineral. The specific rotation of a pure material is an intrinsic property of that material at a given wavelength and temperature.

Racemic mixture

In chemistry, a racemic mixture, is one that has equal amounts of left- and right-handed enantiomers of a chiral molecule. The first known racemic mixture was 'racemic acid', which Louis Pasteur found to be a mixture of the two enantiomeric isomers of tartaric acid.

A racemic mixture is denoted by the prefix (±)- or dl- (for sugars the prefix dl- may be used), indicating an equal (1:1) mixture of dextro and levo isomers.

Racemization

In chemistry, racemization refers to the converting of an enantiomerically pure mixture (one where only one enantiomer is present) into a mixture where more than one of the enantiomers are present. If the racemization results in a mixture where the enantiomers are present in equal quantities, the resulting sample is described as racemic or a racemate.

Chiral molecules have two forms (at each point of asymmetry), which differ in their optical characteristics: The levorotatory form (the (−)-form) will rotate the plane of polarization of a beam of light to the left, whereas the dextrorotatory form (the (+)-form) will rotate the plane of polarization of a beam of light to the right.

Chapter 6. PRINCIPLES OF STEREOCHEMISTRY

CHAPTER HIGHLIGHTS & NOTES: KEY TERMS, PEOPLE, PLACES, CONCEPTS

Thalidomide

Thalidomide is a sedative drug introduced in the late 1950s that was used to treat morning sickness. It was sold from 1957 until 1961, when it was withdrawn after being found to be a cause of birth defects. Modern uses of thalidomide include treating multiple myeloma in combination with dexamethasone, and erythema nodosum leprosum, with strict controls on its use to prevent birth defects.

Meso compound

A meso compound is a non-optically active member of a set of stereoisomers, at least two of which are optically active. This means that despite containing two or more stereocenters (chiral centers) it is not chiral. A meso compound is superimposable on its mirror image, and it does not produce a '(+)' or '(-)' reading when analyzed with a polarimeter.

Electrocyclic reaction

In organic chemistry, an electrocyclic reaction is a type of pericyclic rearrangement where the net result is one pi bond being converted into one sigma bond or vice-versa. These reactions are usually categorized by the following criteria:•Reactions can be either photochemical or thermal.•Reactions can be either ring-opening or ring-closing (electrocyclization).•Depending on the type of reaction (photochemical or thermal) and the number of pi electrons, the reaction can happen through either a conrotatory and disrotatory mechanism.•The type of rotation determines whether the cis or trans isomer of the product will be formed.Classical Examples

The Nazarov cyclization reaction is a named electrocyclic reaction converting divinylketones to cyclopentenones.

A classic example is the thermal ring-opening reaction of 3,4-dimethylcyclobutene.

Sigmatropic reaction

A sigmatropic reaction in organic chemistry is a Pericyclic reaction wherein the net result is one σ-bond is changed to another σ-bond in an uncatalyzed intramolecular process. The name sigmatropic is the result of a compounding of the long-established sigma designation from single carbon-carbon bonds and the Greek word tropos, meaning turn. In this type of rearrangement reaction, a substituent moves from one part of a π-bonded system to another part in an intramolecular reaction with simultaneous rearrangement of the π system.

Tartaric acid

Tartaric acid is a white crystalline diprotic organic acid. It occurs naturally in many plants, particularly grapes, bananas, and tamarinds; is commonly combined with baking soda to function as a leavening agent in recipes, and is one of the main acids found in wine. It is added to other foods to give a sour taste, and is used as an antioxidant.

Steric effects

Steric effects arise from the fact that each atom within a molecule occupies a certain amount of space. If atoms are brought too close together, there is an associated cost in energy due to overlapping electron clouds , and this may affect the molecule's preferred shape (conformation) and reactivity. Steric hindrance

Pseudoephedrine

Pseudoephedrine is a sympathomimetic drug of the phenethylamine and amphetamine chemical classes. It may be used as a nasal/sinus decongestant, as a stimulant, or as a wakefulness-promoting agent.

The salts pseudoephedrine hydrochloride and pseudoephedrine sulfate are found in many over-the-counter preparations, either as a single ingredient or (more commonly) in combination with antihistamines, guaifenesin, dextromethorphan, paracetamol (acetaminophen), or an NSAID (such as aspirin or ibuprofen).

CHAPTER QUIZ: KEY TERMS, PEOPLE, PLACES, CONCEPTS

1. A _________ is a non-optically active member of a set of stereoisomers, at least two of which are optically active. This means that despite containing two or more stereocenters (chiral centers) it is not chiral. A _________ is superimposable on its mirror image, and it does not produce a '(+)' or '(-)' reading when analyzed with a polarimeter.

   a. Mutarotation
   b. Natta projection
   c. Meso compound
   d. Noyori asymmetric hydrogenation

2. A _________ is an atom, bearing groups such that an interchanging of any two groups leads to a stereoisomer.

   A chirality center is a _________ consisting of an atom holding a set of ligands (atoms or groups of atoms) in a spatial arrangement which is not superposable on its mirror image. A chiral center is a generalized extension of an asymmetric carbon atom, which is a carbon atom bonded to four different entities, such that an interchanging of any two groups gives rise to an enantiomer.

   a. Stereoselectivity
   b. Stereospecificity
   c. Stereocenter
   d. Strain

3. . _________ is one of the 20-22 proteinogenic amino acids, and its codons are GAA and GAG. It is a non-essential amino acid. The carboxylate anions and salts of _________ are known as glutamates. In neuroscience, glutamate is an important neurotransmitter that plays a key role in long-term potentiation and is important for learning and memory.

   a. Glutamic acid
   b. Histamine
   c. HTR3A

4. _________, a subdiscipline of chemistry, involves the study of the relative spatial arrangement of atoms within molecules. An important branch of _________ is the study of chiral molecules.

   _________ is also known as 3D chemistry because the prefix 'stereo-' means 'three-dimensionality'.

   a. Bailar twist
   b. Capped square antiprismatic molecular geometry
   c. Chiral auxiliary
   d. Stereochemistry

5. _________ is a carboxylic acid. Its structure is similar to that of glucose. However, _________'s sixth carbon is oxidized to a carboxylic acid.

   _________ is common in carbohydrate chains of proteoglycans. It is part of mucous animal secretions (such as saliva), cell glycocalyx and intercellular matrix (for instance hyaluronan).

   a. 1,2-Dioxetanedione
   b. Allylic strain
   c. Anomer
   d. Glucuronic acid

ANSWER KEY
Chapter 6. PRINCIPLES OF STEREOCHEMISTRY

1. c

2. c

3. a

4. d

5. d

CHAPTER OUTLINE: KEY TERMS, PEOPLE, PLACES, CONCEPTS

______ Cyclic compound

______ Cyclohexane

______ Methylcyclohexane

______ Dimethylallyl pyrophosphate

______ Angle strain

______ Bent bond

______ Cubane

______ Polycyclic compound

______ Tetrahedrane

______ Cholesterol

______ Progesterone

______ Steroid

______ Methyl group

______ Marker degradation

______ Stereochemistry

______ Addition reaction

______ Substitution reaction

______ Heck reaction

Chapter 7. CYCLIC COMPOUNDS STEREOCHEMISTRY OF REACTIONS

CHAPTER HIGHLIGHTS & NOTES: KEY TERMS, PEOPLE, PLACES, CONCEPTS

Cyclic compound

In chemistry, a cyclic compound is a compound in which a series of atoms is connected to form a loop or ring. While the vast majority of cyclic compounds are organic, a few inorganic substances form cyclic compounds as well, including sulfur, silanes, phosphanes, phosphoric acid, and triboric acid. Cyclic compounds may or may not be aromatic.

Cyclohexane

Cyclohexane is a cycloalkane with the molecular formula C_6H_{12}. Cyclohexane is used as a nonpolar solvent for the chemical industry, and also as a raw material for the industrial production of adipic acid and caprolactam, both of which being intermediates used in the production of nylon. On an industrial scale, cyclohexane is produced by reacting benzene with hydrogen.

Methylcyclohexane

Methylcyclohexane is a colourless liquid with a faint benzene-like odour. Its molecular formula is C_7H_{14}. Methylcyclohexane is used in organic synthesis and as a solvent for cellulose ethers.

Dimethylallyl pyrophosphate

Dimethylallyl pyrophosphate (DMAPP) is an intermediate product of both mevalonic acid (MVA) pathway and DOXP/MEP pathway. It is an isomer of isopentenyl pyrophosphate (IPP) and exists in virtually all life forms. The enzyme isopentenyl pyrophosphate isomerase catalyzes the isomerization of DMAPP from IPP.

Precursor of DMAPP in the MVA pathway is mevalonic acid, and 2-C-methyl-D-erythritol-e-P in the MEP/DOXP pathway.

Angle strain

Angle strain, is the resistance associated with bond angle compression or bond angle expansion. It occurs when bond angles deviate from the ideal bond angles to achieve maximum bond strength in a specific chemical conformation. Angle strain typically affects cyclic molecules because non-cyclic molecules will thermodynamically conform to the most favorable stable state.

Bent bond

Bent bond, is a term in organic chemistry that refers to a type of covalent chemical bond with a geometry somewhat reminiscent of a banana. The term itself is a general representation of electron density or configuration resembling a similar 'bent' structure within small ring molecules, such as cyclopropane (C_3H_6) or as a representation of double or triple bonds within a compound that is an alternative to the sigma and pi bond model.

Small cyclic molecules

Bent bonds are a special type of chemical bonding in which the ordinary hybridization state of two atoms making up a chemical bond are modified with increased or decreased s-orbital character in order to accommodate a particular molecular geometry.

Cubane	Cubane is a synthetic hydrocarbon molecule that consists of eight carbon atoms arranged at the corners of a cube, with one hydrogen atom attached to each carbon atom. A solid crystalline substance, cubane is one of the Platonic hydrocarbons. It was first synthesized in 1964 by Philip Eaton, a professor of chemistry at the University of Chicago.
Polycyclic compound	In organic chemistry, a polycyclic compound is a cyclic compound with more than one hydrocarbon loop or ring structures (benzene rings). In general, the term includes all polycyclic aromatic compounds, including the polycyclic aromatic hydrocarbons, the heterocyclic aromatic compounds containing sulfur, nitrogen, oxygen, or another non-carbon atoms, and substituted derivatives of these.
Tetrahedrane	Tetrahedrane is a platonic hydrocarbon with chemical formula C_4H_4 and a tetrahedral structure. Extreme angle strain (carbon bond angles deviate considerably from the tetrahedral bond angle of 109.5°) prevents this molecule from forming naturally. In 1978, Günther Maier prepared a stable tetrahedrane derivative with four tert-butyl substituents.
Cholesterol	Cholesterol is an organic chemical substance classified as a waxy steroid of fat. It is an essential structural component of mammalian cell membranes and is required to establish proper membrane permeability and fluidity. In addition to its importance within cells, cholesterol is an important component in the hormonal systems of the body for the manufacture of bile acids, steroid hormones, and vitamin D. Cholesterol is the principal sterol synthesized by animals; in vertebrates it is formed predominantly in the liver.
Progesterone	Progesterone also known as P4 (pregn-4-ene-3,20-dione) is a C-21 steroid hormone involved in the female menstrual cycle, pregnancy (supports gestation) and embryogenesis of humans and other species. Progesterone belongs to a class of hormones called progestogens, and is the major naturally occurring human progestogen. Progesterone is commonly manufactured from the yam family, Dioscorea.
Steroid	A steroid is a type of organic compound that contains a characteristic arrangement of four cycloalkane rings that are joined to each other. Examples of steroids include the dietary fat cholesterol, the sex hormones estradiol and testosterone, and the anti-inflammatory drug dexamethasone. The core of steroids is composed of twenty carbon atoms bonded together that take the form of four fused rings: three cyclohexane rings (designated as rings A, B, and C in the figure to the right) and one cyclopentane ring (the D ring).

Chapter 7. CYCLIC COMPOUNDS STEREOCHEMISTRY OF REACTIONS

CHAPTER HIGHLIGHTS & NOTES: KEY TERMS, PEOPLE, PLACES, CONCEPTS

Methyl group

Methyl group is an alkyl derived from methane, containing one carbon atom bonded to three hydrogen atoms --CH_3. The group is often abbreviated Me. Such hydrocarbon groups occur in many organic compounds.

Marker degradation

The Marker degradation is a three-step synthetic route in steroid chemistry developed by American chemist Russell Earl Marker in 1938-40. It is used for the production of cortisone and mammalian sex hormones (progesterone, estradiol, etc). from plant steroids, and established Mexico as a world center for steroid production in the years immediately after World War II. The discovery of the Marker degradation allowed the production of substantial quantities of steroid hormones for the first time, and was fundamental in the development of the contraceptive pill and corticosteroid anti-inflammatory drugs. In 1999, the American Chemical Society and the Sociedad Química de México named the route as a National Historic Chemical Landmark.

Stereochemistry

Stereochemistry, a subdiscipline of chemistry, involves the study of the relative spatial arrangement of atoms within molecules. An important branch of stereochemistry is the study of chiral molecules.

Stereochemistry is also known as 3D chemistry because the prefix 'stereo-' means 'three-dimensionality'.

Addition reaction

An addition reaction, in organic chemistry, is in its simplest terms an organic reaction where two or more molecules combine to form a larger one.

Addition reactions are limited to chemical compounds that have multiple bonds, such as molecules with carbon-carbon double bonds (alkenes), or with triple bonds (alkynes). Molecules containing carbon--hetero double bonds like carbonyl (C=O) groups, or imine (C=N) groups, can undergo addition as they too have double bond character.

Substitution reaction

In a substitution reaction, a functional group in a particular chemical compound is replaced by another group. In organic chemistry, the electrophilic and nucleophilic substitution reactions are of prime importance. Organic substitution reactions are classified in several main organic reaction types depending on whether the reagent that brings about the substitution is considered an electrophile or a nucleophile, whether a reactive intermediate involved in the reaction is a carbocation, a carbanion or a free radical or whether the substrate is aliphatic or aromatic.

Heck reaction

The Heck reaction is the chemical reaction of an unsaturated halide (or triflate) with an alkene and a base and palladium catalyst or palladium nanomaterial-based catalyst to form a substituted alkene. Together with the other palladium-catalyzed cross-coupling reactions, this reaction is of great importance, as it allows one to do substitution reactions on planar centers. It is named after Tsutomu Mizoroki and Richard F.

CHAPTER QUIZ: KEY TERMS, PEOPLE, PLACES, CONCEPTS

1. The _________ is a three-step synthetic route in steroid chemistry developed by American chemist Russell Earl Marker in 1938-40. It is used for the production of cortisone and mammalian sex hormones (progesterone, estradiol, etc). from plant steroids, and established Mexico as a world center for steroid production in the years immediately after World War II. The discovery of the _________ allowed the production of substantial quantities of steroid hormones for the first time, and was fundamental in the development of the contraceptive pill and corticosteroid anti-inflammatory drugs. In 1999, the American Chemical Society and the Sociedad Química de México named the route as a National Historic Chemical Landmark.

   a. Strecker degradation
   b. Von Braun amide degradation
   c. Weerman degradation
   d. Marker degradation

2. _________ is a synthetic hydrocarbon molecule that consists of eight carbon atoms arranged at the corners of a cube, with one hydrogen atom attached to each carbon atom. A solid crystalline substance, _________ is one of the Platonic hydrocarbons. It was first synthesized in 1964 by Philip Eaton, a professor of chemistry at the University of Chicago.

   a. Cuneane
   b. Cyclophane
   c. Decyne
   d. Cubane

3. _________ is a cycloalkane with the molecular formula C_6H_{12}. _________ is used as a nonpolar solvent for the chemical industry, and also as a raw material for the industrial production of adipic acid and caprolactam, both of which being intermediates used in the production of nylon. On an industrial scale, _________ is produced by reacting benzene with hydrogen.

   a. Cyclononane
   b. Cyclohexane
   c. 8-Cyclopentyl-1,3-dimethylxanthine
   d. Cycloundecane

4. _________, is the resistance associated with bond angle compression or bond angle expansion. It occurs when bond angles deviate from the ideal bond angles to achieve maximum bond strength in a specific chemical conformation. _________ typically affects cyclic molecules because non-cyclic molecules will thermodynamically conform to the most favorable stable state.

   a. Aroma compound
   b. Arrow pushing
   c. Angle strain
   d. Immobilized enzyme

5. . _________ (DMAPP) is an intermediate product of both mevalonic acid (MVA) pathway and DOXP/MEP pathway. It is an isomer of isopentenyl pyrophosphate (IPP) and exists in virtually all life forms. The enzyme isopentenyl pyrophosphate isomerase catalyzes the isomerization of DMAPP from IPP.

Precursor of DMAPP in the MVA pathway is mevalonic acid, and 2-C-methyl-D-erythritol-e-P in the MEP/DOXP pathway.

a. -4-Hydroxy-3-methyl-but-2-enyl pyrophosphate
b. 3-Methylbutanoic acid
c. Prenol
d. Dimethylallyl pyrophosphate

ANSWER KEY
Chapter 7. CYCLIC COMPOUNDS STEREOCHEMISTRY OF REACTIONS

1. d
2. d
3. b
4. c
5. d

CHAPTER OUTLINE: KEY TERMS, PEOPLE, PLACES, CONCEPTS

_______________ Alcohol

_______________ Gabriel synthesis

_______________ Grignard reaction

_______________ Alkylating antineoplastic agent

_______________ Carboxylic acid

_______________ Allyl group

_______________ Ether

_______________ Phenyl group

_______________ Sulfide

_______________ Thiol

_______________ Iodoacetic acid

_______________ Furan

_______________ Heterocyclic compound

_______________ Styrene oxide

_______________ Thiophene

_______________ Claisen rearrangement

_______________ Dimethyl ether

_______________ Peptide synthesis

_______________ Molecular orbital

______ Dimethylallyl pyrophosphate

______ Ionic compound

______ Solvation

______ Solubility

______ Cell membrane

______ Fatty acid

______ Lipid

______ Phospholipid

______ Phosphatidylethanolamine

______ Choline

______ Lecithin

______ Phosphatidylcholine

______ Phosphatidylserine

______ Partition coefficient

______ Crown ether

______ Ionophore

______ Cryptand

______ Host-guest chemistry

______ Nonactin

CHAPTER OUTLINE: KEY TERMS, PEOPLE, PLACES, CONCEPTS

_______________ Alkoxide

_______________ Ion channel

_______________ Isoelectric point

_______________ Sodium amide

_______________ Sodium hydride

_______________ Thioether

_______________ Polar effect

_______________ Boron trifluoride

_______________ Grignard reagents

_______________ Organolithium reagent

_______________ Carbanion

_______________ Free-radical halogenation

_______________ Clemmensen reduction

_______________ Halothane

_______________ Ozone layer

_______________ Disulfide bond

_______________ Absolute configuration

_______________ Ethylene oxide

CHAPTER HIGHLIGHTS & NOTES: KEY TERMS, PEOPLE, PLACES, CONCEPTS

Alcohol

In chemistry, an alcohol is an organic compound in which the hydroxyl functional group (-OH) is bound to a carbon atom. In particular, this carbon center should be saturated, having single bonds to three other atoms.

An important class of alcohols are the simple acyclic alcohols, the general formula for which is $C_nH_{2n+1}OH$. Of those, ethanol (C_2H_5OH) is the type of alcohol found in alcoholic beverages, and in common speech the word alcohol refers specifically to ethanol.

Gabriel synthesis

The Gabriel synthesis is named for the German chemist Siegmund Gabriel. Traditionally, it is a chemical reaction that transforms primary alkyl halides into primary amines using potassium phthalimide.

The Gabriel reaction has since been generalized to include the alkylation of sulfonamides and imides, followed by deprotection, to obtain amines .

Grignard reaction

The Grignard reaction is an organometallic chemical reaction in which alkyl- or aryl-magnesium halides (Grignard reagents) add to a carbonyl group in an aldehyde or ketone. This reaction is an important tool for the formation of carbon-carbon bonds. The reaction of an organic halide with magnesium is not a Grignard reaction, but provides a Grignard reagent.

Alkylating antineoplastic agent

An alkylating antineoplastic agent is an alkylating agent used in cancer treatment that attaches an alkyl group (C_nH_{2n+1}) to DNA.

The alkyl group is attached to the guanine base of DNA, at the number 7 nitrogen atom of the purine ring.

Since cancer cells, in general, proliferate faster and with less error-correcting than healthy cells, cancer cells are more sensitive to DNA damage -- such as being alkylated. Alkylating agents are used to treat several cancers.

Carboxylic acid

Carboxylic acids ( ) are organic acids characterized by the presence of at least one carboxyl group. The general formula of a carboxylic acid is R-COOH, where R is some monovalent functional group. A carboxyl group (or carboxy) is a functional group consisting of a carbonyl (RR'C=O) and a hydroxyl (R-O-H), which has the formula -C(=O)OH, usually written as -COOH or $-CO_2H$.

Carboxylic acids are Brønsted-Lowry acids because they are proton (H^+) donors.

Allyl group

An allyl group is a substituent with the structural formula $H_2C{=}CH{-}CH_2R$, where R is the connection to the rest of the molecule. It is made up of a methylene ($-CH_2-$), attached to a vinyl group ($-CH{=}CH_2$).

Ether

Wikimedia.org/wikipedia/commons/thumb/5/51/Ether-%28general%29.png/150px-Ether-%28general%29.png' width='150' height='75' />

Ethers ( ) are a class of organic compounds that contain an ether group -- an oxygen atom connected to two alkyl or aryl groups -- of general formula R-O-R'. A typical example is the solvent and anesthetic diethyl ether, commonly referred to simply as 'ether' (CH_3-CH_2-O-CH_2-CH_3). Ethers are common in organic chemistry and pervasive in biochemistry, as they are common linkages in carbohydrates and lignin.

Phenyl group

In organic chemistry, the phenyl group is a cyclic group of atoms with the formula C_6H_5. Phenyl groups are closely related to benzene. Phenyl groups have six carbon atoms bonded together in a hexagonal planar ring, five of which are bonded to individual hydrogen atoms, with the remaining carbon bonded to a substituent.

Sulfide

A sulfide is an anion of sulfur in its lowest oxidation state of 2-. Sulfide is also a slightly archaic term for thioethers, a common type of organosulfur compound that are well known for their bad odors.

The dianion S^{2-} exists only in strongly alkaline aqueous solutions.

Thiol

In organic chemistry, a thiol is an organosulfur compound that contains a carbon-bonded sulfhydryl (-C-SH or R-SH) group (where R represents an alkane, alkene, or other carbon-containing group of atoms). Thiols are the sulfur analogue of alcohols (that is, sulfur takes the place of oxygen in the hydroxyl group of an alcohol), and the word is a portmanteau of 'thio' + 'alcohol,' with the first word deriving from Greek θε?ον ('thion') = 'sulfur'. The -SH functional group itself is referred to as either a thiol group or a sulfhydryl group.

Iodoacetic acid

Iodoacetic acid is a derivative of acetic acid. It is a toxic compound, because, like many alkyl halides, it is an alkylating agent. It reacts with cysteine residues in proteins.

Furan

Furan is a heterocyclic organic compound, consisting of a five-membered aromatic ring with four carbon atoms and one oxygen. The class of compounds containing such rings are also referred to as furans.

Furan is a colorless, flammable, highly volatile liquid with a boiling point close to room temperature.

Heterocyclic compound

A heterocyclic compound is a cyclic compound that has atoms of at least two different elements as members of its ring(s). The counterparts of heterocyclic compounds are homocyclic compounds, the rings of which are made of a single element.

Styrene oxide	Styrene oxide is an epoxide derived from styrene. It may be prepared by epoxidation of styrene with peroxybenzoic acid, in the Prilezhaev reaction: Styrene oxide is a main metabolite of styrene in humans or animals, resulting from oxidation by cytochrome P450. It is considered toxic, mutagenic, and possibly carcinogenic. Styrene oxide is subsequently hydrolyzed in vivo to styrene glycol by epoxide hydrolase.
Thiophene	Thiophene is a heterocyclic compound with the formula C_4H_4S. Consisting of a flat five-membered ring, it is aromatic as indicated by its extensive substitution reactions. Related to thiophene are benzothiophene and dibenzothiophene, containing the thiophene ring fused with one and two benzene rings, respectively. Compounds analogous to thiophene include furan (C_4H_4O) and pyrrole (C_4H_4NH).
Claisen rearrangement	The Claisen rearrangement is a powerful carbon-carbon bond-forming chemical reaction discovered by Rainer Ludwig Claisen. The heating of an allyl vinyl ether will initiate a [3,3]-sigmatropic rearrangement to give a γ,δ-unsaturated carbonyl. Discovered in 1912, the Claisen rearrangement is the first recorded example of a [3,3]-sigmatropic rearrangement.
Dimethyl ether	Dimethyl ether also known as methoxymethane, is the organic compound with the formula CH_3OCH_3. The simplest ether, it is a colourless gas that is a useful precursor to other organic compounds and an aerosol propellant. Today, DME is primarily produced by converting hydrocarbons sourced from natural gas or coal via gasification to synthesis gas (syngas).
Peptide synthesis	In organic chemistry, peptide synthesis is the production of peptides, which are organic compounds in which multiple amino acids are linked via amide bonds which are also known as peptide bonds. The biological process of producing long peptides (proteins) is known as protein biosynthesis. Peptides are synthesized by coupling the carboxyl group or C-terminus of one amino acid to the amino group or N-terminus of another.
Molecular orbital	In chemistry, a molecular orbital is a mathematical function describing the wave-like behavior of an electron in a molecule. This function can be used to calculate chemical and physical properties such as the probability of finding an electron in any specific region. The term 'orbital' was first used in English by Robert S. Mulliken as the English translation of Schrödinger's 'Eigenfunktion'.

Dimethylallyl pyrophosphate	Dimethylallyl pyrophosphate (DMAPP) is an intermediate product of both mevalonic acid (MVA) pathway and DOXP/MEP pathway. It is an isomer of isopentenyl pyrophosphate (IPP) and exists in virtually all life forms. The enzyme isopentenyl pyrophosphate isomerase catalyzes the isomerization of DMAPP from IPP. Precursor of DMAPP in the MVA pathway is mevalonic acid, and 2-C-methyl-D-erythritol-e-P in the MEP/DOXP pathway.
Ionic compound	In chemistry, an ionic compound is a chemical compound in which ions are held together in a lattice structure by ionic bonds. Usually, the positively charged portion consists of metal cations and the negatively charged portion is an anion or polyatomic ion. Ions in ionic compounds are held together by the electrostatic forces between oppositely charged bodies.
Solvation	Solvation, also sometimes called dissolution, is the process of attraction and association of molecules of a solvent with molecules or ions of a solute. As ions dissolve in a solvent they spread out and become surrounded by solvent molecules. By an IUPAC definition, solvation is an interaction of a solute with the solvent, which leads to stabilization of the solute species in the solution.
Solubility	Solubility is the property of a solid, liquid, or gaseous chemical substance called solute to dissolve in a solid, liquid, or gaseous solvent to form a homogeneous solution of the solute in the solvent. The solubility of a substance fundamentally depends on the used solvent as well as on temperature and pressure. The extent of the solubility of a substance in a specific solvent is measured as the saturation concentration where adding more solute does not increase the concentration of the solution.
Cell membrane	The cell membrane is a biological membrane that separates the interior of all cells from the outside environment. The cell membrane is selectively permeable to ions and organic molecules and controls the movement of substances in and out of cells. It basically protects the cell from outside forces.
Fatty acid	In chemistry, especially biochemistry, a fatty acid is a carboxylic acid with a long aliphatic tail (chain), which is either saturated or unsaturated. Most naturally occurring fatty acids have a chain of an even number of carbon atoms, from 4 to 28. Fatty acids are usually derived from triglycerides or phospholipids. When they are not attached to other molecules, they are known as 'free' fatty acids.
Lipid	Lipids constitute a broad group of naturally occurring molecules that include fats, waxes, sterols, fat-soluble vitamins (such as vitamins A, D, E, and K), monoglycerides, diglycerides, triglycerides, phospholipids, and others.

	The main biological functions of lipids include energy storage, as structural components of cell membranes, and as important signaling molecules. Lipids may be broadly defined as hydrophobic or amphiphilic small molecules; the amphiphilic nature of some lipids allows them to form structures such as vesicles, liposomes, or membranes in an aqueous environment.
Phospholipid	Phospholipids are a class of lipids that are a major component of all cell membranes as they can form lipid bilayers. Most phospholipids contain a diglyceride, a phosphate group, and a simple organic molecule such as choline; one exception to this rule is sphingomyelin, which is derived from sphingosine instead of glycerol. The first phospholipid identified as such in biological tissues was lecithin, or phosphatidylcholine, in the egg yolk, by Theodore Nicolas Gobley, a French chemist and pharmacist, in 1847. The structure of the phospholipid molecule generally consists of hydrophobic tails and a hydrophilic head.
Phosphatidylethanolamine	Phosphatidylethanolamine is a lipid found in biological membranes. It is synthesized by the addition of CDP-ethanolamine to diglyceride, releasing CMP. S-adenosyl methionine can subsequently methylate the amine of phosphatidyl ethanolamine to yield phosphatidyl choline. Cephalin is a phospholipid, which is a lipid derivative.
Choline	Choline is a water-soluble essential nutrient. It is usually grouped within the B-complex vitamins. Choline generally refers to the various quaternary ammonium salts containing the N,N,N-trimethylethanolammonium cation.
Lecithin	Lecithin is a generic term to designate any group of yellow-brownish fatty substances occurring in animal and plant tissues composed of phosphoric acid, choline, fatty acids, glycerol, glycolipids, triglycerides, and phospholipids (e.g., phosphatidylcholine, phosphatidylethanolamine, and phosphatidylinositol). Lecithin was first isolated in 1846 by the French chemist and pharmacist Theodore Gobley; in 1850 he named the phosphatidylcholine léchithine. Gobley originally isolated lecithin from egg yolk--λ?κιθος (lekithos) is 'egg yolk' in ancient Greek--and established the complete chemical formula of phosphatidylcholine in 1874; in between, he had demonstrated the presence of lecithin in a variety of biological matters, including venous blood, bile, human brain tissue, fish eggs, fish roe, chicken and sheep brain.
Phosphatidylcholine	Phosphatidylcholines (PC) are a class of phospholipids that incorporate choline as a headgroup. They are a major component of biological membranes and can be easily obtained from a variety of readily available sources such as egg yolk or soy beans from which they are mechanically extracted or chemically extracted using hexane.

Phosphatidylserine

Phosphatidylserine is a phospholipid component, usually kept on the inner-leaflet (the cytosolic side) of cell membranes by an enzyme called flippase. When a cell undergoes apoptosis, phosphatidylserine is no longer restricted to the cytosolic part of the membrane, but becomes exposed on the surface of the cell. Memory and cognition

Early studies of phosphatidylserine distilled the chemical from bovine brain.

Partition coefficient

In chemistry and the pharmaceutical sciences, a partition- (P) or distribution -(D) coefficient is the ratio of concentrations of a compound in the two phases of a mixture of two immiscible solvents at equilibrium. The terms 'gas/liquid partition coefficient' and 'air/water partition coefficient' are sometimes used for dimensionless forms of the Henry's law constant. Hence these coefficients are a measure of differential solubility of the compound between these two solvents.

Crown ether

Crown ethers are cyclic chemical compounds that consist of a ring containing several ether groups. The most common crown ethers are oligomers of ethylene oxide, the repeating unit being ethyleneoxy, i.e., $-CH_2CH_2O-$. Important members of this series are the tetramer (n = 4), the pentamer (n = 5), and the hexamer (n = 6).

Ionophore

An ionophore is a lipid-soluble molecule usually synthesized by microorganisms to transport ions across the lipid bilayer of the cell membrane. There are two broad classifications of ionophores. •Chemical compounds (mobile ion carriers) that bind to a particular ion, shielding its charge from the surrounding environment, and thus facilitating its crossing of the hydrophobic interior of the lipid membrane.•Channel formers that introduce a hydrophilic pore into the membrane, allowing ions to pass through while avoiding contact with the membrane's hydrophobic interior.Mechanism of action

Ionophores disrupt transmembrane ion concentration gradients, required for the proper functioning and survival of microorganisms, and thus have antibiotic properties.

Cryptand

Cryptands are a family of synthetic bi- and polycyclic multidentate ligands for a variety of cations. The Nobel Prize for Chemistry in 1987 was given to Donald J. Cram, Jean-Marie Lehn, and Charles J. Pedersen for their efforts in discovering and determining uses of cryptands and crown ethers, thus launching the now flourishing field of supramolecular chemistry. The term cryptand implies that this ligand binds substrates in a crypt, interring the guest as in a burial.

Host-guest chemistry

In supramolecular chemistry, host-guest chemistry describes complexes that are composed of two or more molecules or ions that are held together in unique structural relationships by forces other than those of full covalent bonds. Host-guest chemistry encompasses the idea of molecular recognition and interactions through noncovalent bonding.

CHAPTER HIGHLIGHTS & NOTES: KEY TERMS, PEOPLE, PLACES, CONCEPTS

Nonactin

Nonactin is a member of a family of naturally occurring cyclic ionophores known as the macrotetrolide antibiotics. The other members of nactins homologous family are monactin, dinactin, trinactin and tetranactin which are all neutral ionophoric substances and higher homologs of nonactin. Collectively, this class is known as the nactins.

Alkoxide

An alkoxide is the conjugate base of an alcohol and therefore consists of an organic group bonded to a negatively charged oxygen atom. They can be written as RO^-, where R is the organic substituent. Alkoxides are strong bases and, when R is not bulky, good nucleophiles and good ligands.

Ion channel

Ion channels are pore-forming proteins that help establish and control the voltage gradient across the plasma membrane of cells by allowing the flow of ions down their electrochemical gradient. They are present in the membranes that surround all biological cells. The study of ion channels involves many scientific techniques such as voltage clamp electrophysiology (in particular patch clamp), immunohistochemistry, and RT-PCR.

Ion channels regulate the flow of ions across the membrane in all cells.

Isoelectric point

The isoelectric point sometimes abbreviated to IEP, is the pH at which a particular molecule or surface carries no net electrical charge.

Amphoteric molecules called zwitterions contain both positive and negative charges depending on the functional groups present in the molecule. The net charge on the molecule is affected by pH of their surrounding environment and can become more positively or negatively charged due to the loss or gain of protons (H^+).

Sodium amide

Sodium amide, commonly called sodamide, is the chemical compound with the formula $NaNH_2$. This solid, which is dangerously reactive toward water, is white when pure, but commercial samples are typically gray due to the presence of small quantities of metallic iron from the manufacturing process. Such impurities do not usually affect the utility of the reagent.

Sodium hydride

Sodium hydride is the chemical compound with the empirical formula NaH. It is primarily used as a strong base in organic synthesis. NaH is representative of the saline hydrides, meaning it is a salt-like hydride, composed of Na^+ and H^- ions, in contrast to the more molecular hydrides such as borane, methane, ammonia and water. It is an ionic material that is insoluble in organic solvents (although soluble in molten Na), consistent with the fact that H^- remains an unknown anion in solution.

Thioether

A thioether is a functional group in organosulfur chemistry with the connectivity C-S-C as shown on right. Like many other sulfur-containing compounds, volatile thioethers have foul odors.

Polar effect

The Polar effect is the effect exerted by a substituent on modifying electrostatic forces operating on a nearby reaction center. The main contributors to the polar effect are the inductive effect, mesomeric effect and the through-space electronic field effect.

An electron withdrawing group or EWG draws electrons away from a reaction center.

Boron trifluoride

Boron trifluoride is the chemical compound with the formula BF_3. This pungent colourless toxic gas forms white fumes in moist air. It is a useful Lewis acid and a versatile building block for other boron compounds.

Grignard reagents

The Grignard reaction is an organometallic chemical reaction in which alkyl- or aryl-magnesium halides (Grignard reagents) add to a carbonyl group in an aldehyde or ketone. This reaction is an important tool for the formation of carbon-carbon bonds. The reaction of an organic halide with magnesium is not a Grignard reaction, but provides a Grignard reagent.

Organolithium reagent

An organolithium reagent is an organometallic compound with a direct bond between a carbon and a lithium atom. As the electropositive nature of lithium puts most of the charge density of the bond on the carbon atom, effectively creating a carbanion, organolithium compounds are extremely powerful bases and nucleophiles. For use as bases, butyllithiums are often used and are commercially available.

Carbanion

A carbanion is an anion in which carbon has an unshared pair of electrons and bears a negative charge usually with three substituents for a total of eight valence electrons . The carbanion exists in a trigonal pyramidal geometry. Formally a carbanion is the conjugate base of a carbon acid.

Free-radical halogenation

In organic chemistry, free-radical halogenation is a type of halogenation. This chemical reaction is typical of alkanes and alkyl-substituted aromatics under application of heat or UV light. The reaction is used for the industrial synthesis of chloroform ($CHCl_3$), dichloromethane (CH_2Cl_2), and hexachlorobutadiene.

Clemmensen reduction

Clemmensen reduction is a chemical reaction described as a reduction of ketones (or aldehydes) to alkanes using zinc amalgam and hydrochloric acid. This reaction is named after Erik Christian Clemmensen, a Danish chemist.

The Clemmensen reduction is particularly effective at reducing aryl-alkyl ketones.

Halothane

Halothane is an inhalational general anesthetic. Its IUPAC name is 2-bromo-2-chloro-1,1,1-trifluoroethane. It is the only inhalational anesthetic agent containing a bromine atom; there are several other halogenated anesthesia agents which lack the bromine atom and do contain the fluorine and chlorine atoms present in halothane.

Ozone layer	The ozone layer is a layer in Earth's atmosphere which contains relatively high concentrations of ozone (O_3). This layer absorbs 97-99% of the Sun's high frequency ultraviolet light, which is damaging to life on Earth. It is mainly located in the lower portion of the stratosphere from approximately 30 to 40 kilometres (19 to 25 mi) above Earth, though the thickness varies seasonally and geographically.
Disulfide bond	In chemistry, a disulfide bond is a covalent bond, usually derived by the coupling of two thiol groups. The linkage is also called an SS-bond or disulfide bridge. The overall connectivity is therefore R-S-S-R. The terminology is widely used in biochemistry.
Absolute configuration	An absolute configuration in stereochemistry is the spatial arrangement of the atoms of a chiral molecular entity and its stereochemical description e.g. R or S. Absolute configurations for a chiral molecule (in pure form) are most often obtained by X-ray crystallography. All enantiomerically pure chiral molecules crystallise in one of the 65 Sohncke Groups (Chiral Space Groups). Alternative techniques are Optical rotatory dispersion, vibrational circular dichroism and the use of chiral shift reagents in proton NMR. When the absolute configuration is obtained the assignment of R or S is based on the Cahn-Ingold-Prelog priority rules.
Ethylene oxide	Ethylene oxide, is the organic compound with the formula C_2H_4O. It is a cyclic ether. This means that it is composed of two alkyl groups attached to an oxygen atom in a cyclic shape (circular).

CHAPTER QUIZ: KEY TERMS, PEOPLE, PLACES, CONCEPTS

1. _________ is a derivative of acetic acid. It is a toxic compound, because, like many alkyl halides, it is an alkylating agent. It reacts with cysteine residues in proteins.

a. Iodobenzamide
b. Iodobenzene
c. Iodoacetic acid
d. Iodoform

2. In chemistry, an _________ is a chemical compound in which ions are held together in a lattice structure by ionic bonds. Usually, the positively charged portion consists of metal cations and the negatively charged portion is an anion or polyatomic ion. Ions in _________s are held together by the electrostatic forces between oppositely charged bodies.

a. Ionic compound
b. 3-Methylbutanoic acid
c. Prenol
d. Quantum chemistry

3. In organic chemistry, _________ is a type of halogenation. This chemical reaction is typical of alkanes and alkyl-substituted aromatics under application of heat or UV light. The reaction is used for the industrial synthesis of chloroform ($CHCl_3$), dichloromethane (CH_2Cl_2), and hexachlorobutadiene.

a. Free-radical reaction
b. Free-radical halogenation
c. Julia olefination
d. Kharasch addition

4. _________s are pore-forming proteins that help establish and control the voltage gradient across the plasma membrane of cells by allowing the flow of ions down their electrochemical gradient. They are present in the membranes that surround all biological cells. The study of _________s involves many scientific techniques such as voltage clamp electrophysiology (in particular patch clamp), immunohistochemistry, and RT-PCR.

_________s regulate the flow of ions across the membrane in all cells.

a. Ion current
b. Ion channel
c. Ultradian
d. Amide

5. . In chemistry, especially biochemistry, a _________ is a carboxylic acid with a long aliphatic tail (chain), which is either saturated or unsaturated. Most naturally occurring _________s have a chain of an even number of carbon atoms, from 4 to 28. _________s are usually derived from triglycerides or phospholipids. When they are not attached to other molecules, they are known as 'free' _________s.

a. Behenic acid
b. Beta oxidation

c. Bosseopentaenoic acid

d. Fatty acid

ANSWER KEY
Chapter 8. INTRODUCTION TO ALKYL HALIDES, ALCOHOLS, ETHERS, THIOLS, AND SULFIDES

1. c
2. a
3. b
4. b
5. d

Chapter 9. THE CHEMISTRY OF ALKYL HALIDES

CHAPTER OUTLINE: KEY TERMS, PEOPLE, PLACES, CONCEPTS

______ Addition reaction

______ Nucleophilic substitution

______ Carbon tetrachloride

______ Substitution reaction

______ Gabriel synthesis

______ Stereochemistry

______ Steric effects

______ Solvent effects

______ Base pair

______ Dimethylallyl pyrophosphate

______ Leaving group

______ Product-determining step

______ Elimination reaction

______ Carbene

______ Dichlorocarbene

______ Carbenoid

______ Methylene

Chapter 9. THE CHEMISTRY OF ALKYL HALIDES

CHAPTER HIGHLIGHTS & NOTES: KEY TERMS, PEOPLE, PLACES, CONCEPTS

Addition reaction

An addition reaction, in organic chemistry, is in its simplest terms an organic reaction where two or more molecules combine to form a larger one.

Addition reactions are limited to chemical compounds that have multiple bonds, such as molecules with carbon-carbon double bonds (alkenes), or with triple bonds (alkynes). Molecules containing carbon--hetero double bonds like carbonyl (C=O) groups, or imine (C=N) groups, can undergo addition as they too have double bond character.

Nucleophilic substitution

In organic and inorganic chemistry, nucleophilic substitution is a fundamental class of reactions in which an electron nucleophile selectively bonds with or attacks the positive or partially positive charge of an atom or a group of atoms called the leaving group; the positive or partially positive atom is referred to as an electrophile.

The most general form for the reaction may be given asNuc: + R-LG → R-Nuc + LG:

The electron pair (:) from the nucleophile (Nuc) attacks the substrate (R-LG) forming a new bond, while the leaving group (LG) departs with an electron pair. The principal product in this case is R-Nuc.

Carbon tetrachloride

Carbon tetrachloride, also known by many other names is the organic compound with the formula CCl_4. It was formerly widely used in fire extinguishers, as a precursor to refrigerants, and as a cleaning agent. It is a colourless liquid with a 'sweet' smell that can be detected at low levels.

Substitution reaction

In a substitution reaction, a functional group in a particular chemical compound is replaced by another group. In organic chemistry, the electrophilic and nucleophilic substitution reactions are of prime importance. Organic substitution reactions are classified in several main organic reaction types depending on whether the reagent that brings about the substitution is considered an electrophile or a nucleophile, whether a reactive intermediate involved in the reaction is a carbocation, a carbanion or a free radical or whether the substrate is aliphatic or aromatic.

Gabriel synthesis

The Gabriel synthesis is named for the German chemist Siegmund Gabriel. Traditionally, it is a chemical reaction that transforms primary alkyl halides into primary amines using potassium phthalimide.

The Gabriel reaction has since been generalized to include the alkylation of sulfonamides and imides, followed by deprotection, to obtain amines .

Stereochemistry

Stereochemistry, a subdiscipline of chemistry, involves the study of the relative spatial arrangement of atoms within molecules.

An important branch of stereochemistry is the study of chiral molecules.

Stereochemistry is also known as 3D chemistry because the prefix 'stereo-' means 'three-dimensionality'.

Steric effects

Steric effects arise from the fact that each atom within a molecule occupies a certain amount of space. If atoms are brought too close together, there is an associated cost in energy due to overlapping electron clouds , and this may affect the molecule's preferred shape (conformation) and reactivity. Steric hindrance

Steric hindrance occurs when the large size of groups within a molecule prevents chemical reactions that are observed in related molecules with smaller groups.

Solvent effects

In chemistry, solvent effects is the group of effects that a solvent has on chemical reactivity. Solvents can have an effect on solubility, stability and reaction rates and choosing the appropriate solvent allows for thermodynamic and kinetic control over a chemical reaction.

A solute dissolves in a solvent when it forms favorable interactions with the solvent.

Base pair

In molecular biology and genetics, the linking between two nitrogenous bases on opposite complementary DNA or certain types of RNA strands that are connected via hydrogen bonds is called a base pair. In the canonical Watson-Crick DNA base pairing, adenine (A) forms a base pair with thymine (T) and guanine (G) forms a base pair with cytosine (C). In RNA, thymine is replaced by uracil (U).

Dimethylallyl pyrophosphate

Dimethylallyl pyrophosphate (DMAPP) is an intermediate product of both mevalonic acid (MVA) pathway and DOXP/MEP pathway. It is an isomer of isopentenyl pyrophosphate (IPP) and exists in virtually all life forms. The enzyme isopentenyl pyrophosphate isomerase catalyzes the isomerization of DMAPP from IPP.

Precursor of DMAPP in the MVA pathway is mevalonic acid, and 2-C-methyl-D-erythritol-e-P in the MEP/DOXP pathway.

Leaving group

In chemistry, a leaving group is a molecular fragment that departs with a pair of electrons in heterolytic bond cleavage. Leaving groups can be anions or neutral molecules. Common anionic leaving groups are halides such as Cl^-, Br^-, and I^-, and sulfonate esters, such as para-toluenesulfonate ('tosylate', TsO^-).

Product-determining step

The product-determining step is the step of a chemical reaction that determines the ratio of products formed via differing reaction mechanisms that start from the same reactants.

Chapter 9. THE CHEMISTRY OF ALKYL HALIDES

CHAPTER HIGHLIGHTS & NOTES: KEY TERMS, PEOPLE, PLACES, CONCEPTS

Elimination reaction

An elimination reaction is a type of organic reaction in which two substituents are removed from a molecule in either a one or two-step mechanism. The one-step mechanism is known as the E2 reaction, and the two-step mechanism is known as the E1 reaction. The numbers do not have to do with the number of steps in the mechanism, but rather the kinetics of the reaction, bimolecular and unimolecular respectively.

Carbene

In chemistry, a carbene is a molecule containing a neutral carbon atom with a valence of two and two unshared valence electrons. The general formula is RR'C:, but the carbon can instead be double-bonded to one group. The term 'carbene' may also merely refer to the compound H_2C:, also called methylene, the parent hydride to which all other carbene compounds are related.

Dichlorocarbene

Dichlorocarbene is a carbene commonly encountered in organic chemistry. This reactive intermediate with chemical formula CCl_2 is easily available by reaction of chloroform and a base such as potassium t-butoxide or sodium hydroxide dissolved in water. A phase transfer catalyst, for instance benzyltriethylammonium bromide, is added to facilitate the migration of the hydroxide in the organic phase.

Carbenoid

In chemistry a carbenoid is a reactive intermediate that shares reaction characteristics with a carbene. In the Simmons-Smith reaction the carbenoid intermediate is a zinc / iodine complex that takes the form ofI-CH_2-Zn-I

This complex reacts with an alkene to form a cyclopropane just as a carbene would do.

Carbenoids appear as intermediates in many other reactions.

Methylene

Methylene is a carbene encountered in organic chemistry. Methylene has a non-linear triplet ground state and is thus paramagnetic. It is not stable in the gaseous state, as it is highly reactive towards itself.

1. _________, a subdiscipline of chemistry, involves the study of the relative spatial arrangement of atoms within molecules. An important branch of _________ is the study of chiral molecules.

   _________ is also known as 3D chemistry because the prefix 'stereo-' means 'three-dimensionality'.

   a. Bailar twist
   b. Stereochemistry
   c. Chiral auxiliary
   d. Chiral column chromatography

2. An _________, in organic chemistry, is in its simplest terms an organic reaction where two or more molecules combine to form a larger one.

   _________s are limited to chemical compounds that have multiple bonds, such as molecules with carbon-carbon double bonds (alkenes), or with triple bonds (alkynes). Molecules containing carbon--hetero double bonds like carbonyl (C=O) groups, or imine (C=N) groups, can undergo addition as they too have double bond character.

   a. Adduct purification
   b. Ammoxidation
   c. Appel reaction
   d. Addition reaction

3. In organic and inorganic chemistry, _________ is a fundamental class of reactions in which an electron nucleophile selectively bonds with or attacks the positive or partially positive charge of an atom or a group of atoms called the leaving group; the positive or partially positive atom is referred to as an electrophile.

   The most general form for the reaction may be given asNuc: + R-LG → R-Nuc + LG:

   The electron pair (:) from the nucleophile (Nuc) attacks the substrate (R-LG) forming a new bond, while the leaving group (LG) departs with an electron pair. The principal product in this case is R-Nuc.

   a. Partial oxidation
   b. Photodegradation
   c. Nucleophilic substitution
   d. Photoinduced electron transfer

4. . In chemistry, a _________ is a molecule containing a neutral carbon atom with a valence of two and two unshared valence electrons. The general formula is RR'C:, but the carbon can instead be double-bonded to one group. The term '_________' may also merely refer to the compound H_2C:, also called methylene, the parent hydride to which all other _________ compounds are related.

   a. Carbene analog
   b. Carbene dimerization
   c. Carbene

5. In chemistry, a _________ is a molecular fragment that departs with a pair of electrons in heterolytic bond cleavage. _________s can be anions or neutral molecules. Common anionic _________s are halides such as Cl^-, Br^-, and I^-, and sulfonate esters, such as para-toluenesulfonate ('tosylate', TsO^-).

   a. Lindemann mechanism
   b. Metamorphic reaction
   c. Migratory insertion
   d. Leaving group

ANSWER KEY
Chapter 9. THE CHEMISTRY OF ALKYL HALIDES

1. b

2. d

3. c

4. c

5. d

Chapter 10. THE CHEMISTRY OF ALCOHOLS AND THIOLS

CHAPTER OUTLINE: KEY TERMS, PEOPLE, PLACES, CONCEPTS

______ Grignard reaction

______ Hydrogen bromide

______ Hydrogen halide

______ Benzenesulfonic acid

______ Methanesulfonic acid

______ Sulfonic acid

______ P-Toluenesulfonic acid

______ Mesylate

______ Alkylating antineoplastic agent

______ Dimethyl sulfate

______ Thionyl chloride

______ Phosphorus tribromide

______ Carboxylic acid

______ Oxidation number

______ Reducing agent

______ Cumene hydroperoxide

______ Chromium trioxide

______ Pyridinium chlorochromate

______ Alcohol oxidation

Chapter 10. THE CHEMISTRY OF ALCOHOLS AND THIOLS

CHAPTER OUTLINE: KEY TERMS, PEOPLE, PLACES, CONCEPTS

______ Chromate ester

______ Ethyl group

______ Stereochemistry

______ Potassium permanganate

______ Breath test

______ Primary alcohol

______ Niacin

______ Substitution reaction

______ Group

______ Free-radical addition

______ Disulfide bond

______ Oxidation state

______ Organic reaction

______ Retrosynthetic analysis

______ Tandem mass spectrometry

______ Mass spectrometry

Grignard reaction

The Grignard reaction is an organometallic chemical reaction in which alkyl- or aryl-magnesium halides (Grignard reagents) add to a carbonyl group in an aldehyde or ketone. This reaction is an important tool for the formation of carbon-carbon bonds. The reaction of an organic halide with magnesium is not a Grignard reaction, but provides a Grignard reagent.

Hydrogen bromide

Hydrogen bromide is the diatomic molecule HBr. HBr is a gas at standard conditions. Hydrobromic acid forms upon dissolving HBr in water.

Hydrogen halide

Hydrogen halides (or hydrohalic acids) are inorganic compounds with the formula HX where X is one of the halogens: fluorine, chlorine, bromine, iodine, and astatine. Hydrogen halides are gases that dissolve in water to give acids.

The hydrogen halides are diatomic molecules with no tendency to ionize in the gas phase.

Benzenesulfonic acid

Benzenesulfonic acid is an organosulfur compound with the formula $C_6H_5SO_3H$. It is the simplest aromatic sulfonic acid. It forms colorless deliquescent sheet crystals or a white waxy solid that is soluble in water and ethanol, slightly soluble in benzene and insoluble in carbon disulfide and diethyl ether. It is often stored in the form of alkali metal salts.

Methanesulfonic acid

Methanesulfonic acid is a colorless liquid with the chemical formula CH_3SO_3H. It is the simplest of the alkylsulfonic acids. Salts and esters of methanesulfonic acid are known as mesylates. Methanesulfonic acid is used as an acid catalyst in organic reactions because it is non-volatile, strong acid that is soluble in organic solvents.

Sulfonic acid

A sulfonic acid refers to a member of the class of organosulfur compounds with the general formula $RS(=O)_2$-OH, where R is an organic alkyl or aryl group and the $S(=O)_2$-OH group a sulfonyl hydroxide. A sulfonic acid can be thought of as sulfuric acid with one hydroxyl group replaced by an organic substituent. The parent compound (with the organic substituent replaced by hydrogen) is the hypothetical compound sulfurous acid.

P-Toluenesulfonic acid

P-Toluenesulfonic acid or tosylic acid (TsOH) is an organic compound with the formula $CH_3C_6H_4SO_3H$. It is a white solid that is soluble in water, alcohols, and other polar organic solvents. The 4-$CH_3C_6H_4SO_2$- group is known as tosyl group and is often abbreviated as Ts or Tos. Most often, TsOH refers to the monohydrate, $TsOH{\cdot}H_2O$.

TsOH is a strong organic acid, about a million times stronger than benzoic acid.

Mesylate

In chemistry, a mesylate is any salt or ester of methanesulfonic acid (CH_3SO_3H). In salts, the mesylate is present as the $CH_3SO_3^-$ anion.

Chapter 10. THE CHEMISTRY OF ALCOHOLS AND THIOLS

CHAPTER HIGHLIGHTS & NOTES: KEY TERMS, PEOPLE, PLACES, CONCEPTS

Alkylating antineoplastic agent	An alkylating antineoplastic agent is an alkylating agent used in cancer treatment that attaches an alkyl group (C_nH_{2n+1}) to DNA. The alkyl group is attached to the guanine base of DNA, at the number 7 nitrogen atom of the purine ring. Since cancer cells, in general, proliferate faster and with less error-correcting than healthy cells, cancer cells are more sensitive to DNA damage -- such as being alkylated. Alkylating agents are used to treat several cancers.
Dimethyl sulfate	Dimethyl sulfate is a chemical compound with formula $(CH_3O)_2SO_2$. As the diester of methanol and sulfuric acid, its formula is often written as $(CH_3)_2SO_4$ or even Me_2SO_4, where CH_3 or Me is methyl. Me_2SO_4 is mainly used as a methylating agent in organic synthesis.
Thionyl chloride	Thionyl chloride is an inorganic compound with the formula $SOCl_2$. It is a reactive chemical reagent used in chlorination reactions. It is a colorless, distillable liquid at room temperature and pressure that decomposes above 140 °C. Thionyl chloride is sometimes confused with sulfuryl chloride, SO_2Cl_2, but the properties of these compounds differ significantly.
Phosphorus tribromide	Phosphorus tribromide is a colourless liquid with the formula PBr_3. It fumes in air due to hydrolysis and has a penetrating odour. It is widely used in the laboratory for the conversion of alcohols to alkyl bromides.
Carboxylic acid	Carboxylic acids ( ) are organic acids characterized by the presence of at least one carboxyl group. The general formula of a carboxylic acid is R-COOH, where R is some monovalent functional group. A carboxyl group (or carboxy) is a functional group consisting of a carbonyl (RR'C=O) and a hydroxyl (R-O-H), which has the formula -C(=O)OH, usually written as -COOH or $-CO_2H$. Carboxylic acids are Brønsted-Lowry acids because they are proton (H^+) donors.
Oxidation number	In coordination chemistry, the oxidation number of a central atom in a coordination compound is the charge that it would have if all the ligands were removed along with the electron pairs that were shared with the central atom. The oxidation number is used in the nomenclature of inorganic compounds. It is represented by a Roman numeral.
Reducing agent	A reducing agent is the element or compound in a reduction-oxidation (redox) reaction that donates an electron to another species; however, since the reducer loses an electron we say it is 'oxidized'.

This means that there must be an 'oxidizer'; because if any chemical is an electron donor (reducer), another must be an electron recipient (oxidizer). Thus reducers are 'oxidized' and oxidizers are 'reduced'.

Cumene hydroperoxide

Cumene hydroperoxide is an intermediate in the cumene process for developing phenol and acetone from benzene and propylene. It is typically used as an oxidising agent. Products of decomposition of cumene hydroperoxide are methylstyrene, acetophenone and cumyl alcohol.

Chromium trioxide

Chromium trioxide is the inorganic compound with the formula CrO_3. It is the acidic anhydride of chromic acid, and is sometimes marketed under the same name. This compound is a dark-red/orange brown solid, which dissolves in water concomitant with hydrolysis.

Pyridinium chlorochromate

Pyridinium chlorochromate is a reddish orange solid reagent used to oxidize primary alcohols to aldehydes and secondary alcohols to ketones. Pyridinium chlorochromate, or PCC, will not fully oxidize a primary alcohol to the carboxylic acid as does the Jones reagent. A disadvantage to using PCC is its toxicity.

Alcohol oxidation

Alcohol oxidation is an important organic reaction. Primary alcohols ($R\text{-}CH_2\text{-}OH$) can be oxidized either to aldehydes (R-CHO) or to carboxylic acids ($R\text{-}CO_2H$), while the oxidation of secondary alcohols ($R^1R^2CH\text{-}OH$) normally terminates at the ketone ($R^1R^2C{=}O$) stage. Tertiary alcohols ($R^1R^2R^3C\text{-}OH$) are resistant to oxidation .

Chromate ester

A chromate ester is a chemical structure that contains a chromium atom in a +6 oxidation state that is connected via an oxygen linkage to a carbon atom. The Cr itself is in its chromate form, with several oxygens attached, and the Cr-O-C attachment makes this chemical group structurally similar to other ester functional groups. They can be synthesized from various chromium(VI) metal compounds, such as CrO_3, chromium chloride complexes, and aqueous chromate ions, and tend to react via redox reactions to liberate chromium(IV).

Ethyl group

In chemistry, an ethyl group is an alkyl substituent derived from ethane (C_2H_6). It has the formula -C_2H_5 and is very often abbreviated -Et. Ethyl is the IUPAC nomenclature of organic chemistry term for an alkane (or alkyl) molecule, using the prefix 'eth-' to indicate the presence of two carbon atoms in the molecule.

Stereochemistry

Stereochemistry, a subdiscipline of chemistry, involves the study of the relative spatial arrangement of atoms within molecules. An important branch of stereochemistry is the study of chiral molecules.

Stereochemistry is also known as 3D chemistry because the prefix 'stereo-' means 'three-dimensionality'.

Potassium permanganate	Potassium permanganate is an inorganic chemical compound with the formula $KMnO_4$. It is a salt consisting of K^+ and MnO_4^- ions. Formerly known as permanganate of potash or Condy's crystals, it is a strong oxidizing agent.
Breath test	A breath test is a type of test performed on air generated from the act of exhalation. Types include:•Breathalyzer - By far the most common usage of this term relates to the legal breath test to determine if a person is driving under the influence of alcohol.•Hydrogen breath test - it is becoming more and more common for people to undertake a medical test for clinical diagnosis of dietary disabilities such as fructose intolerance, fructose malabsorption, lactose intolerance and lactulose intolerance.•The presence of Helicobacter pylori (in peptic ulcer disease) can be tested for with the urea breath test.•Exhaled nitric oxide is a breath test that might signal airway inflammation such as in asthma.•Breath Tests for Diseases have been developed by companies like Menssana Research, Inc. for early detection of Lung Cancer, Breast Cancer, Pulmonary TB and many others, to serve as an adjunct to existing medical tests.
Primary alcohol	A primary alcohol is an alcohol which has the hydroxyl radical connected to a primary carbon. It can also be defined as a molecule containing a '-CH_2OH' group. Examples include ethanol and butanol.
Niacin	'Niacin' redirects here. Niacin is an organic compound with the formula $C_6H_5NO_2$ and, depending on the definition used, one of the forty to eighty essential human nutrients. Niacin is one of five vitamins (when lacking in human diet) associated with a pandemic deficiency disease: niacin deficiency (pellagra), vitamin C deficiency (scurvy), thiamin deficiency (beriberi), vitamin D deficiency (rickets), vitamin A deficiency (night blindness and other symptoms).
Substitution reaction	In a substitution reaction, a functional group in a particular chemical compound is replaced by another group. In organic chemistry, the electrophilic and nucleophilic substitution reactions are of prime importance. Organic substitution reactions are classified in several main organic reaction types depending on whether the reagent that brings about the substitution is considered an electrophile or a nucleophile, whether a reactive intermediate involved in the reaction is a carbocation, a carbanion or a free radical or whether the substrate is aliphatic or aromatic.
Group	In chemistry, a group (also known as a family) is a vertical column in the periodic table of the chemical elements.

There are 18 groups in the standard periodic table, including the d-block elements, but excluding the f-block elements.

The explanation of the pattern of the table is that the elements in a group have similar physical or chemical characteristic of the outermost electron shells of their atoms (i.e. the same core charge), as most chemical properties are dominated by the orbital location of the outermost electron.

Free-radical addition

Free-radical addition is an addition reaction in organic chemistry involving free radicals. The addition may occur between a radical and a non-radical, or between two radicals.

The basic steps with examples of the free radical addition (also known as radical chain mechanism) are:•Initiation by a radical initiator: A radical is created from a non-radical precursor.•Chain propagation: A radical reacts with a non-radical to produce a new radical species•Chain termination: Two radicals react with each other to create a non-radical species

Free radical reactions depend on a reagent having a (relatively) weak bond, allowing it to homolyse to form radicals (often with heat or light).

Disulfide bond

In chemistry, a disulfide bond is a covalent bond, usually derived by the coupling of two thiol groups. The linkage is also called an SS-bond or disulfide bridge. The overall connectivity is therefore R-S-S-R. The terminology is widely used in biochemistry.

Oxidation state

In chemistry, the oxidation state is an indicator of the degree of oxidation of an atom in a chemical compound. The formal oxidation state is the hypothetical charge that an atom would have if all bonds to atoms of different elements were 100% ionic. Oxidation states are typically represented by integers, which can be positive, negative, or zero.

Organic reaction

Organic reactions are chemical reactions involving organic compounds. The basic organic chemistry reaction types are addition reactions, elimination reactions, substitution reactions, pericyclic reactions, rearrangement reactions, photochemical reactions and redox reactions. In organic synthesis, organic reactions are used in the construction of new organic molecules.

Retrosynthetic analysis

Retrosynthetic analysis is a technique for solving problems in the planning of organic syntheses. This is achieved by transforming a target molecule into simpler precursor structures without assumptions regarding starting materials. Each precursor material is examined using the same method.

Tandem mass spectrometry

Tandem mass spectrometry, involves multiple steps of mass spectrometry selection, with some form of fragmentation occurring in between the stages.

CHAPTER HIGHLIGHTS & NOTES: KEY TERMS, PEOPLE, PLACES, CONCEPTS

Tandem MS instruments

Multiple stages of mass analysis separation can be accomplished with individual mass spectrometer elements separated in space or using a single mass spectrometer with the MS steps separated in time.

Tandem in space

In tandem mass spectrometry in space, the separation elements are physically separated and distinct, although there is a physical connection between the elements to maintain high vacuum.

Mass spectrometry — Mass spectrometry is an analytical technique that measures the mass-to-charge ratio of charged particles. It is used for determining masses of particles, for determining the elemental composition of a sample or molecule, and for elucidating the chemical structures of molecules, such as peptides and other chemical compounds. MS works by ionizing chemical compounds to generate charged molecules or molecule fragments and measuring their mass-to-charge ratios.

CHAPTER QUIZ: KEY TERMS, PEOPLE, PLACES, CONCEPTS

1. _________, involves multiple steps of mass spectrometry selection, with some form of fragmentation occurring in between the stages.

   Tandem MS instruments

   Multiple stages of mass analysis separation can be accomplished with individual mass spectrometer elements separated in space or using a single mass spectrometer with the MS steps separated in time.

   Tandem in space

   In _________ in space, the separation elements are physically separated and distinct, although there is a physical connection between the elements to maintain high vacuum.

   a. Mass spectrum
   b. 1,2-Dioxetanedione
   c. Tandem mass spectrometry
   d. Total synthesis

2. . _________ is a colorless liquid with the chemical formula CH_3SO_3H. It is the simplest of the alkylsulfonic acids. Salts and esters of _________ are known as mesylates. _________ is used as an acid catalyst in organic reactions because it is non-volatile, strong acid that is soluble in organic solvents.

a. Mordant red 19
b. Methanesulfonic acid
c. Perfluorobutanesulfonic acid
d. Perfluorooctanesulfonic acid

3. _________s ( ) are organic acids characterized by the presence of at least one carboxyl group. The general formula of a _________ is R-COOH, where R is some monovalent functional group. A carboxyl group (or carboxy) is a functional group consisting of a carbonyl (RR'C=O) and a hydroxyl (R-O-H), which has the formula -C(=O)OH, usually written as -COOH or $-CO_2H$.

_________s are Brønsted-Lowry acids because they are proton (H^+) donors.

a. Carboxylic acid
b. Chloroauric acid
c. Corosolic acid
d. Diprotic acid

4. _________ is the diatomic molecule HBr. HBr is a gas at standard conditions. Hydrobromic acid forms upon dissolving HBr in water.

a. Hydrogen cyanide
b. Lanthanum oxide
c. Hydrogen bromide
d. Lithium hypochlorite

5. _________ is an addition reaction in organic chemistry involving free radicals. The addition may occur between a radical and a non-radical, or between two radicals.

The basic steps with examples of the free radical addition (also known as radical chain mechanism) are:•Initiation by a radical initiator: A radical is created from a non-radical precursor.•Chain propagation: A radical reacts with a non-radical to produce a new radical species•Chain termination: Two radicals react with each other to create a non-radical species

Free radical reactions depend on a reagent having a (relatively) weak bond, allowing it to homolyse to form radicals (often with heat or light).

a. Leaving group
b. Lindemann mechanism
c. Metamorphic reaction
d. Free-radical addition

ANSWER KEY
Chapter 10. THE CHEMISTRY OF ALCOHOLS AND THIOLS

1. c
2. b
3. a
4. c
5. d

Chapter 11. THE CHEMISTRY OF ETHERS, EPDXIDES, GLYCOLS, AND SULI

CHAPTER OUTLINE: KEY TERMS, PEOPLE, PLACES, CONCEPTS

______ Williamson ether synthesis

______ Free-radical addition

______ Alkoxy group

______ Grignard reaction

______ Diethyl ether

______ Addition reaction

______ Claisen condensation

______ McLafferty rearrangement

______ Claisen rearrangement

______ Hydrogen bromide

______ Hydrogen halide

______ Alkylating antineoplastic agent

______ Epoxide

______ Substitution reaction

______ Ethylene oxide

______ Grignard reagents

______ Organolithium reagent

______ Chichibabin reaction

______ Mass spectrum

CHAPTER OUTLINE: KEY TERMS, PEOPLE, PLACES, CONCEPTS

______ Periodic acid

______ Potassium permanganate

______ Carboxylic acid

______ Oxonium ion

______ Activation

______ Effective molarity

______ Sulfone

______ Sulfoxide

______ Nitric acid

______ Hydrogen peroxide

______ Functional group

______ Organic reaction

______ Organic synthesis

______ Oxidation state

______ Diethyl malonate

______ Sharpless epoxidation

Chapter 11. THE CHEMISTRY OF ETHERS, EPDXIDES, GLYCOLS, AND SULFIDES

CHAPTER HIGHLIGHTS & NOTES: KEY TERMS, PEOPLE, PLACES, CONCEPTS

Williamson ether synthesis

The Williamson ether synthesis is an organic reaction, forming an ether from an organohalide and an alcohol. This reaction was developed by Alexander Williamson in 1850. Typically it involves the reaction of an alkoxide ion with a primary alkyl halide via an S_N2 reaction. This reaction is important in the history of organic chemistry because it helped prove the structure of ethers.

Free-radical addition

Free-radical addition is an addition reaction in organic chemistry involving free radicals. The addition may occur between a radical and a non-radical, or between two radicals.

The basic steps with examples of the free radical addition (also known as radical chain mechanism) are:•Initiation by a radical initiator: A radical is created from a non-radical precursor.•Chain propagation: A radical reacts with a non-radical to produce a new radical species•Chain termination: Two radicals react with each other to create a non-radical species

Free radical reactions depend on a reagent having a (relatively) weak bond, allowing it to homolyse to form radicals (often with heat or light).

Alkoxy group

In chemistry, the alkoxy group is an alkyl (carbon and hydrogen chain) group singular bonded to oxygen thus: R--O. The range of alkoxy groups is great, the simplest being methoxy (CH_3O--). An ethoxy group (CH_3CH_2O--) is found in the organic compound phenetol, $C_6H_5OCH_2CH_3$ which is also known as ethoxy benzene. Related to alkoxy groups are aryloxy groups, which have an aryl group singular bonded to oxygen such as the phenoxy group (C_6H_5O--).

Grignard reaction

The Grignard reaction is an organometallic chemical reaction in which alkyl- or aryl-magnesium halides (Grignard reagents) add to a carbonyl group in an aldehyde or ketone. This reaction is an important tool for the formation of carbon-carbon bonds. The reaction of an organic halide with magnesium is not a Grignard reaction, but provides a Grignard reagent.

Diethyl ether

Diethyl ether, simply ether, or ethoxyethane, is an organic compound in the ether class with the formula $(C_2H_5)_2O$. It is a colorless, highly volatile flammable liquid with a characteristic odor. It is commonly used as a solvent and was once used as a general anesthetic.

Addition reaction

An addition reaction, in organic chemistry, is in its simplest terms an organic reaction where two or more molecules combine to form a larger one.

Addition reactions are limited to chemical compounds that have multiple bonds, such as molecules with carbon-carbon double bonds (alkenes), or with triple bonds (alkynes). Molecules containing carbon--hetero double bonds like carbonyl (C=O) groups, or imine (C=N) groups, can undergo addition as they too have double bond character.

Claisen condensation	The Claisen condensation is a carbon-carbon bond forming reaction that occurs between two esters or one ester and another carbonyl compound in the presence of a strong base, resulting in a β-keto ester or a β-diketone. It is named after Rainer Ludwig Claisen, who first published his work on the reaction in 1881 . At least one of the reagents must be enolizable (have an α-proton and be able to undergo deprotonation to form the enolate anion).
McLafferty rearrangement	The McLafferty rearrangement is a reaction observed in mass spectrometry. It is sometimes found that a molecule containing a keto-group undergoes β-cleavage, with the gain of the γ-hydrogen atom. This rearrangement may take place by a radical or ionic mechanism.
Claisen rearrangement	The Claisen rearrangement is a powerful carbon-carbon bond-forming chemical reaction discovered by Rainer Ludwig Claisen. The heating of an allyl vinyl ether will initiate a [3,3]-sigmatropic rearrangement to give a γ,δ-unsaturated carbonyl. Discovered in 1912, the Claisen rearrangement is the first recorded example of a [3,3]-sigmatropic rearrangement.
Hydrogen bromide	Hydrogen bromide is the diatomic molecule HBr. HBr is a gas at standard conditions. Hydrobromic acid forms upon dissolving HBr in water.
Hydrogen halide	Hydrogen halides (or hydrohalic acids) are inorganic compounds with the formula HX where X is one of the halogens: fluorine, chlorine, bromine, iodine, and astatine. Hydrogen halides are gases that dissolve in water to give acids. The hydrogen halides are diatomic molecules with no tendency to ionize in the gas phase.
Alkylating antineoplastic agent	An alkylating antineoplastic agent is an alkylating agent used in cancer treatment that attaches an alkyl group (C_nH_{2n+1}) to DNA. The alkyl group is attached to the guanine base of DNA, at the number 7 nitrogen atom of the purine ring. Since cancer cells, in general, proliferate faster and with less error-correcting than healthy cells, cancer cells are more sensitive to DNA damage -- such as being alkylated. Alkylating agents are used to treat several cancers.
Epoxide	An epoxide is a cyclic ether with three ring atoms. This ring approximately defines an equilateral triangle, which makes it highly strained.

CHAPTER HIGHLIGHTS & NOTES: KEY TERMS, PEOPLE, PLACES, CONCEPTS

Substitution reaction	In a substitution reaction, a functional group in a particular chemical compound is replaced by another group. In organic chemistry, the electrophilic and nucleophilic substitution reactions are of prime importance. Organic substitution reactions are classified in several main organic reaction types depending on whether the reagent that brings about the substitution is considered an electrophile or a nucleophile, whether a reactive intermediate involved in the reaction is a carbocation, a carbanion or a free radical or whether the substrate is aliphatic or aromatic.
Ethylene oxide	Ethylene oxide, is the organic compound with the formula C_2H_4O. It is a cyclic ether. This means that it is composed of two alkyl groups attached to an oxygen atom in a cyclic shape (circular).
Grignard reagents	The Grignard reaction is an organometallic chemical reaction in which alkyl- or aryl-magnesium halides (Grignard reagents) add to a carbonyl group in an aldehyde or ketone. This reaction is an important tool for the formation of carbon-carbon bonds. The reaction of an organic halide with magnesium is not a Grignard reaction, but provides a Grignard reagent.
Organolithium reagent	An organolithium reagent is an organometallic compound with a direct bond between a carbon and a lithium atom. As the electropositive nature of lithium puts most of the charge density of the bond on the carbon atom, effectively creating a carbanion, organolithium compounds are extremely powerful bases and nucleophiles. For use as bases, butyllithiums are often used and are commercially available.
Chichibabin reaction	The Chichibabin reaction (pronounced ' (che')-che-ba-ben) is a method for producing 2-aminopyridine derivatives by the reaction of pyridine with sodium amide. It was reported by Aleksei Chichibabin in 1914. The following is the overall form of the general reaction: The direct amination of pyridine with sodium amide takes place in liquid ammonia. Following the addition elimination mechanism first a nucleophilic NH_2^- is added while a hydride (H^-) is leaving.
Mass spectrum	A mass spectrum is an intensity vs. m/z (mass-to-charge ratio) plot representing a chemical analysis. Hence, the mass spectrum of a sample is a pattern representing the distribution of ions by mass (more correctly: mass-to-charge ratio) in a sample. It is a histogram usually acquired using an instrument called a mass spectrometer.
Periodic acid	Periodic acid is an oxoacid of iodine having chemical formula HIO_4 or H_5IO_6. In dilute aqueous solution, periodic acid exists as discrete hydronium (H_3O^+) and metaperiodate (IO_4^-) ions. When more concentrated, orthoperiodic acid, H_5IO_6, is formed; this dissociates into hydronium and orthoperiodate (IO_6^{5-}) ions.

Potassium permanganate

Potassium permanganate is an inorganic chemical compound with the formula $KMnO_4$. It is a salt consisting of K^+ and MnO_4^- ions. Formerly known as permanganate of potash or Condy's crystals, it is a strong oxidizing agent.

Carboxylic acid

Carboxylic acids ( ) are organic acids characterized by the presence of at least one carboxyl group. The general formula of a carboxylic acid is R-COOH, where R is some monovalent functional group. A carboxyl group (or carboxy) is a functional group consisting of a carbonyl (RR'C=O) and a hydroxyl (R-O-H), which has the formula -C(=O)OH, usually written as -COOH or $-CO_2H$.

Carboxylic acids are Brønsted-Lowry acids because they are proton (H^+) donors.

Oxonium ion

The oxonium ion in chemistry is any oxygen cation with three bonds. The simplest oxonium ion is the hydronium ion H_3O^+. Another oxonium ion frequently encountered in organic chemistry is obtained by protonation or alkylation of a carbonyl group e.g. R-C=O$^+$-R' which forms a resonance structure with the fully fledged carbocation R-C$^+$-O-R' and is therefore especially stable:

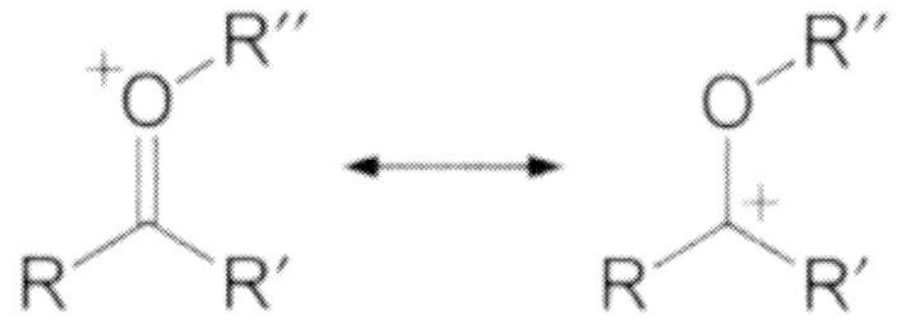

Stable alkyloxonium salts exist; they are extensively used as alkylating agents.

Activation

Activation in (bio-)chemical sciences generally refers to the process whereby something is prepared or excited for a subsequent reaction.

Chemistry

In chemistry, activation of molecules is where the molecules enter a state that avails for a chemical reaction to occur. The phrase energy of activation refers to the energy the reactants must acquire before they can successfully react with each other to produce the products, that is, to reach the transition state.

Effective molarity

In chemistry, the Effective Molarity is defined as the ratio between the first-order rate constant of an intramolecular reaction and the second-order rate constant of the corresponding intermolecular reaction (Kinetic Effective Molarity) or the ratio between the equilibrium constant of an intramolecular reaction and the equilibrium constant of the corresponding intermolecular reaction (Thermodynamic Effective Molarity). It has the dimension of concentration.

Sulfone

A sulfone is a chemical compound containing a sulfonyl functional group attached to two carbon atoms. The central hexavalent sulfur atom is double bonded to each of two oxygen atoms and has a single bond to each of two carbon atoms, usually in two separate hydrocarbon substituents.

The use of the long-standing alternative spelling sulphone is discouraged by IUPAC; it is definitely undesirable to have two spellings in simultaneous common use, and it was agreed to discontinue the ph spelling as the more archaic.

Sulfoxide

A sulfoxide is a chemical compound containing a sulfinyl functional group attached to two carbon atoms. Sulfoxides can be considered as oxidized sulfides. (The use of the alternative spelling sulphoxide is discouraged by IUPAC).

Nitric acid

Nitric acid also known as aqua fortis and spirit of niter, is a highly corrosive and toxic strong mineral acid which is normally colorless but tends to acquire a yellow cast due to the accumulation of oxides of nitrogen if long-stored. Ordinary nitric acid has a concentration of 68%. When the solution contains more than 86% HNO_3, it is referred to as fuming nitric acid.

Hydrogen peroxide

Hydrogen peroxide is the simplest peroxide (a compound with an oxygen-oxygen single bond). It is also a strong oxidizer. Hydrogen peroxide is a clear liquid, slightly more viscous than water.

Functional group

In organic chemistry, functional groups are lexicon specific groups of atoms or bonds within molecules that are responsible for the characteristic chemical reactions of those molecules. The same functional group will undergo the same or similar chemical reaction(s) regardless of the size of the molecule it is a part of. However, its relative reactivity can be modified by nearby functional groups.

Organic reaction

Organic reactions are chemical reactions involving organic compounds. The basic organic chemistry reaction types are addition reactions, elimination reactions, substitution reactions, pericyclic reactions, rearrangement reactions, photochemical reactions and redox reactions. In organic synthesis, organic reactions are used in the construction of new organic molecules.

Organic synthesis

Organic synthesis is a special branch of chemical synthesis and is concerned with the construction of organic compounds via organic reactions. Organic molecules can often contain a higher level of complexity compared to purely inorganic compounds, so the synthesis of organic compounds has developed into one of the most important branches of organic chemistry. There are two main areas of research fields within the general area of organic synthesis: total synthesis and methodology.

Oxidation state

In chemistry, the oxidation state is an indicator of the degree of oxidation of an atom in a chemical compound.

CHAPTER HIGHLIGHTS & NOTES: KEY TERMS, PEOPLE, PLACES, CONCEPTS

The formal oxidation state is the hypothetical charge that an atom would have if all bonds to atoms of different elements were 100% ionic. Oxidation states are typically represented by integers, which can be positive, negative, or zero.

Diethyl malonate: Diethyl malonate, is the diethyl ester of malonic acid. It occurs naturally in grapes and strawberries as a colourless liquid with an apple-like odour, and is used in perfumes. It is also used to synthesize other compounds such as barbiturates, artificial flavourings, vitamin B_1, and vitamin B_6.

Sharpless epoxidation: The Sharpless Epoxidation reaction is an enantioselective chemical reaction to prepare 2,3-epoxyalcohols from primary and secondary allylic alcohols.

The stereochemistry of the resulting epoxide is determined by the diastereomer of the chiral tartrate diester (usually diethyl tartrate or diisopropyl tartrate) employed in the reaction. The oxidizing agent is tert-butyl hydroperoxide.

CHAPTER QUIZ: KEY TERMS, PEOPLE, PLACES, CONCEPTS

1. The _________ is a carbon-carbon bond forming reaction that occurs between two esters or one ester and another carbonyl compound in the presence of a strong base, resulting in a β-keto ester or a β-diketone. It is named after Rainer Ludwig Claisen, who first published his work on the reaction in 1881 .

   At least one of the reagents must be enolizable (have an α-proton and be able to undergo deprotonation to form the enolate anion).

   a. Claisen rearrangement
   b. Claisen condensation
   c. Cope reaction
   d. Cope rearrangement

2. The _________ is an organometallic chemical reaction in which alkyl- or aryl-magnesium halides (Grignard reagents) add to a carbonyl group in an aldehyde or ketone. This reaction is an important tool for the formation of carbon-carbon bonds. The reaction of an organic halide with magnesium is not a _________, but provides a Grignard reagent.

   a. Dimethylmagnesium
   b. Grignard reaction
   c. Phenylmagnesium bromide
   d. Migratory insertion

3. . An _________, in organic chemistry, is in its simplest terms an organic reaction where two or more molecules combine to form a larger one.

_________s are limited to chemical compounds that have multiple bonds, such as molecules with carbon-carbon double bonds (alkenes), or with triple bonds (alkynes). Molecules containing carbon--hetero double bonds like carbonyl (C=O) groups, or imine (C=N) groups, can undergo addition as they too have double bond character.

a. Addition reaction
b. Ammoxidation
c. Appel reaction
d. Arrow pushing

4. The _________ reaction is an enantioselective chemical reaction to prepare 2,3-epoxyalcohols from primary and secondary allylic alcohols.

   The stereochemistry of the resulting epoxide is determined by the diastereomer of the chiral tartrate diester (usually diethyl tartrate or diisopropyl tartrate) employed in the reaction. The oxidizing agent is tert-butyl hydroperoxide.

   a. Sharpless epoxidation
   b. Shi epoxidation
   c. Staudinger reaction
   d. Swern oxidation

5. An _________ is an organometallic compound with a direct bond between a carbon and a lithium atom. As the electropositive nature of lithium puts most of the charge density of the bond on the carbon atom, effectively creating a carbanion, organolithium compounds are extremely powerful bases and nucleophiles. For use as bases, butyllithiums are often used and are commercially available.

   a. Allixin
   b. Organolithium reagent
   c. Hydrindantin
   d. Hypophosphorous acid

ANSWER KEY
Chapter 11. THE CHEMISTRY OF ETHERS, EPDXIDES, GLYCOLS, AND SULFIDES

1. b
2. b
3. a
4. a
5. b

CHAPTER OUTLINE: KEY TERMS, PEOPLE, PLACES, CONCEPTS

______ Absorption spectroscopy

______ Ferulic acid

______ Bond strength

______ Functional group

______ Infrared spectroscopy

______ Inductive effect

______ Mass spectrometry

______ Mass spectrum

______ Base pair

CHAPTER HIGHLIGHTS & NOTES: KEY TERMS, PEOPLE, PLACES, CONCEPTS

Absorption spectroscopy

Absorption spectroscopy refers to spectroscopic techniques that measure the absorption of radiation, as a function of frequency or wavelength, due to its interaction with a sample. The sample absorbs energy, i.e., photons, from the radiating field. The intensity of the absorption varies as a function of frequency, and this variation is the absorption spectrum.

Ferulic acid

Ferulic acid is a hydroxycinnamic acid, a type of organic compound. It is an abundant phenolic phytochemical found in plant cell wall components such as arabinoxylans as covalent side chains. It is related to trans-cinnamic acid.

Bond strength

In chemistry, bond strength is measured between two atoms joined in a chemical bond. It is the degree to which each atom linked to another atom contributes to the valency of this other atom. Bond strength is intimately linked to bond order.

CHAPTER HIGHLIGHTS & NOTES: KEY TERMS, PEOPLE, PLACES, CONCEPTS

Functional group	In organic chemistry, functional groups are lexicon specific groups of atoms or bonds within molecules that are responsible for the characteristic chemical reactions of those molecules. The same functional group will undergo the same or similar chemical reaction(s) regardless of the size of the molecule it is a part of. However, its relative reactivity can be modified by nearby functional groups.
Infrared spectroscopy	Infrared spectroscopy is the spectroscopy that deals with the infrared region of the electromagnetic spectrum, that is light with a longer wavelength and lower frequency than visible light. It covers a range of techniques, mostly based on absorption spectroscopy. As with all spectroscopic techniques, it can be used to identify and study chemicals.
Inductive effect	In chemistry and physics, the inductive effect is an experimentally observable effect of the transmission of charge through a chain of atoms in a molecule by electrostatic induction. The net polar effect exerted by a substituent is a combination of this inductive effect and the mesomeric effect. The electron cloud in a σ-bond between two unlike atoms is not uniform and is slightly displaced towards the more electronegative of the two atoms.
Mass spectrometry	Mass spectrometry is an analytical technique that measures the mass-to-charge ratio of charged particles. It is used for determining masses of particles, for determining the elemental composition of a sample or molecule, and for elucidating the chemical structures of molecules, such as peptides and other chemical compounds. MS works by ionizing chemical compounds to generate charged molecules or molecule fragments and measuring their mass-to-charge ratios.
Mass spectrum	A mass spectrum is an intensity vs. m/z (mass-to-charge ratio) plot representing a chemical analysis. Hence, the mass spectrum of a sample is a pattern representing the distribution of ions by mass (more correctly: mass-to-charge ratio) in a sample. It is a histogram usually acquired using an instrument called a mass spectrometer.
Base pair	In molecular biology and genetics, the linking between two nitrogenous bases on opposite complementary DNA or certain types of RNA strands that are connected via hydrogen bonds is called a base pair. In the canonical Watson-Crick DNA base pairing, adenine (A) forms a base pair with thymine (T) and guanine (G) forms a base pair with cytosine (C). In RNA, thymine is replaced by uracil (U).

1. _________ is the spectroscopy that deals with the infrared region of the electromagnetic spectrum, that is light with a longer wavelength and lower frequency than visible light. It covers a range of techniques, mostly based on absorption spectroscopy. As with all spectroscopic techniques, it can be used to identify and study chemicals.

   a. Allixin
   b. Glycopolymer
   c. Glycorandomization
   d. Infrared spectroscopy

2. In chemistry, _________ is measured between two atoms joined in a chemical bond. It is the degree to which each atom linked to another atom contributes to the valency of this other atom. _________ is intimately linked to bond order.

   a. Bond order
   b. Bond strength
   c. Bond-dissociation energy
   d. 1,2-Dioxetanedione

3. _________ refers to spectroscopic techniques that measure the absorption of radiation, as a function of frequency or wavelength, due to its interaction with a sample. The sample absorbs energy, i.e., photons, from the radiating field. The intensity of the absorption varies as a function of frequency, and this variation is the absorption spectrum.

   a. Absorptivity
   b. Acid dissociation constant
   c. Absorption spectroscopy
   d. Aluminon

4. _________ is a hydroxycinnamic acid, a type of organic compound. It is an abundant phenolic phytochemical found in plant cell wall components such as arabinoxylans as covalent side chains. It is related to trans-cinnamic acid.

   a. 1,2-Dioxetanedione
   b. Acid dissociation constant
   c. Acid value
   d. Ferulic acid

5. In organic chemistry, _________s are lexicon specific groups of atoms or bonds within molecules that are responsible for the characteristic chemical reactions of those molecules. The same _________ will undergo the same or similar chemical reaction(s) regardless of the size of the molecule it is a part of. However, its relative reactivity can be modified by nearby _________s.

   a. Glycopeptide
   b. Glycopolymer
   c. Functional group
   d. Heteroatom

ANSWER KEY
Chapter 12. INTRODUCTION TO SPECTROSCOPY. INFRARED SPECTROSCOPY AND MASS SPECTROMETRY

---

1. d
2. b
3. c
4. d
5. c

Chapter 13. NUCLEAR MAGNETIC RESONANCE SPECTROSCOPY

CHAPTER OUTLINE: KEY TERMS, PEOPLE, PLACES, CONCEPTS

______ Chemical shift

______ Tetramethylsilane

______ Gyromagnetic ratio

______ Substitution reaction

______ Ergocalciferol

CHAPTER HIGHLIGHTS & NOTES: KEY TERMS, PEOPLE, PLACES, CONCEPTS

Chemical shift

In nuclear magnetic resonance (NMR) spectroscopy, the chemical shift is the resonant frequency of a nucleus relative to a standard. Often the position and number of chemical shifts are diagnostic of the structure of a molecule. Chemical shifts are also used to describe signals in other forms of spectroscopy such as photoemission spectroscopy.

Tetramethylsilane

Tetramethylsilane is the chemical compound with the formula $Si(CH_3)_4$. It is the simplest tetraorganosilane. Like all silanes, the TMS framework is tetrahedral.

Gyromagnetic ratio

In physics, the gyromagnetic ratio of a particle or system is the ratio of its magnetic dipole moment to its angular momentum, and it is often denoted by the symbol γ, gamma. Its SI units are radian per second per tesla ($s^{-1} \cdot T^{-1}$) or, equivalently, coulomb per kilogram ($C \cdot kg^{-1}$).

The term 'gyromagnetic ratio' is sometimes used as a synonym for a different but closely related quantity, the g-factor.

Substitution reaction

In a substitution reaction, a functional group in a particular chemical compound is replaced by another group. In organic chemistry, the electrophilic and nucleophilic substitution reactions are of prime importance.

Ergocalciferol	Ergocalciferol is a form of vitamin D, also called vitamin D_2. It has the systematic name '(3β,5Z,7E,22E)-9,10-secoergosta-5,7,10(19),22-tetraen-3-ol'. It is marketed under various names : Deltalin (Eli Lilly and Company), Drisdol (Sanofi-Synthelabo), Calcidol (Patrin Pharma).

CHAPTER QUIZ: KEY TERMS, PEOPLE, PLACES, CONCEPTS

1. In nuclear magnetic resonance (NMR) spectroscopy, the _________ is the resonant frequency of a nucleus relative to a standard. Often the position and number of _________s are diagnostic of the structure of a molecule. _________s are also used to describe signals in other forms of spectroscopy such as photoemission spectroscopy.

   a. Chemical shift
   b. Cosmogenic nuclide
   c. Decay product
   d. FLiNaK

2. In a _________, a functional group in a particular chemical compound is replaced by another group. In organic chemistry, the electrophilic and nucleophilic _________s are of prime importance. Organic _________s are classified in several main organic reaction types depending on whether the reagent that brings about the substitution is considered an electrophile or a nucleophile, whether a reactive intermediate involved in the reaction is a carbocation, a carbanion or a free radical or whether the substrate is aliphatic or aromatic.

   a. Substrate
   b. Substitution reaction
   c. Telomerization
   d. Thermal decomposition

3. _________ is the chemical compound with the formula $Si(CH_3)_4$. It is the simplest tetraorganosilane. Like all silanes, the TMS framework is tetrahedral.

   a. Tetramethylsilane
   b. Cosmogenic nuclide
   c. Decay product
   d. FLiNaK

4. . In physics, the _________ of a particle or system is the ratio of its magnetic dipole moment to its angular momentum, and it is often denoted by the symbol γ, gamma. Its SI units are radian per second per tesla ($s^{-1} \cdot T^{-1}$) or, equivalently, coulomb per kilogram ($C \cdot kg^{-1}$).

   The term '_________' is sometimes used as a synonym for a different but closely related quantity, the g-factor.

a. H-alpha
b. Hanle effect
c. Highly charged ion
d. Gyromagnetic ratio

5. _________ is a form of vitamin D, also called vitamin D_2. It has the systematic name '(3β,5Z,7E,22E)-9,10-secoergosta-5,7,10(19),22-tetraen-3-ol'. It is marketed under various names : Deltalin (Eli Lilly and Company), Drisdol (Sanofi-Synthelabo), Calcidol (Patrin Pharma).

a. Ergocalciferol
b. aldose
c. Acid phosphatase
d. Adamkeiwickz reaction

ANSWER KEY
Chapter 13. NUCLEAR MAGNETIC RESONANCE SPECTROSCOPY

1. a
2. b
3. a
4. d
5. a

Chapter 14. THE CHEMISTRY OF ALKYNES

CHAPTER OUTLINE: KEY TERMS, PEOPLE, PLACES, CONCEPTS

Propargyl chloride

Acetylene

Hydrogen bromide

Hydrogen halide

Alkyne

Enol

Disiamylborane

Lindlar catalyst

Hydrogenation

Solvated electron

Carbanion

Sodium amide

Amadori rearrangement

Grignard reagents

Acetylenic

Gabriel synthesis

Organic synthesis

Pheromone

Vinyl chloride

Chapter 14. THE CHEMISTRY OF ALKYNES

CHAPTER OUTLINE: KEY TERMS, PEOPLE, PLACES, CONCEPTS

Ethylene

CHAPTER HIGHLIGHTS & NOTES: KEY TERMS, PEOPLE, PLACES, CONCEPTS

Propargyl chloride

Propargyl chloride, is a highly toxic and flammable clear brown liquid with chemical formula $CHCCH_2Cl$. It is miscible with benzene or ethanol and insoluble in water. Its refractive index is 1.4350. Common uses for propargyl chloride include soil fumigation, corrosion prevention, and as an intermediate in organic synthesis.

Acetylene

Acetylene is the chemical compound with the formula C_2H_2. It is a hydrocarbon and the simplest alkyne. This colorless gas is widely used as a fuel and a chemical building block.

Hydrogen bromide

Hydrogen bromide is the diatomic molecule HBr. HBr is a gas at standard conditions. Hydrobromic acid forms upon dissolving HBr in water.

Hydrogen halide

Hydrogen halides (or hydrohalic acids) are inorganic compounds with the formula HX where X is one of the halogens: fluorine, chlorine, bromine, iodine, and astatine. Hydrogen halides are gases that dissolve in water to give acids.

The hydrogen halides are diatomic molecules with no tendency to ionize in the gas phase.

Alkyne

Alkynes are hydrocarbons that have a triple bond between two carbon atoms, with the formula C_nH_{2n-2}. Alkynes are traditionally known as acetylenes, although the name acetylene also refers specifically to C_2H_2, known formally as ethyne using IUPAC nomenclature. Like other hydrocarbons, alkynes are generally hydrophobic but tend to be more reactive.

Enol

Enols (also known as alkenols) are alkenes with a hydroxyl group affixed to one of the carbon atoms composing the double bond. Alkenes with a hydroxyl group on both sides of the double bond are called enediols. Deprotonated anions of enols are called enolates.

Disiamylborane

Disiamylborane (bis(1,2-dimethylpropyl)borane) is an organoborane used in organic synthesis. It is used to add water to a terminal alkyne, forming an aldehyde via anti-Markovnikov addition. Disiamylborane is relatively selective for terminal alkynes.

Lindlar catalyst

A Lindlar catalyst is a heterogeneous catalyst that consists of palladium deposited on calcium carbonate and treated with various forms of lead. The lead additive serves to deactivate the palladium sites. A variety of 'catalyst poisons' have been used including lead acetate and lead oxide.

Hydrogenation

Hydrogenation, to treat with hydrogen, also a form of chemical reduction, is a chemical reaction between molecular hydrogen (H_2) and another compound or element, usually in the presence of a catalyst. The process is commonly employed to reduce or saturate organic compounds. Hydrogenation typically constitutes the addition of pairs of hydrogen atoms to a molecule, generally an alkene.

Solvated electron

A solvated electron is a free electron in (solvated in) a solution, and is the smallest possible anion. Solvated electrons occur widely although they are often not observed directly. The deep color of solutions of alkali metals in ammonia arises from the presence of solvated electrons: blue when dilute and copper-colored when more concentrated (> 3 molar).

Carbanion

A carbanion is an anion in which carbon has an unshared pair of electrons and bears a negative charge usually with three substituents for a total of eight valence electrons . The carbanion exists in a trigonal pyramidal geometry. Formally a carbanion is the conjugate base of a carbon acid.

Sodium amide

Sodium amide, commonly called sodamide, is the chemical compound with the formula $NaNH_2$. This solid, which is dangerously reactive toward water, is white when pure, but commercial samples are typically gray due to the presence of small quantities of metallic iron from the manufacturing process. Such impurities do not usually affect the utility of the reagent.

Amadori rearrangement

The Amadori rearrangement is an organic reaction describing the acid or base catalyzed isomerization or rearrangement reaction of the N-glycoside of an aldose or the glycosylamine to the corresponding 1-amino-1-deoxy-ketose. The reaction is important in carbohydrate chemistry.

The reaction mechanism is demonstrated starting from the reaction of D-mannose in its closed (1) and open-form (2) with ammonia to produce the 1,1-amino-alcohol (3), which is unstable and loses water to the glycosylamine (again the open imine (5) and the closed form hemiaminal (4)), which is the starting point for the actual Amadori rearrangement.

Grignard reagents

The Grignard reaction is an organometallic chemical reaction in which alkyl- or aryl-magnesium halides (Grignard reagents) add to a carbonyl group in an aldehyde or ketone. This reaction is an important tool for the formation of carbon-carbon bonds. The reaction of an organic halide with magnesium is not a Grignard reaction, but provides a Grignard reagent.

Chapter 14. THE CHEMISTRY OF ALKYNES

CHAPTER HIGHLIGHTS & NOTES: KEY TERMS, PEOPLE, PLACES, CONCEPTS

Acetylenic

In organic chemistry, the term acetylenic designates•A doubly unsaturated position (sp-hybridized) on a molecular framework, for instance in an alkyne such as acetylene;•An ethynyl fragment, HC ≡ C-, or substituted homologue..

Gabriel synthesis

The Gabriel synthesis is named for the German chemist Siegmund Gabriel. Traditionally, it is a chemical reaction that transforms primary alkyl halides into primary amines using potassium phthalimide.

The Gabriel reaction has since been generalized to include the alkylation of sulfonamides and imides, followed by deprotection, to obtain amines .

Organic synthesis

Organic synthesis is a special branch of chemical synthesis and is concerned with the construction of organic compounds via organic reactions. Organic molecules can often contain a higher level of complexity compared to purely inorganic compounds, so the synthesis of organic compounds has developed into one of the most important branches of organic chemistry. There are two main areas of research fields within the general area of organic synthesis: total synthesis and methodology.

Pheromone

A pheromone is a secreted or excreted chemical factor that triggers a social response in members of the same species. Pheromones are chemicals capable of acting outside the body of the secreting individual to impact the behavior of the receiving individual. There are alarm pheromones, food trail pheromones, sex pheromones, and many others that affect behavior or physiology.

Vinyl chloride

Vinyl chloride is the organochloride with the formula $H_2C{:}CHCl$. It is also called vinyl chloride monomer, or VCM. This colorless compound is an important industrial chemical chiefly used to produce the polymer polyvinyl chloride. At ambient pressure and temperature, vinyl chloride is a gas with a sickly sweet odor.

Ethylene

Ethylene is an organic compound, a hydrocarbon with the formula C_2H_4 or $H_2C{=}CH_2$. It is a colorless flammable gas with a faint 'sweet and musky' odor when pure. It is the simplest alkene (a hydrocarbon with carbon-carbon double bonds), and the simplest unsaturated hydrocarbon after acetylene (C_2H_2).

Chapter 14. THE CHEMISTRY OF ALKYNES

CHAPTER QUIZ: KEY TERMS, PEOPLE, PLACES, CONCEPTS

1. _________s are hydrocarbons that have a triple bond between two carbon atoms, with the formula C_nH_{2n-2}. _________s are traditionally known as acetylenes, although the name acetylene also refers specifically to C_2H_2, known formally as ethyne using IUPAC nomenclature. Like other hydrocarbons, _________s are generally hydrophobic but tend to be more reactive.

   a. Alkyne
   b. Amide
   c. Amidine
   d. Aminal

2. _________, is a highly toxic and flammable clear brown liquid with chemical formula $CHCCH_2Cl$. It is miscible with benzene or ethanol and insoluble in water. Its refractive index is 1.4350. Common uses for _________ include soil fumigation, corrosion prevention, and as an intermediate in organic synthesis.

   a. Pralatrexate
   b. Propiolic acid
   c. Propargyl chloride
   d. QH-II-66

3. _________s (or hydrohalic acids) are inorganic compounds with the formula HX where X is one of the halogens: fluorine, chlorine, bromine, iodine, and astatine. _________s are gases that dissolve in water to give acids. _________ vs hydrohalic acids

   The _________s are diatomic molecules with no tendency to ionize in the gas phase.

   a. Hydrogen halide
   b. Hydrogen isocyanide
   c. Hydrogen peroxide
   d. Hydrogen polonide

4. A _________ is a free electron in (solvated in) a solution, and is the smallest possible anion. _________s occur widely although they are often not observed directly. The deep color of solutions of alkali metals in ammonia arises from the presence of _________s: blue when dilute and copper-colored when more concentrated (> 3 molar).

   a. Spin engineering
   b. Spiro compound
   c. Stacking
   d. Solvated electron

5. . _________ is the diatomic molecule HBr. HBr is a gas at standard conditions. Hydrobromic acid forms upon dissolving HBr in water.

   a. Hydrogen cyanide
   b. Hydrogen bromide
   c. Lead azide

ANSWER KEY
Chapter 14. THE CHEMISTRY OF ALKYNES

1. a
2. c
3. a
4. d
5. b

Chapter 15. DIENES, RESONANCE, AND AROMATICITY

CHAPTER OUTLINE: KEY TERMS, PEOPLE, PLACES, CONCEPTS

______ Cumulene

______ Diene

______ Double bond

______ Molecular orbital

______ Delocalized electron

______ 1,3-Butadiene

______ Molar absorptivity

______ Chromophore

______ Perchloric acid

______ Pericyclic reaction

______ Transition state

______ Stereochemistry

______ Maleic acid

______ Maleic anhydride

______ Hydrogen bromide

______ Hydrogen halide

______ Resonance

______ Copolymer

______ Polybutadiene

Chapter 15. DIENES, RESONANCE, AND AROMATICITY

CHAPTER OUTLINE: KEY TERMS, PEOPLE, PLACES, CONCEPTS

______ Polymer

______ Natural rubber

______ Octet rule

______ Molecular geometry

______ Orbital overlap

______ Methyl radical

______ Methyl salicylate

______ Vanillin

______ Prismane

______ Aromaticity

______ Dewar benzene

______ Heterocyclic compound

______ Addition reaction

______ Ferrocene

______ Grignard reagents

______ Transition metal

______ Electron counting

______ Polycyclic compound

______ Antiaromaticity

Cyclobutadiene

CHAPTER HIGHLIGHTS & NOTES: KEY TERMS, PEOPLE, PLACES, CONCEPTS

Cumulene

A cumulene is a hydrocarbon with three or more cumulative (consecutive) double bonds. A member of this compound class is butatriene (which is also called simply cumulene), $H_2C=C=C=CH_2$. Unlike most alkanes and alkenes, cumulenes tend to be rigid, which makes them appealing for molecular nanotechnology.

Diene

In organic chemistry a diene or diolefin is a hydrocarbon that contains two carbon double bonds. Conjugated dienes are functional groups, with a general formula of C_nH_{2n-2}. Dienes and alkynes are functional isomers.

Double bond

A double bond in chemistry is a chemical bond between two chemical elements involving four bonding electrons instead of the usual two. The most common double bond, that between two carbon atoms, can be found in alkenes. Many types of double bonds between two different elements exist, for example in a carbonyl group with a carbon atom and an oxygen atom.

Molecular orbital

In chemistry, a molecular orbital is a mathematical function describing the wave-like behavior of an electron in a molecule. This function can be used to calculate chemical and physical properties such as the probability of finding an electron in any specific region. The term 'orbital' was first used in English by Robert S. Mulliken as the English translation of Schrödinger's 'Eigenfunktion'.

Delocalized electron

In chemistry, delocalized electrons are electrons in a molecule, ion or solid metal that are not associated with a single atom or one covalent bond. Delocalized electrons are contained within an orbital that extends over several adjacent atoms. Classically, delocalized electrons can be found in conjugated systems and mesoionic compounds.

1,3-Butadiene

1,3-Butadiene is a simple conjugated diene with the formula C_4H_6. It is an important industrial chemical used as a monomer in the production of synthetic rubber. When the word butadiene is used, most of the time it refers to 1,3-butadiene.

Molar absorptivity

The molar absorption coefficient, molar extinction coefficient, or molar absorptivity, is a measurement of how strongly a chemical species absorbs light at a given wavelength.

It is an intrinsic property of the species; the actual absorbance, A, of a sample is dependent on the pathlength, l, and the concentration, c, of the species via the Beer-Lambert law, $A = \epsilon c\ell$.

The SI units for ε are m^2/mol, but in practice, they are usually taken as $M^{-1}\ cm^{-1}$ or L $mol^{-1}\ cm^{-1}$.

Chromophore

A chromophore is the part of a molecule responsible for its color. The color arises when a molecule absorbs certain wavelengths of visible light and transmits or reflects others. The chromophore is a region in the molecule where the energy difference between two different molecular orbitals falls within the range of the visible spectrum.

Perchloric acid

Perchloric acid is the inorganic compound with the formula $HClO_4$. Usually found as an aqueous solution, this colorless compound is a strong acid stronger then sulfuric and nitric acids. It is a powerful oxidizer, but its aqueous solutions up to appr. 70% are remarkably inert, only showing strong acid features and no oxidizing properties.

Pericyclic reaction

In organic chemistry, a pericyclic reaction is a type of organic reaction wherein the transition state of the molecule has a cyclic geometry, and the reaction progresses in a concerted fashion. Pericyclic reactions are usually rearrangement reactions. The major classes of pericyclic reactions are:

In general, these are considered to be equilibrium processes, although it is possible to push the reaction in one direction by designing a reaction by which the product is at a significantly lower energy level; this is due to a unimolecular interpretation of Le Chatelier's principle.

Transition state

The transition state of a chemical reaction is a particular configuration along the reaction coordinate. It is defined as the state corresponding to the highest energy along this reaction coordinate. At this point, assuming a perfectly irreversible reaction, colliding reactant molecules will always go on to form products.

Stereochemistry

Stereochemistry, a subdiscipline of chemistry, involves the study of the relative spatial arrangement of atoms within molecules. An important branch of stereochemistry is the study of chiral molecules.

Stereochemistry is also known as 3D chemistry because the prefix 'stereo-' means 'three-dimensionality'.

Maleic acid

Maleic acid is an organic compound that is a dicarboxylic acid, a molecule with two carboxyl groups. Maleic acid is the cis-isomer of butenedioic acid, whereas fumaric acid is the trans-isomer.

Maleic anhydride

Maleic anhydride is an organic compound with the formula $C_2H_2(CO)_2O$. It is the acid anhydride of maleic acid and in its pure state it is a colourless or white solid with an acrid odour.

Maleic anhydride was traditionally manufactured by the oxidation of benzene or other aromatic compounds. As of 2006, only a few smaller plants continue to use benzene; due to rising benzene prices, most maleic anhydride plants now use n-butane as a feedstock:2 $CH_3CH_2CH_2CH_3 + 7\ O_2 \rightarrow 2\ C_2H_2(CO)_2O + 8\ H_2O$Reactions

The chemistry of maleic anhydride is very rich, reflecting its ready availability and bifunctional reactivity.

Hydrogen bromide

Hydrogen bromide is the diatomic molecule HBr. HBr is a gas at standard conditions. Hydrobromic acid forms upon dissolving HBr in water.

Hydrogen halide

Hydrogen halides (or hydrohalic acids) are inorganic compounds with the formula HX where X is one of the halogens: fluorine, chlorine, bromine, iodine, and astatine. Hydrogen halides are gases that dissolve in water to give acids.

The hydrogen halides are diatomic molecules with no tendency to ionize in the gas phase.

Resonance

In particle physics, a resonance is the peak located around a certain energy found in differential cross sections of scattering experiments. These peaks are associated with subatomic particles (such as nucleons, delta baryons, upsilon mesons) and their excitations. The width of the resonance (Γ) is related to the lifetime (τ) of the particle by the relation $\Gamma = \frac{\hbar}{\tau}$

where h is the reduced Planck constant.

Copolymer

A heteropolymer or copolymer is a polymer derived from two (or more) monomeric species, as opposed to a homopolymer where only one monomer is used. Copolymerization refers to methods used to chemically synthesize a copolymer.

Commercially relevant copolymers include ABS plastic, SBR, Nitrile rubber, styrene-acrylonitrile, styrene-isoprene-styrene (SIS) and ethylene-vinyl acetate.

Polybutadiene

Polybutadiene is a synthetic rubber that is a polymer formed from the polymerization process of the monomer 1,3-butadiene.

It has a high resistance to wear and is used especially in the manufacture of tires, which consumes about 70% of the production.

Chapter 15. DIENES, RESONANCE, AND AROMATICITY

CHAPTER HIGHLIGHTS & NOTES: KEY TERMS, PEOPLE, PLACES, CONCEPTS

Polymer

A polymer is a large molecule (macromolecule) composed of repeating structural units. These sub-units are typically connected by covalent chemical bonds. Although the term polymer is sometimes taken to refer to plastics, it actually encompasses a large class of compounds comprising both natural and synthetic materials with a wide variety of properties.

Natural rubber

Natural rubber, is an elastomer (an elastic hydrocarbon polymer) that was originally derived from latex, a milky colloid produced by some plants. The plants would be 'tapped', that is, an incision made into the bark of the tree and the sticky, milk colored latex sap collected and refined into a usable rubber. The purified form of natural rubber is the chemical polyisoprene, which can also be produced synthetically.

Octet rule

The octet rule is a chemical rule of thumb that states that atoms tend to combine in such a way that they each have eight electrons in their valence shells, giving them the same electronic configuration as a noble gas. The rule is applicable to the main-group elements, especially carbon, nitrogen, oxygen, and the halogens, but also to metals such as sodium or magnesium. In simple terms, molecules or ions tend to be most stable when the outermost electron shells of their constituent atoms contain eight electrons.

Molecular geometry

Molecular geometry is the three-dimensional arrangement of the atoms that constitute a molecule. It determines several properties of a substance including its reactivity, polarity, phase of matter, color, magnetism, and biological activity.

The molecular geometry can be determined by various spectroscopic methods and diffraction methods.

Orbital overlap

Orbital overlap was an idea first introduced by Linus Pauling to explain the molecular bond angles observed through experimentation and is the basis for the concept of orbital hybridisation. s orbitals are spherical and have no directionality while p orbitals are oriented 90° to one another. A theory was needed therefore to explain why molecules such as methane (CH_4) had observed bond angles of 109.5°.

Methyl radical

Methyl radical is a trivalent radical derived from methane, produced by the ultraviolet disassociation of halomethanes.

Methyl salicylate

Methyl salicylate is an organic ester that is naturally produced by many species of plants. Some of the plants which produce it are called wintergreens, hence the common name.

Plants containing methyl salicylate produce this organic ester (a combination of an organic acid with an alcohol) most likely as an anti-herbivore defense.

Vanillin

Vanillin is a phenolic aldehyde, an organic compound with the molecular formula $C_8H_8O_3$.

Its functional groups include aldehyde, ether, and phenol. It is the primary component of the extract of the vanilla bean.

Prismane

Prismane is a polycyclic hydrocarbon with the formula C_6H_6. It is an isomer of benzene, more specific: a valence isomer. Prismane is far less stable than benzene.

Aromaticity

In organic chemistry, aromaticity is a chemical property in which a conjugated ring of unsaturated bonds, lone pairs, or empty orbitals exhibit a stabilization stronger than would be expected by the stabilization of conjugation alone There is no general relationship between aromaticity as a chemical property and the olfactory properties of such compounds.

Aromaticity can also be considered a manifestation of cyclic delocalization and of resonance.

Dewar benzene

Dewar benzene or bicyclo[2.2.0]hexa-2,5-diene is a bicyclic isomer of benzene with the molecular formula C_6H_6. The compound is named after James Dewar who included this structure in a list of possible C_6H_6 structures in 1867. However, he did not propose it as the structure of benzene, and in fact he supported the correct structure previously proposed by August Kekulé in 1865. Synthesis and properties of bicyclo[2.2.0]hexa-2,5-diene

The compound itself was first synthesized in 1962 as a tert-butyl derivative and then as the unsubstituted compound by E.E. van Tamelen in 1963 by photolysis of cis-1,2-dihydro derivative of phthalic anhydride followed by oxidation with lead tetraacetate.

Heterocyclic compound

A heterocyclic compound is a cyclic compound that has atoms of at least two different elements as members of its ring(s). The counterparts of heterocyclic compounds are homocyclic compounds, the rings of which are made of a single element.

Although heterocyclic compounds may be inorganic, most contain at least one carbon atom, and one or more atoms of elements other than carbon within the ring structure, such as sulfur, oxygen, or nitrogen.

Addition reaction

An addition reaction, in organic chemistry, is in its simplest terms an organic reaction where two or more molecules combine to form a larger one.

Addition reactions are limited to chemical compounds that have multiple bonds, such as molecules with carbon-carbon double bonds (alkenes), or with triple bonds (alkynes). Molecules containing carbon--hetero double bonds like carbonyl (C=O) groups, or imine (C=N) groups, can undergo addition as they too have double bond character.

Ferrocene

Ferrocene is an organometallic compound with the formula $Fe(C_5H_5)_2$.

It is the prototypical metallocene, a type of organometallic chemical compound consisting of two cyclopentadienyl rings bound on opposite sides of a central metal atom. Such organometallic compounds are also known as sandwich compounds.

Grignard reagents

The Grignard reaction is an organometallic chemical reaction in which alkyl- or aryl-magnesium halides (Grignard reagents) add to a carbonyl group in an aldehyde or ketone. This reaction is an important tool for the formation of carbon-carbon bonds. The reaction of an organic halide with magnesium is not a Grignard reaction, but provides a Grignard reagent.

Transition metal

In chemistry, the term transition metal has two possible meanings:•The IUPAC definition states that a transition metal is 'an element whose atom has an incomplete d sub-shell, or which can give rise to cations with an incomplete d sub-shell'.•Most scientists describe a 'transition metal' as any element in the d-block of the periodic table, which includes groups 3 to 12 on the periodic table. All elements in the d-block are metals. In actual practice, the f-block is also included in the form of the lanthanide and actinide series.

Jensen has reviewed the history of the terms transition element and d-block.

Electron counting

Electron counting is a formalism used for classifying compounds and for explaining or predicting electronic structure and bonding. Many rules in chemistry rely on electron-counting:•Octet rule is used with Lewis structures for main group elements, especially the lighter ones such as carbon, nitrogen, and oxygen,•Eighteen electron rule in inorganic chemistry and organometallic chemistry of transition metals,•Polyhedral skeletal electron pair theory for cluster compounds, including transition metals and main group elements such as boron including Wade's rules for polyhedral cluster compounds, including transition metals and main group elements and mixtures thereof.

Atoms that do not obey their rule are called 'electron-deficient' when they have too few electrons to achieve a noble gas configuration, or 'hypervalent' when they have too many electrons. Since these compounds tend to be more reactive than compounds that obey their rule, electron counting is an important tool for identifying the reactivity of molecules.

Polycyclic compound

In organic chemistry, a polycyclic compound is a cyclic compound with more than one hydrocarbon loop or ring structures (benzene rings). In general, the term includes all polycyclic aromatic compounds, including the polycyclic aromatic hydrocarbons, the heterocyclic aromatic compounds containing sulfur, nitrogen, oxygen, or another non-carbon atoms, and substituted derivatives of these.

Antiaromaticity

Antiaromatic molecules are cyclic systems containing alternating single and double bonds, where the pi electron energy of antiaromatic compounds is higher than that of its open-chain counterpart.

Therefore antiaromatic compounds are unstable and highly reactive; often antiaromatic compounds distort themselves out of planarity to resolve this instability. Antiaromatic compounds usually fail Hückel's rule of aromaticity.

Examples of antiaromatic systems are cyclobutadiene (A), the cyclopentadienyl cation (B) and the cyclopropenyl anion (C). Cyclooctatetraene is a 4n system but neither aromatic or antiaromatic because the molecule escapes a planar geometry.

By adding or removing an electron pair via a redox reaction, a π system can become aromatic and therefore more stable than the original non- or anti-aromatic compound, for instance the cyclooctatetraenide dianion. The IUPAC criteria for antiaromaticity are as follows:•The molecule must have 4n π electrons where n is any integer.•The molecule must be cyclic.•The molecule must have a conjugated pi electron system.•The molecule must be planar.

However, most chemists agree on the definition based on empirical (or simulated) energetic observations.

Cyclobutadiene

Cyclobutadiene is the smallest [n]-annulene (-annulene), an extremely unstable hydrocarbon having a lifetime shorter than five seconds in the free state. It has chemical formula C_4H_4. It is believed to be in equilibrium between a pair of homologous rectangular/nonplanar ground states and a square, excited triplet state based upon theoretical calculations, and through spectroscopic and crystallographic investigation of substituted cyclobutadienes, in an argon matrix and inside carceplexes.

Chapter 15. DIENES, RESONANCE, AND AROMATICITY

CHAPTER QUIZ: KEY TERMS, PEOPLE, PLACES, CONCEPTS

1. A _________ in chemistry is a chemical bond between two chemical elements involving four bonding electrons instead of the usual two. The most common _________, that between two carbon atoms, can be found in alkenes. Many types of _________s between two different elements exist, for example in a carbonyl group with a carbon atom and an oxygen atom.

   a. formal charge
   b. pi bond
   c. Double bond
   d. triple bond

2. _________ is an organic compound that is a dicarboxylic acid, a molecule with two carboxyl groups. _________ is the cis-isomer of butenedioic acid, whereas fumaric acid is the trans-isomer. It is mainly used as a precursor to fumaric acid, and relative to its parent maleic anhydride, _________ has few applications.

   a. Maleylacetic acid
   b. Malic acid
   c. Malonic acid
   d. Maleic acid

3. _________ is an organic ester that is naturally produced by many species of plants. Some of the plants which produce it are called wintergreens, hence the common name.

   Plants containing _________ produce this organic ester (a combination of an organic acid with an alcohol) most likely as an anti-herbivore defense.

   a. Phenyl salicylate
   b. Methyl salicylate
   c. Salicylmethylecgonine
   d. Salsalate

4. . Antiaromatic molecules are cyclic systems containing alternating single and double bonds, where the pi electron energy of antiaromatic compounds is higher than that of its open-chain counterpart. Therefore antiaromatic compounds are unstable and highly reactive; often antiaromatic compounds distort themselves out of planarity to resolve this instability. Antiaromatic compounds usually fail Hückel's rule of aromaticity.

   Examples of antiaromatic systems are cyclobutadiene (A), the cyclopentadienyl cation (B) and the cyclopropenyl anion (C). Cyclooctatetraene is a 4n system but neither aromatic or antiaromatic because the molecule escapes a planar geometry.

   By adding or removing an electron pair via a redox reaction, a π system can become aromatic and therefore more stable than the original non- or anti-aromatic compound, for instance the cyclooctatetraenide dianion. The IUPAC criteria for _________ are as follows:•The molecule must have 4n π electrons where n is any integer.•The molecule must be cyclic.•The molecule must have a conjugated pi electron system.•The molecule must be planar.

   However, most chemists agree on the definition based on empirical (or simulated) energetic observations.

a. Aromatic transition state theory
b. Aromaticity
c. Effective molarity
d. Antiaromaticity

5. A _________ is a hydrocarbon with three or more cumulative (consecutive) double bonds. A member of this compound class is butatriene (which is also called simply _________), $H_2C=C=C=CH_2$. Unlike most alkanes and alkenes, _________s tend to be rigid, which makes them appealing for molecular nanotechnology.

a. Cyanate ester
b. Cyanimide
c. Cyanohydrin
d. Cumulene

ANSWER KEY
Chapter 15. DIENES, RESONANCE, AND AROMATICITY

---

1. c
2. d
3. b
4. d
5. d

CHAPTER OUTLINE: KEY TERMS, PEOPLE, PLACES, CONCEPTS

______ Anisole

______ Catechol

______ Hydroquinone

______ Resorcinol

______ Styrene

______ Toluene

______ O-Xylene

______ Benzyl chloride

______ Phenyl group

______ Chemical shift

______ Electrophilic addition

______ Benzene

______ Halogenation

______ Electrophilic aromatic substitution

______ Nitric acid

______ Nitro compound

______ Nitration

______ 4-Nitrobenzoic acid

______ Benzenesulfonic acid

Chapter 16. THE CHEMISTRY OF BENZENE AND ITS DERIVATIVES

CHAPTER OUTLINE: KEY TERMS, PEOPLE, PLACES, CONCEPTS

- _______ Nitronium ion
- _______ Oleum
- _______ Sulfuric acid
- _______ Allylic rearrangement
- _______ Acetyl chloride
- _______ Acylation
- _______ Acyl group
- _______ Zinc chloride
- _______ Polar effect
- _______ Alkoxy group
- _______ Molecular orbital
- _______ Activating group
- _______ Deactivating groups
- _______ Orbital overlap
- _______ Organic reaction
- _______ Transition metal
- _______ Fumaric acid
- _______ Bibenzyl
- _______ Carcinogen

CHAPTER OUTLINE: KEY TERMS, PEOPLE, PLACES, CONCEPTS

_______________ Terephthalic acid

_______________ Aromatic hydrocarbon

CHAPTER HIGHLIGHTS & NOTES: KEY TERMS, PEOPLE, PLACES, CONCEPTS

Anisole

Anisole, is the organic compound with the formula $CH_3OC_6H_5$. It is a colorless liquid with a smell reminiscent of anise seed, and in fact many of its derivatives are found in natural and artificial fragrances. The compound is mainly made synthetically and is a precursor to other synthetic compounds.

Catechol

Catechol, also known as pyrocatechol or 1,2-dihydroxybenzene, is an organic compound with the molecular formula $C_6H_4(OH)_2$. It is the ortho isomer of the three isomeric benzenediols. This colorless compound occurs naturally in trace amounts.

Hydroquinone

Hydroquinone, also benzene-1,4-diol or quinol, is an aromatic organic compound that is a type of phenol, having the chemical formula $C_6H_4(OH)_2$. Its chemical structure, shown in the table at right, has two hydroxyl groups bonded to a benzene ring in a para position. It is a white granular solid.

Resorcinol

Resorcinol is a dihydroxy benzene. It is the 1,3-isomer of benzenediol with the formula $C_6H_4(OH)_2$.

Nomenclature

Benzene-1,3-diol is the name recommended by the International Union of Pure and Applied Chemistry (IUPAC) in its 1993 Recommendations for the Nomenclature of Organic Chemistry.

Styrene

Styrene, is an organic compound with the chemical formula $C_6H_5CH=CH_2$. This derivative of benzene is a colorless oily liquid that evaporates easily and has a sweet smell, although high concentrations confer a less pleasant odor. Styrene is the precursor to polystyrene and several copolymers.

Toluene

Toluene, formerly known as toluol, is a clear, water-insoluble liquid with the typical smell of paint thinners. Chemically it is a mono-substituted benzene derivative, i.e.

one in which a single hydrogen atom from the benzene molecule has been replaced by a univalent group, in this case CH_3.

It is an aromatic hydrocarbon that is widely used as an industrial feedstock and as a solvent.

O-Xylene

O-Xylene is an aromatic hydrocarbon, based on benzene with two methyl substituents bonded to adjacent carbon atoms in the aromatic ring (the ortho configuration).

It is a constitutional isomer of m-xylene and p-xylene.

o-Xylene is largely used in the production of phthalic anhydride, and is generally extracted by distillation from a mixed xylene stream in a plant primarily designed for p-xylene production.

Benzyl chloride

Benzyl chloride, is an organic compound with the formula $C_6H_5CH_2Cl$. This colourless liquid is a reactive organochlorine compound that is a widely used chemical building block.

Benzyl chloride is prepared industrially by the gas-phase photochemical reaction of toluene with chlorine:$C_6H_5CH_3 + Cl_2 \rightarrow C_6H_5CH_2Cl + HCl$

In this way, approximately 100,000 tonnes are produced annually.

Phenyl group

In organic chemistry, the phenyl group is a cyclic group of atoms with the formula C_6H_5. Phenyl groups are closely related to benzene. Phenyl groups have six carbon atoms bonded together in a hexagonal planar ring, five of which are bonded to individual hydrogen atoms, with the remaining carbon bonded to a substituent.

Chemical shift

In nuclear magnetic resonance (NMR) spectroscopy, the chemical shift is the resonant frequency of a nucleus relative to a standard. Often the position and number of chemical shifts are diagnostic of the structure of a molecule. Chemical shifts are also used to describe signals in other forms of spectroscopy such as photoemission spectroscopy.

Electrophilic addition

In organic chemistry, an electrophilic addition reaction is an addition reaction where, in a chemical compound, a π bond is broken and two new σ bonds are formed. The substrate of an electrophilic addition reaction must have a double bond or triple bond.

The driving force for this reaction is the formation of an electrophile X^+ that forms a covalent bond with an electron-rich unsaturated C=C bond.

Benzene

Benzene is an organic chemical compound. It is composed of 6 carbon atoms in a ring, with 1 hydrogen atom attached to each carbon atom, with the molecular formula C_6H_6.

Halogenation

Halogenation is a chemical reaction that involves the reaction of a compound, usually an organic compound, with a halogen. Dehalogenation is the reverse, the removal of a halogen from a molecule. The pathway and stoichiometry of halogenation depends on the structural features and functional groups of the organic substrate as well as the halogen.

Electrophilic aromatic substitution

Electrophilic aromatic substitution is an organic reaction in which an atom that is attached to an aromatic system (usually hydrogen) is replaced by an electrophile. Some of the most important electrophilic aromatic substitutions are aromatic nitration, aromatic halogenation, aromatic sulfonation, and acylation and alkylating Friedel-Crafts reactions.

The most widely practiced example of this reaction is the ethylation of benzene.

Nitric acid

Nitric acid also known as aqua fortis and spirit of niter, is a highly corrosive and toxic strong mineral acid which is normally colorless but tends to acquire a yellow cast due to the accumulation of oxides of nitrogen if long-stored. Ordinary nitric acid has a concentration of 68%. When the solution contains more than 86% HNO_3, it is referred to as fuming nitric acid.

Nitro compound

Nitro compounds are organic compounds that contain one or more nitro functional groups ($-NO_2$). They are often highly explosive, especially when the compound contains more than one nitro group and is impure. The nitro group is one of the most common explosophores (functional group that makes a compound explosive) used globally.

Nitration

Nitration is a general chemical process for the introduction of a nitro group into a chemical compound. The dominant application of nitration is for the production of nitrobenzene, the precursor to methylene diphenyl diisocyanate. Nitrations are famously used for the production of explosives, for example the conversion of glycerin to nitroglycerin and the conversion of toluene to trinitrotoluene.

4-Nitrobenzoic acid

4-Nitrobenzoic acid is an organic compound with the formula $C_6H_4(NO_2)CO_2H$. It is a precursor to 4-nitrobenzoyl chloride, the precursor to the anestheic Procaine and folic acid. It is also a precursor to 4-aminobenzoic acid.

4-Nitrobenzoic acid is prepared by oxidation of 4-nitrotoluene using oxygen or nitric acid as oxidants.

Benzenesulfonic acid

Benzenesulfonic acid is an organosulfur compound with the formula $C_6H_5SO_3H$. It is the simplest aromatic sulfonic acid. It forms colorless deliquescent sheet crystals or a white waxy solid that is soluble in water and ethanol, slightly soluble in benzene and insoluble in carbon disulfide and diethyl ether. It is often stored in the form of alkali metal salts.

Nitronium ion

The nitronium ion is not a radical), NO

+2, is a generally reactive cation created by the removal of an electron from the paramagnetic nitrogen dioxide molecule, or the protonation of nitric acid.

It is reactive enough to exist in normal conditions, but it is used extensively as an electrophile in the nitration of other substances. The ion is generated in situ for this purpose by mixing concentrated sulfuric acid and concentrated nitric acid according to the equilibrium:2 H_2SO_4 + HNO_3 → 2 HSO−4 + NO+2 + H_3O^+

Historically, the nitronium ion was detected by Raman Spectroscopy, since its symmetric stretch is Raman active but Infrared inactive.

Oleum

Oleum, or fuming sulfuric acid refers to a solution of various compositions of sulfur trioxide in sulfuric acid or sometimes more specifically to disulfuric acid (also known as pyrosulfuric acid).

Oleums can be described by the formula $ySO_3.H_2O$ where y is the total molar sulfur trioxide content. The value of y can be varied, to include different oleums.

Sulfuric acid

Sulfuric acid is a highly caustic strong mineral acid with the molecular formula H_2SO_4. It is a colorless to slightly yellow viscous liquid which is soluble in water at all concentrations. The historical name of this acid is oil of vitriol.

Allylic rearrangement

An allylic rearrangement is an organic reaction in which the double bond in an allyl chemical compound shifts to the next carbon atom. It is encountered in nucleophilic substitution.

In reaction conditions that favor a S_N1 reaction mechanism the intermediate is a carbocation for which several resonance structures are possible.

Acetyl chloride

Acetyl chloride, CH_3COCl, also known as ethanoyl chloride or acyl chloride, is an acid chloride derived from acetic acid. It belongs to the class of organic compounds called acyl halides. It is a colorless liquid.

Acylation

In chemistry, acylation is the process of adding an acyl group to a compound. The compound providing the acyl group is called the acylating agent.

Because they form a strong electrophile when treated with some metal catalysts, acyl halides are commonly used as acylating agents.

Acyl group

An acyl group is a functional group derived by the removal of one or more hydroxyl groups from an oxoacid, including inorganic acids.

In organic chemistry, the acyl group is usually derived from a carboxylic acid (IUPAC name: alkanoyl). Therefore, it has the formula RCO-, where R represents an alkyl group that is attached to the CO group with a single bond.

Zinc chloride

Zinc chloride is the name of chemical compound with the formula $ZnCl_2$ and its hydrates. Zinc chlorides, of which nine crystalline forms are known, are colorless or white, and are highly soluble in water. $ZnCl_2$ itself is hygroscopic and even deliquescent.

Polar effect

The Polar effect is the effect exerted by a substituent on modifying electrostatic forces operating on a nearby reaction center. The main contributors to the polar effect are the inductive effect, mesomeric effect and the through-space electronic field effect.

An electron withdrawing group or EWG draws electrons away from a reaction center.

Alkoxy group

In chemistry, the alkoxy group is an alkyl (carbon and hydrogen chain) group singular bonded to oxygen thus: R--O. The range of alkoxy groups is great, the simplest being methoxy (CH_3O--). An ethoxy group (CH_3CH_2O--) is found in the organic compound phenetol, $C_6H_5OCH_2CH_3$ which is also known as ethoxy benzene. Related to alkoxy groups are aryloxy groups, which have an aryl group singular bonded to oxygen such as the phenoxy group (C_6H_5O--).

Molecular orbital

In chemistry, a molecular orbital is a mathematical function describing the wave-like behavior of an electron in a molecule. This function can be used to calculate chemical and physical properties such as the probability of finding an electron in any specific region. The term 'orbital' was first used in English by Robert S. Mulliken as the English translation of Schrödinger's 'Eigenfunktion'.

Activating group

In organic chemistry, a functional group is called an activating group if a benzene molecule to which it is attached more readily participates in electrophilic substitution reactions. Benzene itself will normally undergo substitutions by electrophiles, but additional substituents can alter the reaction rate or products by electronically or sterically affecting the interaction of the two reactants.

Activating groups are generally ortho/para directing for electrophilic aromatic substitution (though the deactivating halogens are also ortho/para directing as they have unshared lone pairs of electrons that are shared with the aromatic ring)

Functional groups are typically divided into three levels of activating ability.

Chapter 16. THE CHEMISTRY OF BENZENE AND ITS DERIVATIVES

CHAPTER HIGHLIGHTS & NOTES: KEY TERMS, PEOPLE, PLACES, CONCEPTS

Deactivating groups

In organic chemistry, a deactivating group (or electron withdrawing group) is a functional group attached to a benzene molecule that removes electron density from the benzene ring, making electrophilic aromatic substitution reactions slower and more complex relative to benzene. Depending on their relative strengths, deactivating groups also determine the positions (relative to themselves) on the benzene ring where substitutions must take place; this property is therefore important in processes of organic synthesis.

Deactivating groups are generally sorted into three categories.

Orbital overlap

Orbital overlap was an idea first introduced by Linus Pauling to explain the molecular bond angles observed through experimentation and is the basis for the concept of orbital hybridisation. s orbitals are spherical and have no directionality while p orbitals are oriented 90° to one another. A theory was needed therefore to explain why molecules such as methane (CH_4) had observed bond angles of 109.5°.

Organic reaction

Organic reactions are chemical reactions involving organic compounds. The basic organic chemistry reaction types are addition reactions, elimination reactions, substitution reactions, pericyclic reactions, rearrangement reactions, photochemical reactions and redox reactions. In organic synthesis, organic reactions are used in the construction of new organic molecules.

Transition metal

In chemistry, the term transition metal has two possible meanings:•The IUPAC definition states that a transition metal is 'an element whose atom has an incomplete d sub-shell, or which can give rise to cations with an incomplete d sub-shell'.•Most scientists describe a 'transition metal' as any element in the d-block of the periodic table, which includes groups 3 to 12 on the periodic table. All elements in the d-block are metals. In actual practice, the f-block is also included in the form of the lanthanide and actinide series.

Jensen has reviewed the history of the terms transition element and d-block.

Fumaric acid

Fumaric acid is the chemical compound with the formula $HO_2CCH=CHCO_2H$. This white crystalline compound is one of two isomeric unsaturated dicarboxylic acids, the other being maleic acid. In fumaric acid the carboxylic acid groups are trans (E) and in maleic acid they are cis (Z). Fumaric acid has a fruit-like taste.

Bibenzyl

Bibenzyl is an aromatic chemical compound that can be considered a derivative of ethane in which one phenyl group is attached to each carbon atom.

Bibenzyl forms the central core of some stilbenoid natural products and isoquinoline alkaloids.

Carcinogen

A carcinogen is any substance, radionuclide, or radiation that is an agent directly involved in causing cancer.

This may be due to the ability to damage the genome or to the disruption of cellular metabolic processes. Several radioactive substances are considered carcinogens, but their carcinogenic activity is attributed to the radiation, for example gamma rays and alpha particles, which they emit.

Terephthalic acid	Terephthalic acid is the organic compound with formula $C_6H_4(COOH)_2$. This colourless solid is a commodity chemical, used principally as a precursor to the polyester PET, used to make clothing and plastic bottles. Several billion kilograms are produced annually.
Aromatic hydrocarbon	An aromatic hydrocarbon is a hydrocarbon with alternating double and single bonds between carbon atoms. The term 'aromatic' was assigned before the physical mechanism determining aromaticity was discovered, and was derived from the fact that many of the compounds have a sweet scent. The configuration of six carbon atoms in aromatic compounds is known as a benzene ring, after the simplest possible such hydrocarbon, benzene.

CHAPTER QUIZ: KEY TERMS, PEOPLE, PLACES, CONCEPTS

1. _________, also benzene-1,4-diol or quinol, is an aromatic organic compound that is a type of phenol, having the chemical formula $C_6H_4(OH)_2$. Its chemical structure, shown in the table at right, has two hydroxyl groups bonded to a benzene ring in a para position. It is a white granular solid.

   a. Bromoethane
   b. Hydroquinone
   c. 1,2-Dioxetanedione
   d. Crown ether

2. _________, or fuming sulfuric acid refers to a solution of various compositions of sulfur trioxide in sulfuric acid or sometimes more specifically to disulfuric acid (also known as pyrosulfuric acid).

   _________s can be described by the formula $ySO_3.H_2O$ where y is the total molar sulfur trioxide content. The value of y can be varied, to include different _________s.

   a. Ortho acid
   b. Orthocarbonic acid
   c. Oxoacid
   d. Oleum

3. . _________ is an organic compound with the formula $C_6H_4(NO_2)CO_2H$. It is a precursor to 4-nitrobenzoyl chloride, the precursor to the anestheic Procaine and folic acid. It is also a precursor to 4-aminobenzoic acid.

   _________ is prepared by oxidation of 4-nitrotoluene using oxygen or nitric acid as oxidants.

a. 3-Nitrobenzyl alcohol
b. -3-Nitrobiphenyline
c. 4-Nitrobenzoic acid
d. 2-Nitrocinnamaldehyde

4. _________ is the name of chemical compound with the formula $ZnCl_2$ and its hydrates. _________s, of which nine crystalline forms are known, are colorless or white, and are highly soluble in water. $ZnCl_2$ itself is hygroscopic and even deliquescent.

a. Zinc chloride
b. Zintl phase
c. Zirconium tungstate
d. 1,2-Dioxetanedione

5. In chemistry, _________ is the process of adding an acyl group to a compound. The compound providing the acyl group is called the acylating agent.

Because they form a strong electrophile when treated with some metal catalysts, acyl halides are commonly used as acylating agents.

a. Adamkeiwickz reaction
b. Adams decarboxylation
c. Acylation
d. Alkylation

ANSWER KEY
Chapter 16. THE CHEMISTRY OF BENZENE AND ITS DERIVATIVES

1. b
2. d
3. c
4. a
5. c

Chapter 17. ALLYLIC AND BENZYLIC REACTIVITY

CHAPTER OUTLINE: KEY TERMS, PEOPLE, PLACES, CONCEPTS

Alkoxy group

Polar effect

Molecular orbital

Orbital overlap

Hydrogen halide

Clemmensen reduction

Free-radical addition

Mass spectrum

Carbon tetrachloride

Phenyl group

Grignard reagents

Hofmann rearrangement

Allylic rearrangement

Benzyl chloride

Chromium trioxide

Potassium permanganate

Benzoic acid

Carboxylic acid

Phenyl isothiocyanate

Essential oil

Terpene

Diterpene

Limonene

Monoterpene

Biosynthesis

Isopentenyl pyrophosphate

Pyrophosphoric acid

Geranyl pyrophosphate

CHAPTER HIGHLIGHTS & NOTES: KEY TERMS, PEOPLE, PLACES, CONCEPTS

Alkoxy group

In chemistry, the alkoxy group is an alkyl (carbon and hydrogen chain) group singular bonded to oxygen thus: R--O. The range of alkoxy groups is great, the simplest being methoxy (CH_3O--). An ethoxy group (CH_3CH_2O--) is found in the organic compound phenetol, $C_6H_5OCH_2CH_3$ which is also known as ethoxy benzene. Related to alkoxy groups are aryloxy groups, which have an aryl group singular bonded to oxygen such as the phenoxy group (C_6H_5O--).

Polar effect

The Polar effect is the effect exerted by a substituent on modifying electrostatic forces operating on a nearby reaction center. The main contributors to the polar effect are the inductive effect, mesomeric effect and the through-space electronic field effect.

An electron withdrawing group or EWG draws electrons away from a reaction center.

Molecular orbital

In chemistry, a molecular orbital is a mathematical function describing the wave-like behavior of an electron in a molecule.

This function can be used to calculate chemical and physical properties such as the probability of finding an electron in any specific region. The term 'orbital' was first used in English by Robert S. Mulliken as the English translation of Schrödinger's 'Eigenfunktion'.

Orbital overlap

Orbital overlap was an idea first introduced by Linus Pauling to explain the molecular bond angles observed through experimentation and is the basis for the concept of orbital hybridisation. s orbitals are spherical and have no directionality while p orbitals are oriented 90° to one another. A theory was needed therefore to explain why molecules such as methane (CH_4) had observed bond angles of 109.5°.

Hydrogen halide

Hydrogen halides (or hydrohalic acids) are inorganic compounds with the formula HX where X is one of the halogens: fluorine, chlorine, bromine, iodine, and astatine. Hydrogen halides are gases that dissolve in water to give acids.

The hydrogen halides are diatomic molecules with no tendency to ionize in the gas phase.

Clemmensen reduction

Clemmensen reduction is a chemical reaction described as a reduction of ketones (or aldehydes) to alkanes using zinc amalgam and hydrochloric acid. This reaction is named after Erik Christian Clemmensen, a Danish chemist.

The Clemmensen reduction is particularly effective at reducing aryl-alkyl ketones.

Free-radical addition

Free-radical addition is an addition reaction in organic chemistry involving free radicals. The addition may occur between a radical and a non-radical, or between two radicals.

The basic steps with examples of the free radical addition (also known as radical chain mechanism) are:•Initiation by a radical initiator: A radical is created from a non-radical precursor.•Chain propagation: A radical reacts with a non-radical to produce a new radical species•Chain termination: Two radicals react with each other to create a non-radical species

Free radical reactions depend on a reagent having a (relatively) weak bond, allowing it to homolyse to form radicals (often with heat or light).

Mass spectrum

A mass spectrum is an intensity vs. m/z (mass-to-charge ratio) plot representing a chemical analysis. Hence, the mass spectrum of a sample is a pattern representing the distribution of ions by mass (more correctly: mass-to-charge ratio) in a sample. It is a histogram usually acquired using an instrument called a mass spectrometer.

Carbon tetrachloride

Carbon tetrachloride, also known by many other names is the organic compound with the formula CCl_4. It was formerly widely used in fire extinguishers, as a precursor to refrigerants, and as a cleaning agent.

Chapter 17. ALLYLIC AND BENZYLIC REACTIVITY

CHAPTER HIGHLIGHTS & NOTES: KEY TERMS, PEOPLE, PLACES, CONCEPTS

Phenyl group

In organic chemistry, the phenyl group is a cyclic group of atoms with the formula C_6H_5. Phenyl groups are closely related to benzene. Phenyl groups have six carbon atoms bonded together in a hexagonal planar ring, five of which are bonded to individual hydrogen atoms, with the remaining carbon bonded to a substituent.

Grignard reagents

The Grignard reaction is an organometallic chemical reaction in which alkyl- or aryl-magnesium halides (Grignard reagents) add to a carbonyl group in an aldehyde or ketone. This reaction is an important tool for the formation of carbon-carbon bonds. The reaction of an organic halide with magnesium is not a Grignard reaction, but provides a Grignard reagent.

Hofmann rearrangement

The Hofmann rearrangement is the organic reaction of a primary amide to a primary amine with one fewer carbon atom.

This reaction is also sometimes called the Hofmann degradation or the Harmon Process, and should not be confused with the Hofmann elimination. Mechanism

The reaction of bromine with sodium hydroxide forms sodium hypobromite in situ, which transforms the primary amide into an intermediate isocyanate.

Allylic rearrangement

An allylic rearrangement is an organic reaction in which the double bond in an allyl chemical compound shifts to the next carbon atom. It is encountered in nucleophilic substitution.

In reaction conditions that favor a S_N1 reaction mechanism the intermediate is a carbocation for which several resonance structures are possible.

Benzyl chloride

Benzyl chloride, is an organic compound with the formula $C_6H_5CH_2Cl$. This colourless liquid is a reactive organochlorine compound that is a widely used chemical building block.

Benzyl chloride is prepared industrially by the gas-phase photochemical reaction of toluene with chlorine:$C_6H_5CH_3 + Cl_2 \rightarrow C_6H_5CH_2Cl + HCl$

In this way, approximately 100,000 tonnes are produced annually.

Chromium trioxide

Chromium trioxide is the inorganic compound with the formula CrO_3. It is the acidic anhydride of chromic acid, and is sometimes marketed under the same name. This compound is a dark-red/orange brown solid, which dissolves in water concomitant with hydrolysis.

Potassium permanganate

Potassium permanganate is an inorganic chemical compound with the formula $KMnO_4$. It is a salt consisting of K^+ and MnO_4^- ions. Formerly known as permanganate of potash or Condy's crystals, it is a strong oxidizing agent.

Benzoic acid

Benzoic acid, $C_7H_6O_2$ (or C_6H_5COOH), is a colorless crystalline solid and the simplest aromatic carboxylic acid. The name derived from gum benzoin, which was for a long time the only source for benzoic acid. Its salts are used as a food preservative and benzoic acid is an important precursor for the synthesis of many other organic substances.

Carboxylic acid

Carboxylic acids ( ) are organic acids characterized by the presence of at least one carboxyl group. The general formula of a carboxylic acid is R-COOH, where R is some monovalent functional group. A carboxyl group (or carboxy) is a functional group consisting of a carbonyl (RR'C=O) and a hydroxyl (R-O-H), which has the formula -C(=O)OH, usually written as -COOH or $-CO_2H$.

Carboxylic acids are Brønsted-Lowry acids because they are proton (H^+) donors.

Phenyl isothiocyanate

Phenyl isothiocyanate is a reagent used in reversed phase HPLC. PITC is less sensitive than o-phthaldehyde (OPA) and cannot be fully automated. PITC can be used for analysing secondary amines, unlike OPA.

It is also known as Edman's reagent and is used in Edman degradation.

Commercially available, this compound may be synthesized by reacting aniline with carbon disulfide and concentrated ammonia to give the ammonium dithiocarbamate salt.

Essential oil

An essential oil is a concentrated hydrophobic liquid containing volatile aroma compounds from plants. Essential oils are also known as volatile oils, ethereal oils or aetherolea, or simply as the 'oil of' the plant from which they were extracted, such as oil of clove. An oil is 'essential' in the sense that it carries a distinctive scent, or essence, of the plant.

Terpene

Terpenes (-peen) are a large and diverse class of organic compounds, produced by a variety of plants, particularly conifers, though also by some insects such as termites or swallowtail butterflies, which emit terpenes from their osmeterium. They are often strong smelling and thus may have had a protective function.

They are the major components of resin, and of turpentine produced from resin.

Diterpene

Diterpene, a type of terpene, is an organic compound composed of four isoprene units and has the molecular formula $C_{20}H_{32}$. They derive from geranylgeranyl pyrophosphate. Diterpenes form the basis for biologically important compounds such as retinol, retinal, and phytol.

Limonene

Limonene is a colourless liquid hydrocarbon classified as a cyclic terpene. The more common D isomer possesses a strong smell of oranges.

Chapter 17. ALLYLIC AND BENZYLIC REACTIVITY

CHAPTER HIGHLIGHTS & NOTES: KEY TERMS, PEOPLE, PLACES, CONCEPTS

Monoterpene	Monoterpenes are a class of terpenes that consist of two isoprene units and have the molecular formula $C_{10}H_{16}$. Monoterpenes may be linear (acyclic) or contain rings. Biochemical modifications such as oxidation or rearrangement produce the related monoterpenoids.
Biosynthesis	Biosynthesis is an enzyme-catalyzed process in cells of living organisms by which substrates are converted to more complex products. The biosynthesis process often consists of several enzymatic steps in which the product of one step is used as substrate in the following step. Examples for such multi-step biosynthetic pathways are those for the production of amino acids, fatty acids, and natural products.
Isopentenyl pyrophosphate	Isopentenyl pyrophosphate is an intermediate in the classical, HMG-CoA reductase pathway used by organisms in the biosynthesis of terpenes and terpenoids. IPP is formed from acetyl-CoA via mevalonic acid. IPP can then be isomerized to dimethylallyl pyrophosphate by the enzyme isopentenyl pyrophosphate isomerase.
Pyrophosphoric acid	Pyrophosphoric acid, also known under the name diphosphoric acid, is colorless, odorless, hygroscopic and is soluble in water, diethyl ether, and ethyl alcohol. It is produced from phosphoric acid by dehydration. Pyrophosphoric acid slowly hydrolyzes in the presence of water into phosphoric acid.
Geranyl pyrophosphate	Geranyl pyrophosphate is an intermediate in the HMG-CoA reductase pathway used by organisms in the biosynthesis of farnesyl pyrophosphate, geranylgeranyl pyrophosphate, cholesterol, terpenes and terpenoids. •Geraniol•Farnesyl pyrophosphate•Geranylgeranyl pyrophosphate.

Chapter 17. ALLYLIC AND BENZYLIC REACTIVITY

CHAPTER QUIZ: KEY TERMS, PEOPLE, PLACES, CONCEPTS

1. In chemistry, the _________ is an alkyl (carbon and hydrogen chain) group singular bonded to oxygen thus: R--O. The range of _________s is great, the simplest being methoxy (CH_3O--). An ethoxy group (CH_3CH_2O--) is found in the organic compound phenetol, $C_6H_5OCH_2CH_3$ which is also known as ethoxy benzene. Related to _________s are aryloxy groups, which have an aryl group singular bonded to oxygen such as the phenoxy group (C_6H_5O--).

   a. Ethylenedioxy
   b. Alkoxy group
   c. Rot-proof
   d. Smoke point

2. _________, $C_7H_6O_2$ (or C_6H_5COOH), is a colorless crystalline solid and the simplest aromatic carboxylic acid. The name derived from gum benzoin, which was for a long time the only source for _________. Its salts are used as a food preservative and _________ is an important precursor for the synthesis of many other organic substances.

   a. lactose
   b. mannitol
   c. Benzoic acid
   d. 1,2-Dioxetanedione

3. _________ is a colourless liquid hydrocarbon classified as a cyclic terpene. The more common D isomer possesses a strong smell of oranges. It is used in chemical synthesis as a precursor to carvone and as a renewably-based solvent in cleaning products.

   a. Linalool
   b. Linalyl acetate
   c. Lineatin
   d. Limonene

4. The _________ is the effect exerted by a substituent on modifying electrostatic forces operating on a nearby reaction center. The main contributors to the _________ are the inductive effect, mesomeric effect and the through-space electronic field effect.

   An electron withdrawing group or EWG draws electrons away from a reaction center.

   a. Ring strain
   b. Polar effect
   c. Walsh diagram
   d. Smoke point

5. . In chemistry, a _________ is a mathematical function describing the wave-like behavior of an electron in a molecule. This function can be used to calculate chemical and physical properties such as the probability of finding an electron in any specific region. The term 'orbital' was first used in English by Robert S. Mulliken as the English translation of Schrödinger's 'Eigenfunktion'.

   a. Molecular orbital

b. Monte Carlo molecular modeling

c. Physical and Theoretical Chemistry Laboratory

d. Quantum chemistry

ANSWER KEY
Chapter 17. ALLYLIC AND BENZYLIC REACTIVITY

1. b
2. c
3. d
4. b
5. a

CHAPTER OUTLINE: KEY TERMS, PEOPLE, PLACES, CONCEPTS

Aryl halide

Vinyl chloride

Catechol

Hydroquinone

Phenol

Resorcinol

P-Cresol

Steric effects

Addition reaction

Heck reaction

Nucleophilic aromatic substitution

Meisenheimer complex

Polar effect

Molecular orbital

Transition metal

Dansyl chloride

Oxidation state

Functional group

18-Electron rule

Chapter 18. THE CHEMISTRY OF ARYL HALIDES, VINYLIC HALIDES, AND PHENOLS

CHAPTER OUTLINE: KEY TERMS, PEOPLE, PLACES, CONCEPTS

______ Electron counting

______ Substitution reaction

______ Grignard reagents

______ Oxidative addition

______ Reductive elimination

______ Insertion

______ Boronic acid

______ Suzuki reaction

______ Catecholborane

______ Ground state

______ Metallacycle

______ Green chemistry

______ Ziegler-Natta catalyst

______ Catalyst

______ Hydroformylation

______ Phenyl group

______ Picric acid

______ Stille reaction

______ Anthranilic acid

CHAPTER OUTLINE: KEY TERMS, PEOPLE, PLACES, CONCEPTS

______ Free-radical reaction

______ Reaction inhibitor

______ Vitamin E

______ Sandmeyer reaction

______ Claisen rearrangement

______ Autoxidation

______ Cumene hydroperoxide

______ Cumene

CHAPTER HIGHLIGHTS & NOTES: KEY TERMS, PEOPLE, PLACES, CONCEPTS

Aryl halide

In organic chemistry, an aryl halide is an aromatic compound in which one or more hydrogen atoms directly bonded to an aromatic ring are replaced by a halide. The haloarene are distinguished from haloalkanes because they exhibit many differences in methods of preparation and properties. The most important members are the aryl chlorides, but the class of compounds is so broad that many derivatives enjoy niche applications.

Vinyl chloride

Vinyl chloride is the organochloride with the formula H_2C:CHCl. It is also called vinyl chloride monomer, or VCM. This colorless compound is an important industrial chemical chiefly used to produce the polymer polyvinyl chloride. At ambient pressure and temperature, vinyl chloride is a gas with a sickly sweet odor.

Catechol

Catechol, also known as pyrocatechol or 1,2-dihydroxybenzene, is an organic compound with the molecular formula $C_6H_4(OH)_2$. It is the ortho isomer of the three isomeric benzenediols. This colorless compound occurs naturally in trace amounts.

Chapter 18. THE CHEMISTRY OF ARYL HALIDES, VINYLIC HALIDES, AND PHENOLS

CHAPTER HIGHLIGHTS & NOTES: KEY TERMS, PEOPLE, PLACES, CONCEPTS

Hydroquinone

Hydroquinone, also benzene-1,4-diol or quinol, is an aromatic organic compound that is a type of phenol, having the chemical formula $C_6H_4(OH)_2$. Its chemical structure, shown in the table at right, has two hydroxyl groups bonded to a benzene ring in a para position. It is a white granular solid.

Phenol

Phenol, is an organic compound with the chemical formula C_6H_5OH. It is a white crystalline solid at room temperature. The molecule consists of a phenyl group ($-C_6H_5$) bonded to a hydroxyl group (-OH). It is mildly acidic, but requires careful handling due to its propensity to cause burns.

Resorcinol

Resorcinol is a dihydroxy benzene. It is the 1,3-isomer of benzenediol with the formula $C_6H_4(OH)_2$.

Nomenclature

Benzene-1,3-diol is the name recommended by the International Union of Pure and Applied Chemistry (IUPAC) in its 1993 Recommendations for the Nomenclature of Organic Chemistry.

P-Cresol

P-Cresol, also 4-methylphenol, is a phenol, with formula $(CH_3)C_6H_4(OH)$.

It is a positional isomer; the other two are m-cresol and o-cresol. P-cresol is a major component in pig odor.

Steric effects

Steric effects arise from the fact that each atom within a molecule occupies a certain amount of space. If atoms are brought too close together, there is an associated cost in energy due to overlapping electron clouds , and this may affect the molecule's preferred shape (conformation) and reactivity. Steric hindrance

Steric hindrance occurs when the large size of groups within a molecule prevents chemical reactions that are observed in related molecules with smaller groups.

Addition reaction

An addition reaction, in organic chemistry, is in its simplest terms an organic reaction where two or more molecules combine to form a larger one.

Addition reactions are limited to chemical compounds that have multiple bonds, such as molecules with carbon-carbon double bonds (alkenes), or with triple bonds (alkynes). Molecules containing carbon--hetero double bonds like carbonyl (C=O) groups, or imine (C=N) groups, can undergo addition as they too have double bond character.

CHAPTER HIGHLIGHTS & NOTES: KEY TERMS, PEOPLE, PLACES, CONCEPTS

Heck reaction

The Heck reaction is the chemical reaction of an unsaturated halide (or triflate) with an alkene and a base and palladium catalyst or palladium nanomaterial-based catalyst to form a substituted alkene. Together with the other palladium-catalyzed cross-coupling reactions, this reaction is of great importance, as it allows one to do substitution reactions on planar centers. It is named after Tsutomu Mizoroki and Richard F. Heck.

Nucleophilic aromatic substitution

A nucleophilic aromatic substitution is a substitution reaction in organic chemistry in which the nucleophile displaces a good leaving group, such as a halide, on an aromatic ring. There are 6 nucleophilic substitution mechanisms encountered with aromatic systems:•the S_NAr (addition-elimination) mechanism•the aromatic SN1 mechanism encountered with diazonium salts•the benzyne mechanism•the free radical $S_{RN}1$ mechanism•the ANRORC mechanism•Vicarious nucleophilic substitution.

The most important of these is the S_NAr mechanism, where electron withdrawing groups activate the ring towards nucleophilic attack, for example if there are nitro functional groups positioned ortho or para to the halide leaving group. S_NAr reaction mechanism

Aryl halides cannot undergo S_N2 reaction.The C-Br bond is in the plane of the ring as the carbon atom is trigonal.

Meisenheimer complex

A Meisenheimer complex is a 1:1 reaction adduct between an arene carrying electron withdrawing groups and nucleophile. These complexes are found as reactive intermediates in nucleophilic aromatic substitution but stable and isolated Meisenheimer salts are also known.

The early development of this type of complex takes place around the turn of the 19th century.

Polar effect

The Polar effect is the effect exerted by a substituent on modifying electrostatic forces operating on a nearby reaction center. The main contributors to the polar effect are the inductive effect, mesomeric effect and the through-space electronic field effect.

An electron withdrawing group or EWG draws electrons away from a reaction center.

Molecular orbital

In chemistry, a molecular orbital is a mathematical function describing the wave-like behavior of an electron in a molecule. This function can be used to calculate chemical and physical properties such as the probability of finding an electron in any specific region. The term 'orbital' was first used in English by Robert S. Mulliken as the English translation of Schrödinger's 'Eigenfunktion'.

Chapter 18. THE CHEMISTRY OF ARYL HALIDES, VINYLIC HALIDES, AND PHENOLS

CHAPTER HIGHLIGHTS & NOTES: KEY TERMS, PEOPLE, PLACES, CONCEPTS

Transition metal	In chemistry, the term transition metal has two possible meanings:•The IUPAC definition states that a transition metal is 'an element whose atom has an incomplete d sub-shell, or which can give rise to cations with an incomplete d sub-shell'.•Most scientists describe a 'transition metal' as any element in the d-block of the periodic table, which includes groups 3 to 12 on the periodic table. All elements in the d-block are metals. In actual practice, the f-block is also included in the form of the lanthanide and actinide series. Jensen has reviewed the history of the terms transition element and d-block.
Dansyl chloride	Dansyl chloride is a reagent that reacts with primary amino groups in both aliphatic and aromatic amines to produce stable blue- or blue-green-fluorescent sulfonamide adducts. It can also be made to react with secondary amines. Dansyl chloride is widely used to modify amino acids; specifically, protein sequencing and amino acid analysis.
Oxidation state	In chemistry, the oxidation state is an indicator of the degree of oxidation of an atom in a chemical compound. The formal oxidation state is the hypothetical charge that an atom would have if all bonds to atoms of different elements were 100% ionic. Oxidation states are typically represented by integers, which can be positive, negative, or zero.
Functional group	In organic chemistry, functional groups are lexicon specific groups of atoms or bonds within molecules that are responsible for the characteristic chemical reactions of those molecules. The same functional group will undergo the same or similar chemical reaction(s) regardless of the size of the molecule it is a part of. However, its relative reactivity can be modified by nearby functional groups.
18-Electron rule	The 18-electron rule is a rule used primarily for predicting formulae for stable metal complexes. The rule rests on the fact that valence shells of a transition metal consists of nine valence orbitals, which collectively can accommodate 18 electrons either as nonbonding electron pairs or as bonding electron pairs. Stated differently, the combination of these nine atomic orbitals with ligand orbitals gives rise to nine molecular orbitals that are either metal-ligand bonding or non-bonding.
Electron counting	Electron counting is a formalism used for classifying compounds and for explaining or predicting electronic structure and bonding. Many rules in chemistry rely on electron-counting:•Octet rule is used with Lewis structures for main group elements, especially the lighter ones such as carbon, nitrogen, and oxygen,•Eighteen electron rule in inorganic chemistry and organometallic chemistry of transition metals,•Polyhedral skeletal electron pair theory for cluster compounds, including transition metals and main group elements such as boron including Wade's rules for polyhedral cluster compounds, including transition metals and main group elements and mixtures thereof.

Atoms that do not obey their rule are called 'electron-deficient' when they have too few electrons to achieve a noble gas configuration, or 'hypervalent' when they have too many electrons. Since these compounds tend to be more reactive than compounds that obey their rule, electron counting is an important tool for identifying the reactivity of molecules.

Substitution reaction

In a substitution reaction, a functional group in a particular chemical compound is replaced by another group. In organic chemistry, the electrophilic and nucleophilic substitution reactions are of prime importance. Organic substitution reactions are classified in several main organic reaction types depending on whether the reagent that brings about the substitution is considered an electrophile or a nucleophile, whether a reactive intermediate involved in the reaction is a carbocation, a carbanion or a free radical or whether the substrate is aliphatic or aromatic.

Grignard reagents

The Grignard reaction is an organometallic chemical reaction in which alkyl- or aryl-magnesium halides (Grignard reagents) add to a carbonyl group in an aldehyde or ketone. This reaction is an important tool for the formation of carbon-carbon bonds. The reaction of an organic halide with magnesium is not a Grignard reaction, but provides a Grignard reagent.

Oxidative addition

Oxidative addition and reductive elimination are two important and related classes of reactions in organometallic chemistry. Oxidative addition is a process that increases both the oxidation state and coordination number of a metal centre. Oxidative addition is often a step in catalytic cycles, in conjunction with its reverse reaction, reductive elimination.

Reductive elimination

Oxidative addition and reductive elimination are two important and related classes of reactions in organometallic chemistry. Oxidative addition is a process that increases both the oxidation state and coordination number of a metal centre. Oxidative addition is often a step in catalytic cycles, in conjunction with its reverse reaction, reductive elimination.

Insertion

In genetics, an insertion (also called an insertion mutation) is the addition of one or more nucleotide base pairs into a DNA sequence. This can often happen in microsatellite regions due to the DNA polymerase slipping. Insertions can be anywhere in size from one base pair incorrectly inserted into a DNA sequence to a section of one chromosome inserted into another.

Boronic acid

A boronic acid is an alkyl or aryl substituted boric acid containing a carbon-boron bond belonging to the larger class of organoboranes. Boronic acids act as Lewis acids. Their unique feature is that they are capable of forming reversible covalent complexes with sugars, amino acids, hydroxamic acids, etc.

CHAPTER HIGHLIGHTS & NOTES: KEY TERMS, PEOPLE, PLACES, CONCEPTS

Suzuki reaction

The Suzuki reaction is the organic reaction of an aryl- or vinyl-boronic acid with an aryl- or vinyl-halide catalyzed by a palladium(0) complex, which can also be in the form of a nanomaterial-based catalyst. It is widely used to synthesize poly-olefins, styrenes, and substituted biphenyls, and has been extended to incorporate alkyl bromides. Several reviews have been published.

Catecholborane

Catecholborane is an organoboron compound that is useful in organic synthesis. This colourless liquid is a derivative of catechol and a borane, having the formula $C_6H_4O_2BH$.

Traditionally catecholborane is produced by treating catechol with borane (BH_3) in a cooled solution of THF. However, this method results in a loss of 2 mole equivalents of the hydride. Nöth and Männig devised a more economical method involves the reaction of alkali-metal boron hydride ($LiBH_4$, $NaBH_4$, of KBH_4) with tris(catecholato)bisborane in an ethereal solvent such as diethyl ether.

Ground state

The ground state of a quantum mechanical system is its lowest-energy state; the energy of the ground state is known as the zero-point energy of the system. An excited state is any state with energy greater than the ground state. The ground state of a quantum field theory is usually called the vacuum state or the vacuum.

Metallacycle

In organometallic chemistry, a metallacycle is a derivative of a carbocyclic compound wherein a metal has replaced at least one carbon center. Metallacycles appear frequently as reactive intermediates in catalysis, e.g. olefin metathesis and alkyne trimerization. In organic synthesis, directed ortho metalation is widely used for the functionalization of arene rings via C-H activation.

Green chemistry

Green chemistry, is a philosophy of chemical research and engineering that encourages the design of products and processes that minimize the use and generation of hazardous substances. Whereas environmental chemistry is the chemistry of the natural environment, and of pollutant chemicals in nature, green chemistry seeks to reduce and prevent pollution at its source. In 1990 the Pollution Prevention Act was passed in the United States.

Ziegler-Natta catalyst

A Ziegler-Natta catalyst is a catalyst used in the synthesis of polymers of 1-alkenes (α-olefins). Three types of Ziegler-Natta catalysts are currently employed:•Solid and supported catalysts based on titanium compounds. They are used in polymerization reactions in combination with cocatalysts, organoaluminum compounds such as triethylaluminium, $Al(C_2H_5)_3$.•Metallocene catalysts, combination of various mono- and bis-metallocene, in particular ansa- (or bridged) metallocene complexes of Ti, Zr or Hf.

Catalyst

Catalysis is the change in rate of a chemical reaction due to the participation of a substance called a catalyst. Unlike other reagents that participate in the chemical reaction, a catalyst is not consumed by the reaction itself. A catalyst may participate in multiple chemical transformations.

Hydroformylation

Hydroformylation, is an important industrial process for the production of aldehydes from alkenes. This chemical reaction entails the addition of a formyl group (CHO) and a hydrogen atom to a carbon-carbon double bond. This process has undergone continuous growth since its invention in the 1930s: Production capacity reached 6.6×10^6 tons in 1995. It is important because the resulting aldehydes are easily converted into many secondary products.

Phenyl group

In organic chemistry, the phenyl group is a cyclic group of atoms with the formula C_6H_5. Phenyl groups are closely related to benzene. Phenyl groups have six carbon atoms bonded together in a hexagonal planar ring, five of which are bonded to individual hydrogen atoms, with the remaining carbon bonded to a substituent.

Picric acid

Picric acid is the chemical compound formally called 2,4,6-trinitrophenol (TNP). This yellow crystalline solid is one of the most acidic phenols. Like other highly nitrated compounds such as TNT, picric acid is an explosive.

Stille reaction

The Stille reaction is a chemical reaction coupling an organotin compound with an sp^2-hybridized organic halide catalyzed by palladium. The reaction is widely used in organic synthesis.

X is typically a halide, such as Cl, Br, I. Additionally, X can be a pseudohalide such as a triflate, $CF_3SO_3^-$.

Anthranilic acid

Anthranilic acid is the organic compound with the formula $C_6H_4(NH_2)COOH$. This amino acid is a white solid when pure, although commercial samples may appear yellow. The molecule consists of a benzene ring with two adjacent functional groups, a carboxylic acid and an amine. It is sometimes referred to as vitamin L. it has a sweetish taste, it is flammable and will produce nitrogen oxide fumes when burning, it maybe sensitive to prolonged exposure to air and light.

Free-radical reaction

A free-radical reaction is any chemical reaction involving free radicals. This reaction type is abundant in organic reactions.

Two pioneering studies into free radical reactions have been the discovery of the triphenylmethyl radical by Moses Gomberg (1900) and the lead-mirror experiment described by Friedrich Paneth in 1927. In this last experiment tetramethyllead is decomposed at elevated temperatures to methyl radicals and elemental lead in a quartz tube.

Reaction inhibitor

A reaction inhibitor is a substance that decreases the rate of, or prevents, a chemical reaction.
•Added acetanilide slows the decomposition of drug-store hydrogen peroxide solution, inhibiting the reaction

$2H_2O_2 \rightarrow 2H_2O + O_2$, which is catalyzed by heat, light, and impurities. Inhibition of a catalyst

Chapter 18. THE CHEMISTRY OF ARYL HALIDES, VINYLIC HALIDES, AND PHENOLS

CHAPTER HIGHLIGHTS & NOTES: KEY TERMS, PEOPLE, PLACES, CONCEPTS

Vitamin E	Vitamin E is used to refer to a group of fat-soluble compounds that include both tocopherols and tocotrienols. There are many different forms of vitamin E, of which γ-tocopherol is the most common in the North American diet. γ-Tocopherol can be found in corn oil, soybean oil, margarine and dressings.
Sandmeyer reaction	The Sandmeyer reaction is a chemical reaction used to synthesize aryl halides from aryl diazonium salts. he Swiss chemist Traugott Sandmeyer. An aromatic (or heterocyclic) amine quickly reacts with a nitrite to form an aryl diazonium salt, which decomposes in the presence of copper(I) salts, such as copper(I) chloride, to form the desired aryl halide.
Claisen rearrangement	The Claisen rearrangement is a powerful carbon-carbon bond-forming chemical reaction discovered by Rainer Ludwig Claisen. The heating of an allyl vinyl ether will initiate a [3,3]-sigmatropic rearrangement to give a γ,δ-unsaturated carbonyl. Discovered in 1912, the Claisen rearrangement is the first recorded example of a [3,3]-sigmatropic rearrangement.
Autoxidation	Autoxidation is any oxidation that occurs in open air or in presence of oxygen and/or UV radiation and forms peroxides and hydroperoxides. A classic example of autoxidation is that of simple ethers like diethyl ether, whose peroxides can be dangerously explosive. It can be considered to be a slow, flameless combustion of materials by reaction with oxygen.
Cumene hydroperoxide	Cumene hydroperoxide is an intermediate in the cumene process for developing phenol and acetone from benzene and propylene. It is typically used as an oxidising agent. Products of decomposition of cumene hydroperoxide are methylstyrene, acetophenone and cumyl alcohol.
Cumene	Cumene is the common name for isopropylbenzene, an organic compound that is an aromatic hydrocarbon. It is a constituent of crude oil and refined fuels. It is a flammable colorless liquid that has a boiling point of 152 °C. Nearly all the cumene that is produced as a pure compound on an industrial scale is converted to cumene hydroperoxide, which is an intermediate in the synthesis of other industrially important chemicals, primarily phenol and acetone.

CHAPTER QUIZ: KEY TERMS, PEOPLE, PLACES, CONCEPTS

1. _________, is an organic compound with the chemical formula C_6H_5OH. It is a white crystalline solid at room temperature. The molecule consists of a phenyl group ($-C_6H_5$) bonded to a hydroxyl group (-OH). It is mildly acidic, but requires careful handling due to its propensity to cause burns.

a. Phrixotoxin
b. Polyacrylamide
c. Phenol
d. Psalmotoxin

2. The _________ is a rule used primarily for predicting formulae for stable metal complexes. The rule rests on the fact that valence shells of a transition metal consists of nine valence orbitals, which collectively can accommodate 18 electrons either as nonbonding electron pairs or as bonding electron pairs. Stated differently, the combination of these nine atomic orbitals with ligand orbitals gives rise to nine molecular orbitals that are either metal-ligand bonding or non-bonding.

a. Bioceramic
b. 18-Electron rule
c. Bioorganometallic chemistry
d. Calcareous sinter

3. The Grignard reaction is an organometallic chemical reaction in which alkyl- or aryl-magnesium halides (_________) add to a carbonyl group in an aldehyde or ketone. This reaction is an important tool for the formation of carbon-carbon bonds. The reaction of an organic halide with magnesium is not a Grignard reaction, but provides a Grignard reagent.

a. Hexamethylenetetramine
b. Hexyllithium
c. Hydrindantin
d. Grignard reagents

4. _________ is the organochloride with the formula $H_2C{:}CHCl$. It is also called _________ monomer, or VCM. This colorless compound is an important industrial chemical chiefly used to produce the polymer polyvinyl chloride. At ambient pressure and temperature, _________ is a gas with a sickly sweet odor.

a. Vinyl chloride
b. 1,2-Dioxetanedione
c. Fluorinert
d. Etacrynic acid

5. . A _________ is any chemical reaction involving free radicals. This reaction type is abundant in organic reactions.

Two pioneering studies into free radical reactions have been the discovery of the triphenylmethyl radical by Moses Gomberg (1900) and the lead-mirror experiment described by Friedrich Paneth in 1927. In this last experiment tetramethyllead is decomposed at elevated temperatures to methyl radicals and elemental lead in a quartz tube.

a. Free-radical reaction
b. Glycopeptide

c. Glycopolymer

d. Glycorandomization

ANSWER KEY
Chapter 18. THE CHEMISTRY OF ARYL HALIDES, VINYLIC HALIDES, AND PHENOLS

1. c

2. b

3. d

4. a

5. a

Chapter 19. THE CHEMISTRY OF ALDEHYDES AND KETONES. CARBONYL-/

CHAPTER OUTLINE: KEY TERMS, PEOPLE, PLACES, CONCEPTS

- Aldehyde
- Carboxylic acid
- Aldol condensation
- Molecular orbital
- Benzophenone
- Acyl group
- Carbon tetrachloride
- Furfural
- Propanoic acid
- Mass spectrometry
- McLafferty rearrangement
- Clemmensen reduction
- Pimelic acid
- Pinacol rearrangement
- Cyanohydrin
- Dimethylallyl pyrophosphate
- Hydrogen bromide
- Hydrogen halide
- Stereochemistry

______ Chloral

______ Chloral hydrate

______ Polar effect

______ Steric effects

______ Grignard reaction

______ Sodium borohydride

______ Reducing agent

______ Nitro compound

______ Reductive amination

______ Grignard reagents

______ Organolithium reagent

______ Acetal

______ Ketal

______ Hemiacetal

______ Hydrolysis

______ Paraldehyde

______ Absolute configuration

______ Protecting group

______ Imine

CHAPTER OUTLINE: KEY TERMS, PEOPLE, PLACES, CONCEPTS

_______________ Amine

_______________ Triethylene glycol

_______________ Gabriel synthesis

_______________ Triphenylphosphine oxide

_______________ Transition metal

_______________ Bakelite

_______________ Acetone cyanohydrin

CHAPTER HIGHLIGHTS & NOTES: KEY TERMS, PEOPLE, PLACES, CONCEPTS

Aldehyde

An aldehyde is an organic compound containing a formyl group. This functional group, with the structure R-CHO, consists of a carbonyl center (a carbon double bonded to oxygen) bonded to hydrogen and an R group, which is any generic alkyl or side chain. The group without R is called the aldehyde group or formyl group.

Carboxylic acid

Carboxylic acids ( ) are organic acids characterized by the presence of at least one carboxyl group. The general formula of a carboxylic acid is R-COOH, where R is some monovalent functional group. A carboxyl group (or carboxy) is a functional group consisting of a carbonyl (RR'C=O) and a hydroxyl (R-O-H), which has the formula -C(=O)OH, usually written as -COOH or $-CO_2H$.

Carboxylic acids are Brønsted-Lowry acids because they are proton (H^+) donors.

Aldol condensation

An aldol condensation is an organic reaction in which an enol or an enolate ion reacts with a carbonyl compound to form a β-hydroxyaldehyde or β-hydroxyketone, followed by a dehydration to give a conjugated enone.

Aldol condensations are important in organic synthesis, providing a good way to form carbon-carbon bonds. The Robinson annulation reaction sequence features an aldol condensation; the Wieland-Miescher ketone product is an important starting material for many organic syntheses.

Molecular orbital

In chemistry, a molecular orbital is a mathematical function describing the wave-like behavior of an electron in a molecule. This function can be used to calculate chemical and physical properties such as the probability of finding an electron in any specific region. The term 'orbital' was first used in English by Robert S. Mulliken as the English translation of Schrödinger's 'Eigenfunktion'.

Benzophenone

Benzophenone is the organic compound with the formula $(C_6H_5)_2CO$, generally abbreviated Ph_2CO. Benzophenone is a widely used building block in organic chemistry, being the parent diarylketone.

Benzophenone can be used as a photo initiator in UV-curing applications such as inks, imaging, and clear coatings in the printing industry. Benzophenone prevents ultraviolet (UV) light from damaging scents and colors in products such as perfumes and soaps.

Acyl group

An acyl group is a functional group derived by the removal of one or more hydroxyl groups from an oxoacid, including inorganic acids.

In organic chemistry, the acyl group is usually derived from a carboxylic acid (IUPAC name: alkanoyl). Therefore, it has the formula RCO-, where R represents an alkyl group that is attached to the CO group with a single bond.

Carbon tetrachloride

Carbon tetrachloride, also known by many other names is the organic compound with the formula CCl_4. It was formerly widely used in fire extinguishers, as a precursor to refrigerants, and as a cleaning agent. It is a colourless liquid with a 'sweet' smell that can be detected at low levels.

Furfural

Furfural is an organic compound derived from a variety of agricultural byproducts, including corncobs, oat, wheat bran, and sawdust. The name furfural comes from the Latin word furfur, meaning bran, referring to its usual source.

Furfural is an heterocyclic aldehyde, with the ring structure shown at right.

Propanoic acid

Propanoic acid is a naturally occurring carboxylic acid with chemical formula CH_3CH_2COOH. It is a clear liquid with a pungent odor. The anion $CH_3CH_2COO^-$ as well as the salts and esters of propanoic acid are known as propanoates (or propionates).

Mass spectrometry	Mass spectrometry is an analytical technique that measures the mass-to-charge ratio of charged particles. It is used for determining masses of particles, for determining the elemental composition of a sample or molecule, and for elucidating the chemical structures of molecules, such as peptides and other chemical compounds. MS works by ionizing chemical compounds to generate charged molecules or molecule fragments and measuring their mass-to-charge ratios.
McLafferty rearrangement	The McLafferty rearrangement is a reaction observed in mass spectrometry. It is sometimes found that a molecule containing a keto-group undergoes β-cleavage, with the gain of the γ-hydrogen atom. This rearrangement may take place by a radical or ionic mechanism.
Clemmensen reduction	Clemmensen reduction is a chemical reaction described as a reduction of ketones (or aldehydes) to alkanes using zinc amalgam and hydrochloric acid. This reaction is named after Erik Christian Clemmensen, a Danish chemist. The Clemmensen reduction is particularly effective at reducing aryl-alkyl ketones.
Pimelic acid	Pimelic acid is the organic compound with the formula $HO_2C(CH_2)_5CO_2H$. Derivatives of pimelic acid are involved in the biosynthesis of the amino acid called lysine. Pimelic acid is one methylene longer than a related dicarboxylic acid, adipic acid, a precursor to many polyesters and polyamides. It is the final member of the mnemonic used to aid recollection of the order of the first six dicarboxylic acids using their common (not IUPAC) nomenclature: Dicarboxylic acid Pimelic acid has been synthesized from cyclohexanone and from salicylic acid.
Pinacol rearrangement	The pinacol rearrangement is a method for converting a 1,2-diol to a carbonyl compound in organic chemistry. This 1,2-rearrangement takes place under acidic conditions. The name of the reaction comes from the rearrangement of pinacol to pinacolone.
Cyanohydrin	A cyanohydrin is a functional group found in organic compounds. Cyanohydrins have the formula $R_2C(OH)CN$, where R is H, alkyl, or aryl. Cyanohydrins are industrially important precursors to carboxylic acids and some amino acids.
Dimethylallyl pyrophosphate	Dimethylallyl pyrophosphate (DMAPP) is an intermediate product of both mevalonic acid (MVA) pathway and DOXP/MEP pathway. It is an isomer of isopentenyl pyrophosphate (IPP) and exists in virtually all life forms. The enzyme isopentenyl pyrophosphate isomerase catalyzes the isomerization of DMAPP from IPP. Precursor of DMAPP in the MVA pathway is mevalonic acid, and 2-C-methyl-D-erythritol-e-P in the MEP/DOXP pathway.

CHAPTER HIGHLIGHTS & NOTES: KEY TERMS, PEOPLE, PLACES, CONCEPTS

Hydrogen bromide	Hydrogen bromide is the diatomic molecule HBr. HBr is a gas at standard conditions. Hydrobromic acid forms upon dissolving HBr in water.
Hydrogen halide	Hydrogen halides (or hydrohalic acids) are inorganic compounds with the formula HX where X is one of the halogens: fluorine, chlorine, bromine, iodine, and astatine. Hydrogen halides are gases that dissolve in water to give acids. The hydrogen halides are diatomic molecules with no tendency to ionize in the gas phase.
Stereochemistry	Stereochemistry, a subdiscipline of chemistry, involves the study of the relative spatial arrangement of atoms within molecules. An important branch of stereochemistry is the study of chiral molecules. Stereochemistry is also known as 3D chemistry because the prefix 'stereo-' means 'three-dimensionality'.
Chloral	Chloral, is the organic compound with the formula Cl_3CCHO. This aldehyde is a colourless oily liquid that is soluble in a wide range of solvents. It reacts with water to form chloral hydrate, a once widely used sedative and hypnotic substance. Chloral can be produced by chlorination of ethanol, as reported in 1832 by Justus von Liebig.
Chloral hydrate	Chloral hydrate is a sedative and hypnotic drug as well as a chemical reagent and precursor. The name chloral hydrate indicates that it is formed from chloral (trichloroacetaldehyde) by the addition of one molecule of water. Its chemical formula is $C_2H_3Cl_3O_2$.
Polar effect	The Polar effect is the effect exerted by a substituent on modifying electrostatic forces operating on a nearby reaction center. The main contributors to the polar effect are the inductive effect, mesomeric effect and the through-space electronic field effect. An electron withdrawing group or EWG draws electrons away from a reaction center.
Steric effects	Steric effects arise from the fact that each atom within a molecule occupies a certain amount of space. If atoms are brought too close together, there is an associated cost in energy due to overlapping electron clouds , and this may affect the molecule's preferred shape (conformation) and reactivity. Steric hindrance Steric hindrance occurs when the large size of groups within a molecule prevents chemical reactions that are observed in related molecules with smaller groups.

Grignard reaction

The Grignard reaction is an organometallic chemical reaction in which alkyl- or aryl-magnesium halides (Grignard reagents) add to a carbonyl group in an aldehyde or ketone. This reaction is an important tool for the formation of carbon-carbon bonds. The reaction of an organic halide with magnesium is not a Grignard reaction, but provides a Grignard reagent.

Sodium borohydride

Sodium borohydride, is an inorganic compound with the formula $NaBH_4$. This white solid, usually encountered as a powder, is a versatile reducing agent that finds wide application in chemistry, both in the laboratory and on a technical scale. Large amounts are used for bleaching wood pulp.

Reducing agent

A reducing agent is the element or compound in a reduction-oxidation (redox) reaction that donates an electron to another species; however, since the reducer loses an electron we say it is 'oxidized'. This means that there must be an 'oxidizer'; because if any chemical is an electron donor (reducer), another must be an electron recipient (oxidizer). Thus reducers are 'oxidized' and oxidizers are 'reduced'.

Nitro compound

Nitro compounds are organic compounds that contain one or more nitro functional groups ($-NO_2$). They are often highly explosive, especially when the compound contains more than one nitro group and is impure. The nitro group is one of the most common explosophores (functional group that makes a compound explosive) used globally.

Reductive amination

Reductive amination is a form of amination that involves the conversion of a carbonyl group to an amine via an intermediate imine. The carbonyl group is most commonly a ketone or an aldehyde.

In this organic reaction, the amine first reacts with the carbonyl group to form a hemiaminal species, which subsequently loses one molecule of water in a reversible manner by alkylimino-de-oxo-bisubstitution, to form the imine.

Grignard reagents

The Grignard reaction is an organometallic chemical reaction in which alkyl- or aryl-magnesium halides (Grignard reagents) add to a carbonyl group in an aldehyde or ketone. This reaction is an important tool for the formation of carbon-carbon bonds. The reaction of an organic halide with magnesium is not a Grignard reaction, but provides a Grignard reagent.

Organolithium reagent

An organolithium reagent is an organometallic compound with a direct bond between a carbon and a lithium atom. As the electropositive nature of lithium puts most of the charge density of the bond on the carbon atom, effectively creating a carbanion, organolithium compounds are extremely powerful bases and nucleophiles. For use as bases, butyllithiums are often used and are commercially available.

CHAPTER HIGHLIGHTS & NOTES: KEY TERMS, PEOPLE, PLACES, CONCEPTS

Acetal	An acetal is a molecule with two single-bonded oxygen atoms attached to the same carbon atom. Traditional usages distinguish ketals from acetals (whereas a ketal has two carbon-bonded R groups and is formally derived from a ketone, an acetal has one or both carbon-bonded R groups as a hydrogen and is formally derived from an aldehyde). Current IUPAC terminology classifies ketals as a subset of acetals.
Ketal	A ketal is a functional group or molecule containing a carbon bonded to two -OR groups, where O is oxygen and R represents any alkyl group. It is essentially equivalent to an acetal, and often the term acetal is used instead. Acetals traditionally derive from the product of the reaction of an aldehyde with excess of alcohol, whereas the name ketal derives from the product of the reaction of a ketone with excess alcohol.
Hemiacetal	Hemiacetals and hemiketals are compounds that are derived from aldehydes and ketones respectively. The Greek word hèmi means half. These compounds are formed by formal addition of an alcohol to the carbonyl group.
Hydrolysis	Hydrolysis usually means the rupture of chemical bonds by the action of water. Generally, hydrolysis is a step in the degradation of a substance. In terms of the word's derivation, hydrolysis comes from Greek roots hydro 'water' + lysis 'separation'.
Paraldehyde	Paraldehyde is the cyclic trimer of acetaldehyde molecules. Formally, it is a derivative of 1,3,5-trioxane. The corresponding tetramer is metaldehyde.
Absolute configuration	An absolute configuration in stereochemistry is the spatial arrangement of the atoms of a chiral molecular entity and its stereochemical description e.g. R or S. Absolute configurations for a chiral molecule (in pure form) are most often obtained by X-ray crystallography. All enantiomerically pure chiral molecules crystallise in one of the 65 Sohncke Groups (Chiral Space Groups). Alternative techniques are Optical rotatory dispersion, vibrational circular dichroism and the use of chiral shift reagents in proton NMR. When the absolute configuration is obtained the assignment of R or S is based on the Cahn-Ingold-Prelog priority rules.
Protecting group	A protecting group is introduced into a molecule by chemical modification of a functional group in order to obtain chemoselectivity in a subsequent chemical reaction. It plays an important role in multistep organic synthesis.

Imine	An imine is a functional group or chemical compound containing a carbon-nitrogen double bond, with the nitrogen attached to a hydrogen atom (H) or an organic group. If this group is not a hydrogen atom, then the compound is known as a Schiff base. The carbon has two additional single bonds.
Amine	Amines are organic compounds and functional groups that contain a basic nitrogen atom with a lone pair. Amines are derivatives of ammonia, wherein one or more hydrogen atoms have been replaced by a substituent such as an alkyl or aryl group. Important amines include amino acids, biogenic amines, trimethylamine, and aniline; see Category:Amines for a list of amines.
Triethylene glycol	Triethylene glycol, TEG, or triglycol is a colorless odorless viscous liquid with molecular formula $HOCH_2CH_2OCH_2CH_2OCH_2CH_2OH$. It is used as a plasticizer for vinyl. It is also used in air sanitizer products, such as 'Oust' or 'Clean and Pure.' When aerosolized it acts as a disinfectant. Glycols are also used as liquid desiccants for natural gas and in air conditioning systems.
Gabriel synthesis	The Gabriel synthesis is named for the German chemist Siegmund Gabriel. Traditionally, it is a chemical reaction that transforms primary alkyl halides into primary amines using potassium phthalimide. The Gabriel reaction has since been generalized to include the alkylation of sulfonamides and imides, followed by deprotection, to obtain amines .
Triphenylphosphine oxide	Triphenylphosphine oxide is the chemical compound with the formula $OP(C_6H_5)_3$. Often chemists abbreviate the formula by writing Ph_3PO or PPh_3O (Ph = C_6H_5). This white crystalline compound is a common side product in reactions involving triphenylphosphine.
Transition metal	In chemistry, the term transition metal has two possible meanings:•The IUPAC definition states that a transition metal is 'an element whose atom has an incomplete d sub-shell, or which can give rise to cations with an incomplete d sub-shell'.•Most scientists describe a 'transition metal' as any element in the d-block of the periodic table, which includes groups 3 to 12 on the periodic table. All elements in the d-block are metals. In actual practice, the f-block is also included in the form of the lanthanide and actinide series. Jensen has reviewed the history of the terms transition element and d-block.
Bakelite	Bakelite or polyoxybenzylmethylenglycolanhydride, is an early plastic. It is a thermosetting phenol formaldehyde resin, formed from an elimination reaction of phenol with formaldehyde, usually with a wood flour filler. It was developed in 1907 by Belgian chemist Leo Baekeland.
Acetone cyanohydrin	Acetone cyanohydrin is an organic compound used in the production of methyl methacrylate, the monomer of the transparent plastic polymethyl methacrylate (PMMA), also known as acrylic.

CHAPTER HIGHLIGHTS & NOTES: KEY TERMS, PEOPLE, PLACES, CONCEPTS

The compound is generated as part of the acetone cyanohydrin route to methyl methacrylate. It is treated with sulfuric acid to give the sulfate ester of the methacrylamide, methanolysis of which gives ammonium bisulfate and MMA. In the laboratory, this compound may be prepared by reacting sodium cyanide with acetone, followed by acidification:

A simplified procedure involves the action of sodium or potassium cyanide on the sodium bisulfite adduct of acetone prepared in situ.

CHAPTER QUIZ: KEY TERMS, PEOPLE, PLACES, CONCEPTS

1. _________s and hemiketals are compounds that are derived from aldehydes and ketones respectively. The Greek word hèmi means half. These compounds are formed by formal addition of an alcohol to the carbonyl group.

   a. Hemiaminal
   b. Hemithioacetal
   c. Hemiacetal
   d. Hydrazone

2. An _________ is an organometallic compound with a direct bond between a carbon and a lithium atom. As the electropositive nature of lithium puts most of the charge density of the bond on the carbon atom, effectively creating a carbanion, organolithium compounds are extremely powerful bases and nucleophiles. For use as bases, butyllithiums are often used and are commercially available.

   a. Allixin
   b. Hexyllithium
   c. Hydrindantin
   d. Organolithium reagent

3. _________ is an analytical technique that measures the mass-to-charge ratio of charged particles. It is used for determining masses of particles, for determining the elemental composition of a sample or molecule, and for elucidating the chemical structures of molecules, such as peptides and other chemical compounds. MS works by ionizing chemical compounds to generate charged molecules or molecule fragments and measuring their mass-to-charge ratios.

   a. Mass spectrometry
   b. Nucleotidase
   c. Polyol pathway
   d. Pro-oxidant

4. . _________ is the organic compound with the formula $(C_6H_5)_2CO$, generally abbreviated Ph_2CO.

_________ is a widely used building block in organic chemistry, being the parent diarylketone.

_________ can be used as a photo initiator in UV-curing applications such as inks, imaging, and clear coatings in the printing industry. _________ prevents ultraviolet (UV) light from damaging scents and colors in products such as perfumes and soaps.

a. Bromfenac
b. CB-13
c. Benzophenone
d. Ciclobendazole

5. _________, a subdiscipline of chemistry, involves the study of the relative spatial arrangement of atoms within molecules. An important branch of _________ is the study of chiral molecules.

_________ is also known as 3D chemistry because the prefix 'stereo-' means 'three-dimensionality'.

a. Stereochemistry
b. Capped square antiprismatic molecular geometry
c. Chiral auxiliary
d. Chiral column chromatography

ANSWER KEY

Chapter 19. THE CHEMISTRY OF ALDEHYDES AND KETONES. CARBONYL-ADDITION REACTIONS

1. c

2. d

3. a

4. c

5. a

Chapter 20. THE CHEMISTRY OF CARBOXYLIC ACIDS

CHAPTER OUTLINE: KEY TERMS, PEOPLE, PLACES, CONCEPTS

______ Carboxylic acid

______ Sulfonic acid

______ Benzoic acid

______ Phthalic acid

______ Cinnamic acid

______ Salicylic acid

______ Tartaric acid

______ Polar effect

______ Molecular orbital

______ Diethylene glycol

______ Fluoroacetic acid

______ Trifluoroacetic acid

______ Dimethyl ether

______ Fatty acid

______ Olefin metathesis

______ Surfactant

______ Benzalkonium chloride

______ Critical micelle concentration

______ Decarboxylation

CHAPTER OUTLINE: KEY TERMS, PEOPLE, PLACES, CONCEPTS

Alkylating antineoplastic agent

Gabriel synthesis

Diazomethane

Methanesulfonyl chloride

Thionyl chloride

Phosphorus pentoxide

Grignard reaction

Primary alcohol

Aldol condensation

Carbamic acid

Carbon dioxide

Carbonic acid

Dimethyl carbonate

Maleic acid

Maleic anhydride

Phosgene

Urea

Malonic acid

Organolithium reagent

Chapter 20. THE CHEMISTRY OF CARBOXYLIC ACIDS

CHAPTER HIGHLIGHTS & NOTES: KEY TERMS, PEOPLE, PLACES, CONCEPTS

Carboxylic acid

Carboxylic acids ( ) are organic acids characterized by the presence of at least one carboxyl group. The general formula of a carboxylic acid is R-COOH, where R is some monovalent functional group. A carboxyl group (or carboxy) is a functional group consisting of a carbonyl (RR'C=O) and a hydroxyl (R-O-H), which has the formula -C(=O)OH, usually written as -COOH or $-CO_2H$.

Carboxylic acids are Brønsted-Lowry acids because they are proton (H^+) donors.

Sulfonic acid

A sulfonic acid refers to a member of the class of organosulfur compounds with the general formula $RS(=O)_2$-OH, where R is an organic alkyl or aryl group and the $S(=O)_2$-OH group a sulfonyl hydroxide. A sulfonic acid can be thought of as sulfuric acid with one hydroxyl group replaced by an organic substituent. The parent compound (with the organic substituent replaced by hydrogen) is the hypothetical compound sulfurous acid.

Benzoic acid

Benzoic acid, $C_7H_6O_2$ (or C_6H_5COOH), is a colorless crystalline solid and the simplest aromatic carboxylic acid. The name derived from gum benzoin, which was for a long time the only source for benzoic acid. Its salts are used as a food preservative and benzoic acid is an important precursor for the synthesis of many other organic substances.

Phthalic acid

Phthalic acid is an aromatic dicarboxylic acid, with formula $C_6H_4(CO_2H)_2$. It is an isomer of isophthalic acid and terephthalic acid. Although phthalic acid is of modest commercial importance, the closely related derivative phthalic anhydride is a commodity chemical produced on a large scale.

Cinnamic acid

Cinnamic acid is a white crystalline organic acid, which is slightly soluble in water.

It is obtained from oil of cinnamon, or from balsams such as storax. It is also found in shea butter and is the best indication of its environmental history and post-extraction conditions.

Salicylic acid

Salicylic acid is a monohydroxybenzoic acid, a type of phenolic acid and a beta hydroxy acid. This colorless crystalline organic acid is widely used in organic synthesis and functions as a plant hormone. It is derived from the metabolism of salicin.

Tartaric acid

Tartaric acid is a white crystalline diprotic organic acid. It occurs naturally in many plants, particularly grapes, bananas, and tamarinds; is commonly combined with baking soda to function as a leavening agent in recipes, and is one of the main acids found in wine. It is added to other foods to give a sour taste, and is used as an antioxidant.

Polar effect

The Polar effect is the effect exerted by a substituent on modifying electrostatic forces operating on a nearby reaction center. The main contributors to the polar effect are the inductive effect, mesomeric effect and the through-space electronic field effect.

Molecular orbital

In chemistry, a molecular orbital is a mathematical function describing the wave-like behavior of an electron in a molecule. This function can be used to calculate chemical and physical properties such as the probability of finding an electron in any specific region. The term 'orbital' was first used in English by Robert S. Mulliken as the English translation of Schrödinger's 'Eigenfunktion'.

Diethylene glycol

Diethylene glycol is an organic compound with the formula $(HOCH_2CH_2)_2O$. It is a colorless, practically odorless, poisonous, and hygroscopic liquid with a sweetish taste. It is miscible in water, alcohol, ether, acetone and ethylene glycol. DEG is a widely used solvent.

Fluoroacetic acid

Fluoroacetic acid is a chemical compound with formula CH_2FCOOH. The sodium salt, sodium fluoroacetate is used as a pesticide.

Trifluoroacetic acid

Trifluoroacetic acid is the simplest stable perfluorinated carboxylic acid chemical compound, with the formula CF_3CO_2H. It is a strong carboxylic acid due to the influence of the electronegative trifluoromethyl group. TFA is almost 100,000-fold more acidic than acetic acid. TFA is widely used in organic chemistry.

Dimethyl ether

Dimethyl ether also known as methoxymethane, is the organic compound with the formula CH_3OCH_3. The simplest ether, it is a colourless gas that is a useful precursor to other organic compounds and an aerosol propellant.

Today, DME is primarily produced by converting hydrocarbons sourced from natural gas or coal via gasification to synthesis gas (syngas).

Fatty acid

In chemistry, especially biochemistry, a fatty acid is a carboxylic acid with a long aliphatic tail (chain), which is either saturated or unsaturated. Most naturally occurring fatty acids have a chain of an even number of carbon atoms, from 4 to 28. Fatty acids are usually derived from triglycerides or phospholipids. When they are not attached to other molecules, they are known as 'free' fatty acids.

Olefin metathesis

Olefin metathesis is an organic reaction that entails the redistribution of fragments of alkenes (olefins) by the scission and regeneration of carbon - carbon double bonds. Catalysts for this reaction have evolved rapidly for the past few decades. Because of the relative simplicity of olefin metathesis it often creates fewer undesired by-products and hazardous wastes than alternate organic reactions.

Surfactant

Surfactants are compounds that lower the surface tension of a liquid, the interfacial tension between two liquids, or that between a liquid and a solid. Surfactants may act as detergents, wetting agents, emulsifiers, foaming agents, and dispersants.

Benzalkonium chloride

Benzalkonium chloride, is a mixture of alkylbenzyldimethylammonium chlorides of various even-numbered alkyl chain lengths. This product is a nitrogenous cationic surface-acting agent belonging to the quaternary ammonium group. It has three main categories of use: as a biocide, a cationic surfactant and phase transfer agent in the chemical industry.

Critical micelle concentration

In colloidal and surface chemistry, the critical micelle concentration is defined as the concentration of surfactants above which micelles form and almost all additional surfactants added to the system go to micelles.

The CMC is an important characteristic of a surfactant. Before reaching the CMC, the surface tension changes strongly with the concentration of the surfactant.

Decarboxylation

Decarboxylation is a chemical reaction that releases carbon dioxide (CO_2). Usually, decarboxylation refers to a reaction of carboxylic acids, removing a carbon atom from a carbon chain. The reverse process, which is the first chemical step in photosynthesis, is called carbonation, the addition of CO_2 to a compound.

Alkylating antineoplastic agent

An alkylating antineoplastic agent is an alkylating agent used in cancer treatment that attaches an alkyl group (C_nH_{2n+1}) to DNA.

The alkyl group is attached to the guanine base of DNA, at the number 7 nitrogen atom of the purine ring.

Since cancer cells, in general, proliferate faster and with less error-correcting than healthy cells, cancer cells are more sensitive to DNA damage -- such as being alkylated. Alkylating agents are used to treat several cancers.

Gabriel synthesis

The Gabriel synthesis is named for the German chemist Siegmund Gabriel. Traditionally, it is a chemical reaction that transforms primary alkyl halides into primary amines using potassium phthalimide.

The Gabriel reaction has since been generalized to include the alkylation of sulfonamides and imides, followed by deprotection, to obtain amines .

Diazomethane

Diazomethane is the chemical compound CH_2N_2. It is the simplest of diazo compounds. In the pure form at room temperature, it is an extremely sensitive explosive yellow gas, thus it is almost universally used as a solution in diethyl ether.

Methanesulfonyl chloride

Methanesulfonyl chloride is a compound containing a sulfonyl chloride used to make methanesulfonates and to generate sulfene.

Methanesulfonyl chloride is highly toxic, moisture sensitive, corrosive, and a lachrymator. It should be stored in a dry location, preferably in a desiccator.

Thionyl chloride

Thionyl chloride is an inorganic compound with the formula $SOCl_2$. It is a reactive chemical reagent used in chlorination reactions. It is a colorless, distillable liquid at room temperature and pressure that decomposes above 140 °C. Thionyl chloride is sometimes confused with sulfuryl chloride, SO_2Cl_2, but the properties of these compounds differ significantly.

Phosphorus pentoxide

Phosphorus pentoxide is a chemical compound with molecular formula P_4O_{10} (with its common name derived from its empirical formula, P_2O_5). This white crystalline solid is the anhydride of phosphoric acid. It is a powerful desiccant.

Grignard reaction

The Grignard reaction is an organometallic chemical reaction in which alkyl- or aryl-magnesium halides (Grignard reagents) add to a carbonyl group in an aldehyde or ketone. This reaction is an important tool for the formation of carbon-carbon bonds. The reaction of an organic halide with magnesium is not a Grignard reaction, but provides a Grignard reagent.

Primary alcohol

A primary alcohol is an alcohol which has the hydroxyl radical connected to a primary carbon. It can also be defined as a molecule containing a '-CH_2OH' group.

Examples include ethanol and butanol.

Aldol condensation

An aldol condensation is an organic reaction in which an enol or an enolate ion reacts with a carbonyl compound to form a β-hydroxyaldehyde or β-hydroxyketone, followed by a dehydration to give a conjugated enone.

Aldol condensations are important in organic synthesis, providing a good way to form carbon-carbon bonds. The Robinson annulation reaction sequence features an aldol condensation; the Wieland-Miescher ketone product is an important starting material for many organic syntheses.

Carbamic acid

Carbamic acid is a compound that is unstable under normal circumstances. It is technically the simplest amino acid, though its instability (and the unique nature of the carboxyl-nitrogen bond) allows glycine to assume this title. Its importance is due more to its relevance in identifying the names of larger compounds.

Carbon dioxide

Carbon dioxide is a naturally occurring chemical compound composed of two oxygen atoms covalently bonded to a single carbon atom. It is a gas at standard temperature and pressure and exists in Earth's atmosphere in this state, as a trace gas at a concentration of 0.039% by volume.

Chapter 20. THE CHEMISTRY OF CARBOXYLIC ACIDS

CHAPTER HIGHLIGHTS & NOTES: KEY TERMS, PEOPLE, PLACES, CONCEPTS

Carbonic acid

Carbonic acid is the organic compound with the formula H_2CO_3 (equivalently $OC(OH)_2$). It is also a name sometimes given to solutions of carbon dioxide in water, because such solutions contain small amounts of H_2CO_3. Carbonic acid forms two kinds of salts, the carbonates and the bicarbonates.

Dimethyl carbonate

Dimethyl carbonate is an organic compound with the formula $OC(OCH_3)_2$. It is a colourless, flammable liquid. It is classified as a carbonate ester.

Maleic acid

Maleic acid is an organic compound that is a dicarboxylic acid, a molecule with two carboxyl groups. Maleic acid is the cis-isomer of butenedioic acid, whereas fumaric acid is the trans-isomer. It is mainly used as a precursor to fumaric acid, and relative to its parent maleic anhydride, maleic acid has few applications.

Maleic anhydride

Maleic anhydride is an organic compound with the formula $C_2H_2(CO)_2O$. It is the acid anhydride of maleic acid and in its pure state it is a colourless or white solid with an acrid odour.

Maleic anhydride was traditionally manufactured by the oxidation of benzene or other aromatic compounds. As of 2006, only a few smaller plants continue to use benzene; due to rising benzene prices, most maleic anhydride plants now use n-butane as a feedstock:2 $CH_3CH_2CH_2CH_3$ + 7 O_2 → 2 $C_2H_2(CO)_2O$ + 8 H_2OReactions

The chemistry of maleic anhydride is very rich, reflecting its ready availability and bifunctional reactivity.

Phosgene

Phosgene is the chemical compound with the formula $COCl_2$. This colorless gas gained infamy as a chemical weapon during World War I. It is also a valued industrial reagent and building block in synthesis of pharmaceuticals and other organic compounds. In low concentrations, its odor resembles freshly cut hay or grass.

Urea

Urea is an organic compound with the chemical formula $CO(NH_2)_2$. The molecule has two --NH_2 groups joined by a carbonyl (C=O) functional group.

Urea serves an important role in the metabolism of nitrogen-containing compounds by animals and is the main nitrogen-containing substance in the urine of mammals.

Malonic acid

Malonic acid is a dicarboxylic acid with structure $CH_2(COOH)_2$. The ionized form of malonic acid, as well as its esters and salts, are known as malonates. For example, diethyl malonate is malonic acid's diethyl ester.

Organolithium reagent

An organolithium reagent is an organometallic compound with a direct bond between a carbon and a lithium atom.

As the electropositive nature of lithium puts most of the charge density of the bond on the carbon atom, effectively creating a carbanion, organolithium compounds are extremely powerful bases and nucleophiles. For use as bases, butyllithiums are often used and are commercially available.

CHAPTER QUIZ: KEY TERMS, PEOPLE, PLACES, CONCEPTS

1. _________ is a monohydroxybenzoic acid, a type of phenolic acid and a beta hydroxy acid. This colorless crystalline organic acid is widely used in organic synthesis and functions as a plant hormone. It is derived from the metabolism of salicin.

a. Salicylic acid
b. CRL-40,941
c. Cupferron
d. Cycrimine

2. _________, $C_7H_6O_2$ (or C_6H_5COOH), is a colorless crystalline solid and the simplest aromatic carboxylic acid. The name derived from gum benzoin, which was for a long time the only source for _________. Its salts are used as a food preservative and _________ is an important precursor for the synthesis of many other organic substances.

a. lactose
b. Benzoic acid
c. 1,1,1-Trichloroethane
d. 1,2-Dioxetanedione

3. _________ is a chemical compound with formula CH_2FCOOH. The sodium salt, sodium fluoroacetate is used as a pesticide.

a. Fluvastatin
b. Fluoroacetic acid
c. Foscarnet
d. Furantetracarboxylic acid

4. . _________s ( ) are organic acids characterized by the presence of at least one carboxyl group. The general formula of a _________ is R-COOH, where R is some monovalent functional group. A carboxyl group (or carboxy) is a functional group consisting of a carbonyl (RR'C=O) and a hydroxyl (R-O-H), which has the formula -C(=O)OH, usually written as -COOH or $-CO_2H$.

_________s are Brønsted-Lowry acids because they are proton (H^+) donors.

a. Chiral Lewis acid

b. Carboxylic acid
c. Corosolic acid
d. Diprotic acid

5. An _________ is an organometallic compound with a direct bond between a carbon and a lithium atom. As the electropositive nature of lithium puts most of the charge density of the bond on the carbon atom, effectively creating a carbanion, organolithium compounds are extremely powerful bases and nucleophiles. For use as bases, butyllithiums are often used and are commercially available.

a. Allixin
b. Uric acid
c. Organolithium reagent
d. Methacrylic acid

ANSWER KEY
Chapter 20. THE CHEMISTRY OF CARBOXYLIC ACIDS

1. a
2. b
3. b
4. b
5. c

Chapter 21. THE CHEMISTRY OF CARBOXYLIC ACID DERIVATIVES

CHAPTER OUTLINE: KEY TERMS, PEOPLE, PLACES, CONCEPTS

- Carboxylic acid
- Lactone
- Phthalimide
- Amide
- Carbamic acid
- Dimethyl carbonate
- Methyl carbamate
- Phosgene
- Urea
- Bond length
- Triple bond
- Butyric acid
- Dimethyl sulfide
- Acid anhydride
- Claisen condensation
- Grignard reaction
- Saponification
- Addition reaction
- Nucleophilic acyl substitution

Chapter 21. THE CHEMISTRY OF CARBOXYLIC ACID DERIVATIVES

CHAPTER OUTLINE: KEY TERMS, PEOPLE, PLACES, CONCEPTS

_______________ Stereochemistry

_______________ Hydrolysis

_______________ Imidic acid

_______________ Sandmeyer reaction

_______________ Molecular orbital

_______________ Polar effect

_______________ Rosenmund reduction

_______________ Stille reaction

_______________ Aspirin

_______________ Hydroxamic acid

_______________ Maleic acid

_______________ Maleic anhydride

_______________ Transesterification

_______________ Sodium borohydride

_______________ Nitrile

_______________ Organolithium reagent

_______________ Grignard reagents

_______________ Aldol condensation

_______________ Carbon dioxide

CHAPTER OUTLINE: KEY TERMS, PEOPLE, PLACES, CONCEPTS

________ Gabriel synthesis

________ Hydrogen cyanide

________ Condensation polymer

________ Amine

________ Ethylene glycol

________ Polyester

________ Terephthalic acid

________ Farnesyl pyrophosphate

________ Phospholipid

CHAPTER HIGHLIGHTS & NOTES: KEY TERMS, PEOPLE, PLACES, CONCEPTS

Carboxylic acid

Carboxylic acids ( ) are organic acids characterized by the presence of at least one carboxyl group. The general formula of a carboxylic acid is R-COOH, where R is some monovalent functional group. A carboxyl group (or carboxy) is a functional group consisting of a carbonyl (RR'C=O) and a hydroxyl (R-O-H), which has the formula -C(=O)OH, usually written as -COOH or $-CO_2H$.

Carboxylic acids are Brønsted-Lowry acids because they are proton (H^+) donors.

Lactone

In chemistry, a lactone is a cyclic ester which can be seen as the condensation product of an alcohol group -OH and a carboxylic acid group -COOH in the same molecule. It is characterized by a closed ring consisting of two or more carbon atoms and a single oxygen atom, with a ketone group =O in one of the carbons adjacent to the other oxygen.

Chapter 21. THE CHEMISTRY OF CARBOXYLIC ACID DERIVATIVES

CHAPTER HIGHLIGHTS & NOTES: KEY TERMS, PEOPLE, PLACES, CONCEPTS

Phthalimide

Phthalimide is an imide, which is a chemical compound with two carbonyl groups bound to a secondary amine or ammonia. It is a white solid at room temperature.

Phthalimide can be prepared by heating phthalic anhydride with aqueous ammonia giving 95-97% yield.

Amide

Amide refers to compounds with the functional group $R_nE(O)_xNR'_2$ (R and R' refer to H or organic groups). Most common are 'organic amides' (n = 1, E = C, x = 1), but many other important types of amides are known including phosphor amides (n = 2, E = P, x = 1 and many related formulas) and sulfonamides (E = S, x= 2). The term amide refers both to classes of compounds and to the functional group ($R_nE(O)_xNR'_2$) within those compounds.

Carbamic acid

Carbamic acid is a compound that is unstable under normal circumstances. It is technically the simplest amino acid, though its instability (and the unique nature of the carboxyl-nitrogen bond) allows glycine to assume this title. Its importance is due more to its relevance in identifying the names of larger compounds.

Dimethyl carbonate

Dimethyl carbonate is an organic compound with the formula $OC(OCH_3)_2$. It is a colourless, flammable liquid. It is classified as a carbonate ester.

Methyl carbamate

Methyl carbamate is an organic compound and the simplest ester of the hypothetical carbamic acid (NH_2COOH). Its sum formula is $C_2H_5NO_2$.

Methyl carbamate is formed by the reaction of ammonia with methyl chloroformate or methyl carbonate.

Phosgene

Phosgene is the chemical compound with the formula $COCl_2$. This colorless gas gained infamy as a chemical weapon during World War I. It is also a valued industrial reagent and building block in synthesis of pharmaceuticals and other organic compounds. In low concentrations, its odor resembles freshly cut hay or grass.

Urea

Urea is an organic compound with the chemical formula $CO(NH_2)_2$. The molecule has two $--NH_2$ groups joined by a carbonyl (C=O) functional group.

Urea serves an important role in the metabolism of nitrogen-containing compounds by animals and is the main nitrogen-containing substance in the urine of mammals.

Bond length

In molecular geometry, bond length is the average distance between nuclei of two bonded atoms in a molecule.

Bond length is related to bond order, when more electrons participate in bond formation the bond will get shorter. Bond length is also inversely related to bond strength and the bond dissociation energy, as (all other things being equal) a stronger bond will be shorter.

Triple bond

A triple bond in chemistry is a chemical bond between two chemical elements involving six bonding electrons instead of the usual two in a covalent single bond. The most common triple bond, that between two carbon atoms, can be found in alkynes. Other functional groups containing a triple bond are cyanides and isocyanides.

Butyric acid

Butyric acid, also known under the systematic name butanoic acid, is a carboxylic acid with the structural formula $CH_3CH_2CH_2$-COOH. Salts and esters of butyric acid are known as butyrates or butanoates. Butyric acid is found in milk, especially goat, sheep and buffalo's milk, butter, Parmesan cheese, and vomit, and as a product of anaerobic fermentation (including in the colon and as body odor). It has an unpleasant smell and acrid taste, with a sweetish aftertaste (similar to ether).

Dimethyl sulfide

Dimethyl sulfide or methylthiomethane is an organosulfur compound with the formula $(CH_3)_2S$. Dimethyl sulfide is a water-insoluble flammable liquid that boils at 37 °C (99 °F) and has a characteristic disagreeable odor. It is a component of the smell produced from cooking of certain vegetables, notably maize, cabbage, beetroot and seafoods. It is also an indication of bacterial infection in malt production and brewing.

Acid anhydride

'Anhydride' redirects here.

An acid anhydride is an organic compound that has two acyl groups bound to the same oxygen atom. Most commonly, the acyl groups are derived from the same carboxylic acid, the formula of the anhydride being $(RC(O))_2O$. Symmetrical acid anhydrides of this type are named by replacing the word acid in the name of the parent carboxylic acid by the word anhydride.

Claisen condensation

The Claisen condensation is a carbon-carbon bond forming reaction that occurs between two esters or one ester and another carbonyl compound in the presence of a strong base, resulting in a β-keto ester or a β-diketone. It is named after Rainer Ludwig Claisen, who first published his work on the reaction in 1881 .

At least one of the reagents must be enolizable (have an α-proton and be able to undergo deprotonation to form the enolate anion).

Grignard reaction

The Grignard reaction is an organometallic chemical reaction in which alkyl- or aryl-magnesium halides (Grignard reagents) add to a carbonyl group in an aldehyde or ketone. This reaction is an important tool for the formation of carbon-carbon bonds.

Chapter 21. THE CHEMISTRY OF CARBOXYLIC ACID DERIVATIVES

CHAPTER HIGHLIGHTS & NOTES: KEY TERMS, PEOPLE, PLACES, CONCEPTS

Saponification

Saponification is a process that produces soap, usually from fats and lye. In technical terms, saponification involves base (usually caustic soda NaOH) hydrolysis of triglycerides, which are esters of fatty acids, to form the sodium salt of a carboxylate. In addition to soap, such traditional saponification processes produces glycerol.

Addition reaction

An addition reaction, in organic chemistry, is in its simplest terms an organic reaction where two or more molecules combine to form a larger one.

Addition reactions are limited to chemical compounds that have multiple bonds, such as molecules with carbon-carbon double bonds (alkenes), or with triple bonds (alkynes). Molecules containing carbon--hetero double bonds like carbonyl (C=O) groups, or imine (C=N) groups, can undergo addition as they too have double bond character.

Nucleophilic acyl substitution

Nucleophilic acyl substitution describes the substitution reaction involving nucleophiles and acyl compounds. Acyl compounds are carboxylic acid derivatives including esters, amides and acid halides. Nucleophiles include anionic reagents such as alkoxide compounds and enolates or species of high basicity, such as amines.

Stereochemistry

Stereochemistry, a subdiscipline of chemistry, involves the study of the relative spatial arrangement of atoms within molecules. An important branch of stereochemistry is the study of chiral molecules.

Stereochemistry is also known as 3D chemistry because the prefix 'stereo-' means 'three-dimensionality'.

Hydrolysis

Hydrolysis usually means the rupture of chemical bonds by the action of water. Generally, hydrolysis is a step in the degradation of a substance. In terms of the word's derivation, hydrolysis comes from Greek roots hydro 'water' + lysis 'separation'.

Imidic acid

In chemistry, an imidic acid is any molecule that contains the -C(=NH)-OH functional group. It is the tautomer of an amide.

The term 'imino acid' is an obsolete term for this group that should not be used in this context because an imino acid actually has a different technical meaning.

Sandmeyer reaction

The Sandmeyer reaction is a chemical reaction used to synthesize aryl halides from aryl diazonium salts. he Swiss chemist Traugott Sandmeyer.

Molecular orbital	In chemistry, a molecular orbital is a mathematical function describing the wave-like behavior of an electron in a molecule. This function can be used to calculate chemical and physical properties such as the probability of finding an electron in any specific region. The term 'orbital' was first used in English by Robert S. Mulliken as the English translation of Schrödinger's 'Eigenfunktion'.
Polar effect	The Polar effect is the effect exerted by a substituent on modifying electrostatic forces operating on a nearby reaction center. The main contributors to the polar effect are the inductive effect, mesomeric effect and the through-space electronic field effect. An electron withdrawing group or EWG draws electrons away from a reaction center.
Rosenmund reduction	The Rosenmund reduction is a chemical reaction that reduces an acid halide to an aldehyde using hydrogen gas over palladium-on-carbon poisoned with barium sulfate. The reaction was named after Karl Wilhelm Rosenmund. The catalyst must be poisoned because otherwise the catalyst is too active and will reduce the acid chloride to a primary alcohol.
Stille reaction	The Stille reaction is a chemical reaction coupling an organotin compound with an sp^2-hybridized organic halide catalyzed by palladium. The reaction is widely used in organic synthesis. X is typically a halide, such as Cl, Br, I. Additionally, X can be a pseudohalide such as a triflate, $CF_3SO_3^-$.
Aspirin	Aspirin also known as acetylsalicylic acid , is a salicylate drug, often used as an analgesic to relieve minor aches and pains, as an antipyretic to reduce fever, and as an anti-inflammatory medication. It was first isolated by Felix Hoffmann, a chemist with the German company Bayer, under the direction of Arthur Eichengrün. Salicylic acid, the main metabolite of aspirin, is an integral part of human and animal metabolism.
Hydroxamic acid	A hydroxamic acid is a class of chemical compounds sharing the same functional group in which an hydroxylamine is inserted into a carboxylic acid. Its general structure is R-CO-NH-OH, with an R as an organic residue, a CO as a carbonyl group, and a hydroxylamine as NH_2-OH. They are used as metal chelators in industry, e.g. benzohydroxamic acid and others in the reprocessing of irradiated fuel.

Chapter 21. THE CHEMISTRY OF CARBOXYLIC ACID DERIVATIVES

CHAPTER HIGHLIGHTS & NOTES: KEY TERMS, PEOPLE, PLACES, CONCEPTS

Maleic acid

Maleic acid is an organic compound that is a dicarboxylic acid, a molecule with two carboxyl groups. Maleic acid is the cis-isomer of butenedioic acid, whereas fumaric acid is the trans-isomer. It is mainly used as a precursor to fumaric acid, and relative to its parent maleic anhydride, maleic acid has few applications.

Maleic anhydride

Maleic anhydride is an organic compound with the formula $C_2H_2(CO)_2O$. It is the acid anhydride of maleic acid and in its pure state it is a colourless or white solid with an acrid odour.

Maleic anhydride was traditionally manufactured by the oxidation of benzene or other aromatic compounds. As of 2006, only a few smaller plants continue to use benzene; due to rising benzene prices, most maleic anhydride plants now use n-butane as a feedstock:2 $CH_3CH_2CH_2CH_3$ + 7 O_2 → 2 $C_2H_2(CO)_2O$ + 8 H_2OReactions

The chemistry of maleic anhydride is very rich, reflecting its ready availability and bifunctional reactivity.

Transesterification

In organic chemistry, transesterification is the process of exchanging the organic group R″ of an ester with the organic group R′ of an alcohol. These reactions are often catalyzed by the addition of an acid or base catalyst. The reaction can also be accomplished with the help of enzymes (biocatalysts) particularly lipases (E.C.3.1.1.3).

Sodium borohydride

Sodium borohydride, is an inorganic compound with the formula $NaBH_4$. This white solid, usually encountered as a powder, is a versatile reducing agent that finds wide application in chemistry, both in the laboratory and on a technical scale. Large amounts are used for bleaching wood pulp.

Nitrile

A nitrile is any organic compound that has a -C≡N functional group. The prefix cyano- is used interchangeably with the term nitrile in industrial literature. Nitriles are found in many useful compounds, including methyl cyanoacrylate, used in super glue, and nitrile butadiene rubber, a nitrile-containing polymer used in latex-free laboratory and medical gloves.

Organolithium reagent

An organolithium reagent is an organometallic compound with a direct bond between a carbon and a lithium atom. As the electropositive nature of lithium puts most of the charge density of the bond on the carbon atom, effectively creating a carbanion, organolithium compounds are extremely powerful bases and nucleophiles. For use as bases, butyllithiums are often used and are commercially available.

Grignard reagents

The Grignard reaction is an organometallic chemical reaction in which alkyl- or aryl-magnesium halides (Grignard reagents) add to a carbonyl group in an aldehyde or ketone. This reaction is an important tool for the formation of carbon-carbon bonds.

Aldol condensation	An aldol condensation is an organic reaction in which an enol or an enolate ion reacts with a carbonyl compound to form a β-hydroxyaldehyde or β-hydroxyketone, followed by a dehydration to give a conjugated enone. Aldol condensations are important in organic synthesis, providing a good way to form carbon-carbon bonds. The Robinson annulation reaction sequence features an aldol condensation; the Wieland-Miescher ketone product is an important starting material for many organic syntheses.
Carbon dioxide	Carbon dioxide is a naturally occurring chemical compound composed of two oxygen atoms covalently bonded to a single carbon atom. It is a gas at standard temperature and pressure and exists in Earth's atmosphere in this state, as a trace gas at a concentration of 0.039% by volume. As part of the carbon cycle known as photosynthesis, plants, algae, and cyanobacteria absorb carbon dioxide, light, and water to produce carbohydrate energy for themselves and oxygen as a waste product.
Gabriel synthesis	The Gabriel synthesis is named for the German chemist Siegmund Gabriel. Traditionally, it is a chemical reaction that transforms primary alkyl halides into primary amines using potassium phthalimide. The Gabriel reaction has since been generalized to include the alkylation of sulfonamides and imides, followed by deprotection, to obtain amines .
Hydrogen cyanide	Hydrogen cyanide is a chemical compound with chemical formula HCN. It is a colorless, extremely poisonous liquid that boils slightly above room temperature at 26 °C (79 °F). Hydrogen cyanide is a linear molecule, with a triple bond between carbon and nitrogen. A minor tautomer of HCN is HNC, hydrogen isocyanide.
Condensation polymer	Condensation polymers are any kind of polymers formed through a condensation reaction--where molecules join together--losing small molecules as by-products such as water or methanol, as opposed to addition polymers which involve the reaction of unsaturated monomers. Types of condensation polymers include polyamides, polyacetals and polyesters. Condensation polymerization, a form of step-growth polymerization, is a process by which two molecules join together, resulting loss of small molecules which is often water.
Amine	Amines are organic compounds and functional groups that contain a basic nitrogen atom with a lone pair. Amines are derivatives of ammonia, wherein one or more hydrogen atoms have been replaced by a substituent such as an alkyl or aryl group.

Chapter 21. THE CHEMISTRY OF CARBOXYLIC ACID DERIVATIVES

CHAPTER HIGHLIGHTS & NOTES: KEY TERMS, PEOPLE, PLACES, CONCEPTS

Ethylene glycol	Ethylene glycol is an organic compound widely used as an automotive antifreeze and a precursor to polymers. In its pure form, it is an odorless, colorless, syrupy, sweet-tasting liquid. Ethylene glycol is toxic, and ingestion can result in death.
Polyester	Polyester is a category of polymers which contain the ester functional group in their main chain. Although there are many polyesters, the term 'polyester' as a specific material most commonly refers to polyethylene terephthalate (PET). Polyesters include naturally occurring chemicals, such as in the cutin of plant cuticles, as well as synthetics through step-growth polymerization such as polycarbonate and polybutyrate.
Terephthalic acid	Terephthalic acid is the organic compound with formula $C_6H_4(COOH)_2$. This colourless solid is a commodity chemical, used principally as a precursor to the polyester PET, used to make clothing and plastic bottles. Several billion kilograms are produced annually.
Farnesyl pyrophosphate	Farnesyl pyrophosphate also known as farnesyl diphosphate (FDP), is an intermediate in the HMG-CoA reductase pathway used by organisms in the biosynthesis of terpenes, terpenoids, and sterols. It is the immediate precursor of squalene (via the enzyme squalene synthase), dehydrodolichol diphosphate (a precursor of dolichol), and geranylgeranyl pyrophosphate (GGPP). Biosynthesis Farnesyl pyrophosphate synthase (a prenyl transferase) catalyzes sequential condensation reactions of dimethylallyl pyrophosphate with 2 units of 3-isopentenyl pyrophosphate to form farnesyl pyrophosphate, as is shown in the following two steps:•Dimethylallyl pyrophosphate reacts with 3-isopentenyl pyrophosphate to form geranyl pyrophosphate:•Geranyl pyrophosphate then reacts with another molecule of 3-isopentenyl pyrophosphate to form farnesyl pyrophosphate The above reactions are inhibited by bisphosphonates (used for osteoporosis).
Phospholipid	Phospholipids are a class of lipids that are a major component of all cell membranes as they can form lipid bilayers. Most phospholipids contain a diglyceride, a phosphate group, and a simple organic molecule such as choline; one exception to this rule is sphingomyelin, which is derived from sphingosine instead of glycerol. The first phospholipid identified as such in biological tissues was lecithin, or phosphatidylcholine, in the egg yolk, by Theodore Nicolas Gobley, a French chemist and pharmacist, in 1847. The structure of the phospholipid molecule generally consists of hydrophobic tails and a hydrophilic head.

1. _________s ( ) are organic acids characterized by the presence of at least one carboxyl group. The general formula of a _________ is R-COOH, where R is some monovalent functional group. A carboxyl group (or carboxy) is a functional group consisting of a carbonyl (RR'C=O) and a hydroxyl (R-O-H), which has the formula -C(=O)OH, usually written as -COOH or -CO_2H.

   _________s are Brønsted-Lowry acids because they are proton (H^+) donors.

   a. Chiral Lewis acid
   b. Carboxylic acid
   c. Corosolic acid
   d. Diprotic acid

2. In molecular geometry, _________ is the average distance between nuclei of two bonded atoms in a molecule.

   _________ is related to bond order, when more electrons participate in bond formation the bond will get shorter. _________ is also inversely related to bond strength and the bond dissociation energy, as (all other things being equal) a stronger bond will be shorter.

   a. Cyclic compound
   b. Diatomic molecule
   c. Bond length
   d. Linear molecular geometry

3. The Grignard reaction is an organometallic chemical reaction in which alkyl- or aryl-magnesium halides (_________) add to a carbonyl group in an aldehyde or ketone. This reaction is an important tool for the formation of carbon-carbon bonds. The reaction of an organic halide with magnesium is not a Grignard reaction, but provides a Grignard reagent.

   a. Hexamethylenetetramine
   b. Grignard reagents
   c. Hydrindantin
   d. Hypophosphorous acid

4. In chemistry, a _________ is a cyclic ester which can be seen as the condensation product of an alcohol group -OH and a carboxylic acid group -COOH in the same molecule. It is characterized by a closed ring consisting of two or more carbon atoms and a single oxygen atom, with a ketone group =O in one of the carbons adjacent to the other oxygen.

   _________s are usually named according to the precursor acid molecule (aceto = 2 carbons, propio = 3, butyro = 4, valero = 5, capro = 6, etc)., with a -_________ suffix and a Greek letter prefix that specifies the number of carbons in the heterocyle -- that is, the distance between the relevant -OH and the -COOH groups along said backbone.

   a. Methine
   b. Lactone
   c. Nitrate
   d. Nitrile ylide

5. The _________ is the effect exerted by a substituent on modifying electrostatic forces operating on a nearby reaction center. The main contributors to the _________ are the inductive effect, mesomeric effect and the through-space electronic field effect.

   An electron withdrawing group or EWG draws electrons away from a reaction center.

   a. Polar effect
   b. Taft equation
   c. Walsh diagram
   d. Quantum chemistry

ANSWER KEY
Chapter 21. THE CHEMISTRY OF CARBOXYLIC ACID DERIVATIVES

1. b
2. c
3. b
4. b
5. a

CHAPTER OUTLINE: KEY TERMS, PEOPLE, PLACES, CONCEPTS

______ Enol

______ Carboxylic acid

______ Ethyl acetate

______ Polar effect

______ Molecular orbital

______ Claisen condensation

______ Dihydroxyacetone phosphate

______ Tautomer

______ Grignard reagents

______ Haloform reaction

______ Carbon dioxide

______ Phosphorus tribromide

______ Nucleophilic substitution

______ Substitution reaction

______ Aldol reaction

______ Aldol condensation

______ Condensation

______ Mesityl oxide

______ Organic reaction

______ Organic synthesis

______ Dieckmann condensation

______ Diethyl carbonate

______ Fatty acid

______ Biosynthesis

______ Acyl carrier protein

______ Malonyl-CoA

______ Carrier protein

______ Diethyl malonate

______ Gabriel synthesis

______ Malonic ester synthesis

______ Alkylation

______ Maleic acid

______ Maleic anhydride

______ Acetoacetic ester synthesis

______ Lithium diisopropylamide

______ Acetoacetic acid

______ Hydrogen bromide

______ Hydrogen cyanide

CHAPTER OUTLINE: KEY TERMS, PEOPLE, PLACES, CONCEPTS

_______________ Hydrogen halide

_______________ Oxidation state

_______________ Robinson annulation

_______________ Periodic acid

_______________ Grignard reaction

_______________ Nitro compound

_______________ Organolithium reagent

CHAPTER HIGHLIGHTS & NOTES: KEY TERMS, PEOPLE, PLACES, CONCEPTS

Enol

Enols (also known as alkenols) are alkenes with a hydroxyl group affixed to one of the carbon atoms composing the double bond. Alkenes with a hydroxyl group on both sides of the double bond are called enediols. Deprotonated anions of enols are called enolates.

Carboxylic acid

Carboxylic acids ( ) are organic acids characterized by the presence of at least one carboxyl group. The general formula of a carboxylic acid is R-COOH, where R is some monovalent functional group. A carboxyl group (or carboxy) is a functional group consisting of a carbonyl (RR'C=O) and a hydroxyl (R-O-H), which has the formula -C(=O)OH, usually written as -COOH or $-CO_2H$.

Carboxylic acids are Brønsted-Lowry acids because they are proton (H^+) donors.

Ethyl acetate

Ethyl acetate is the organic compound with the formula $CH_3COOCH_2CH_3$. This colorless liquid has a characteristic sweet smell (similar to pear drops) and is used in glues, nail polish removers, and cigarettes . Ethyl acetate is the ester of ethanol and acetic acid; it is manufactured on a large scale for use as a solvent.

CHAPTER HIGHLIGHTS & NOTES: KEY TERMS, PEOPLE, PLACES, CONCEPTS

Polar effect	The Polar effect is the effect exerted by a substituent on modifying electrostatic forces operating on a nearby reaction center. The main contributors to the polar effect are the inductive effect, mesomeric effect and the through-space electronic field effect. An electron withdrawing group or EWG draws electrons away from a reaction center.
Molecular orbital	In chemistry, a molecular orbital is a mathematical function describing the wave-like behavior of an electron in a molecule. This function can be used to calculate chemical and physical properties such as the probability of finding an electron in any specific region. The term 'orbital' was first used in English by Robert S. Mulliken as the English translation of Schrödinger's 'Eigenfunktion'.
Claisen condensation	The Claisen condensation is a carbon-carbon bond forming reaction that occurs between two esters or one ester and another carbonyl compound in the presence of a strong base, resulting in a β-keto ester or a β-diketone. It is named after Rainer Ludwig Claisen, who first published his work on the reaction in 1881 . At least one of the reagents must be enolizable (have an α-proton and be able to undergo deprotonation to form the enolate anion).
Dihydroxyacetone phosphate	Dihydroxyacetone phosphate is a biochemical compound involved in many reactions, from the Calvin cycle in plants to the ether-lipid biosynthesis process in Leishmania mexicana. Its major biochemical role is in the glycolysis metabolic pathway. DHAP may be referred to as glycerone phosphate in older texts.
Tautomer	Tautomers are isomers (structural isomers) of organic compounds that readily interconvert by a chemical reaction called tautomerization. This reaction commonly results in the formal migration of a hydrogen atom or proton, accompanied by a switch of a single bond and adjacent double bond. The concept of tautomerizations is called tautomerism.
Grignard reagents	The Grignard reaction is an organometallic chemical reaction in which alkyl- or aryl-magnesium halides (Grignard reagents) add to a carbonyl group in an aldehyde or ketone. This reaction is an important tool for the formation of carbon-carbon bonds. The reaction of an organic halide with magnesium is not a Grignard reaction, but provides a Grignard reagent.
Haloform reaction	The haloform reaction is a chemical reaction where a haloform (CHX_3, where X is a halogen) is produced by the exhaustive halogenation of a methyl ketone (a molecule containing the R-CO-CH_3 group) in the presence of a base. R may be H, alkyl or aryl. The reaction can be used to produce chloroform ($CHCl_3$), bromoform ($CHBr_3$), or iodoform (CHI_3).

Carbon dioxide

Carbon dioxide is a naturally occurring chemical compound composed of two oxygen atoms covalently bonded to a single carbon atom. It is a gas at standard temperature and pressure and exists in Earth's atmosphere in this state, as a trace gas at a concentration of 0.039% by volume.

As part of the carbon cycle known as photosynthesis, plants, algae, and cyanobacteria absorb carbon dioxide, light, and water to produce carbohydrate energy for themselves and oxygen as a waste product.

Phosphorus tribromide

Phosphorus tribromide is a colourless liquid with the formula PBr_3. It fumes in air due to hydrolysis and has a penetrating odour. It is widely used in the laboratory for the conversion of alcohols to alkyl bromides.

Nucleophilic substitution

In organic and inorganic chemistry, nucleophilic substitution is a fundamental class of reactions in which an electron nucleophile selectively bonds with or attacks the positive or partially positive charge of an atom or a group of atoms called the leaving group; the positive or partially positive atom is referred to as an electrophile.

The most general form for the reaction may be given asNuc: + R-LG → R-Nuc + LG:

The electron pair (:) from the nucleophile (Nuc) attacks the substrate (R-LG) forming a new bond, while the leaving group (LG) departs with an electron pair. The principal product in this case is R-Nuc.

Substitution reaction

In a substitution reaction, a functional group in a particular chemical compound is replaced by another group. In organic chemistry, the electrophilic and nucleophilic substitution reactions are of prime importance. Organic substitution reactions are classified in several main organic reaction types depending on whether the reagent that brings about the substitution is considered an electrophile or a nucleophile, whether a reactive intermediate involved in the reaction is a carbocation, a carbanion or a free radical or whether the substrate is aliphatic or aromatic.

Aldol reaction

The aldol reaction is a powerful means of forming carbon-carbon bonds in organic chemistry. Discovered independently by Charles-Adolphe Wurtz and Alexander Borodin in 1872, the reaction combines two carbonyl compounds (the original experiments used aldehydes) to form a new β-hydroxy carbonyl compound. These products are known as aldols, from the aldehyde + alcohol, a structural motif seen in many of the products.

Aldol condensation

An aldol condensation is an organic reaction in which an enol or an enolate ion reacts with a carbonyl compound to form a β-hydroxyaldehyde or β-hydroxyketone, followed by a dehydration to give a conjugated enone.

Aldol condensations are important in organic synthesis, providing a good way to form carbon-carbon bonds. The Robinson annulation reaction sequence features an aldol condensation; the Wieland-Miescher ketone product is an important starting material for many organic syntheses.

Condensation

Condensation is the change of the physical state of matter from gaseous phase into liquid phase, and is the reverse of vaporization. When the transition happens from the gaseous phase into the solid phase directly, the change is called deposition.

Condensation is initiated by the formation of atomic/molecular clusters of that species within its gaseous volume--like rain drop or snow-flake formation within clouds--or at the contact between such gaseous phase and a (solvent) liquid or solid surface.

Mesityl oxide

Mesityl oxide is a α,β-Unsaturated ketone with the formula $CH_3C(O)CH=C(CH_3)_2$. This compound is a colorless, volatile liquid with a strong peppermint odor.

It is prepared by the aldol condensation of acetone to give diacetone alcohol, which readily dehydrates to give this compound.

Organic reaction

Organic reactions are chemical reactions involving organic compounds. The basic organic chemistry reaction types are addition reactions, elimination reactions, substitution reactions, pericyclic reactions, rearrangement reactions, photochemical reactions and redox reactions. In organic synthesis, organic reactions are used in the construction of new organic molecules.

Organic synthesis

Organic synthesis is a special branch of chemical synthesis and is concerned with the construction of organic compounds via organic reactions. Organic molecules can often contain a higher level of complexity compared to purely inorganic compounds, so the synthesis of organic compounds has developed into one of the most important branches of organic chemistry. There are two main areas of research fields within the general area of organic synthesis: total synthesis and methodology.

Dieckmann condensation

The Dieckmann condensation is the intramolecular chemical reaction of diesters with base to give β-ketoesters. he German chemist Walter Dieckmann (1869-1925). The equivalent intermolecular reaction is the Claisen condensation.

Diethyl carbonate

Diethyl carbonate is a carbonate ester of carbonic acid and ethanol. At room temperature (25 °C) diethyl carbonate is a clear liquid with a low flash point.

Diethyl carbonate is used as a solvent such as in erythromycin I.M injections.

Fatty acid

In chemistry, especially biochemistry, a fatty acid is a carboxylic acid with a long aliphatic tail (chain), which is either saturated or unsaturated. Most naturally occurring fatty acids have a chain of an even number of carbon atoms, from 4 to 28. Fatty acids are usually derived from triglycerides or phospholipids. When they are not attached to other molecules, they are known as 'free' fatty acids.

Biosynthesis

Biosynthesis is an enzyme-catalyzed process in cells of living organisms by which substrates are converted to more complex products. The biosynthesis process often consists of several enzymatic steps in which the product of one step is used as substrate in the following step. Examples for such multi-step biosynthetic pathways are those for the production of amino acids, fatty acids, and natural products.

Acyl carrier protein

The acyl carrier protein is an important component in both fatty acid and polyketide biosynthesis with the growing chain bound during synthesis as a thiol ester at the distal thiol of a 4'-phosphopantethiene moiety. The protein is expressed in the inactive apo form and the 4'-phosphopantetheine moiety must be post-translationally attached to a conserved serine residue on the ACP by the action of holo-acyl carrier protein synthase (ACPS), a phosphopantetheinyl transferase.

4'-Phosphopantetheine is an essential prosthetic group of several acyl carrier proteins involved in pathways of primary and secondary metabolism including the acyl carrier proteins (ACP) of fatty acid synthases, ACPs of polyketide synthases, and peptidyl carrier proteins (PCP) and aryl carrier proteins (ArCP) of nonribosomal peptide synthetases (NRPS).

Malonyl-CoA

Malonyl-CoA is a coenzyme A derivative of malonic acid.

It plays a key role in chain elongation in fatty acid biosynthesis and polyketide biosynthesis.

Malonyl-CoA is also used in transporting alpha-ketoglutarate across the mitochondrial membrane into the mitochondrial matrix.

Carrier protein

Carrier proteins are proteins involved in the movement of ions, small molecules, or macromolecules, such as another protein, across a biological membrane. Carrier proteins are integral membrane proteins; that is they exist within and span the membrane across which they transport substances. The proteins may assist in the movement of substances by facilitated diffusion or active transport.

Diethyl malonate

Diethyl malonate, is the diethyl ester of malonic acid. It occurs naturally in grapes and strawberries as a colourless liquid with an apple-like odour, and is used in perfumes.

CHAPTER HIGHLIGHTS & NOTES: KEY TERMS, PEOPLE, PLACES, CONCEPTS

Gabriel synthesis

The Gabriel synthesis is named for the German chemist Siegmund Gabriel. Traditionally, it is a chemical reaction that transforms primary alkyl halides into primary amines using potassium phthalimide.

The Gabriel reaction has since been generalized to include the alkylation of sulfonamides and imides, followed by deprotection, to obtain amines .

Malonic ester synthesis

The malonic ester synthesis is a chemical reaction where diethyl malonate or another ester of malonic acid is alkylated at the carbon alpha (directly adjacent) to both carbonyl groups, and then converted to a substituted acetic acid. The major drawback of malonic ester synthesis is that the alkylation stage can also produce dialkylated structures. This makes separation of products difficult and yields lower.

Alkylation

Alkylation is the transfer of an alkyl group from one molecule to another. The alkyl group may be transferred as an alkyl carbocation, a free radical, a carbanion or a carbene . Alkylating agents are widely used in chemistry because the alkyl group is probably the most common group encountered in organic molecules.

Maleic acid

Maleic acid is an organic compound that is a dicarboxylic acid, a molecule with two carboxyl groups. Maleic acid is the cis-isomer of butenedioic acid, whereas fumaric acid is the trans-isomer. It is mainly used as a precursor to fumaric acid, and relative to its parent maleic anhydride, maleic acid has few applications.

Maleic anhydride

Maleic anhydride is an organic compound with the formula $C_2H_2(CO)_2O$. It is the acid anhydride of maleic acid and in its pure state it is a colourless or white solid with an acrid odour.

Maleic anhydride was traditionally manufactured by the oxidation of benzene or other aromatic compounds. As of 2006, only a few smaller plants continue to use benzene; due to rising benzene prices, most maleic anhydride plants now use n-butane as a feedstock:2 $CH_3CH_2CH_2CH_3$ + 7 O_2 → 2 $C_2H_2(CO)_2O$ + 8 H_2OReactions

The chemistry of maleic anhydride is very rich, reflecting its ready availability and bifunctional reactivity.

Acetoacetic ester synthesis

Acetoacetic ester synthesis is a chemical reaction where ethyl acetoacetate is alkylated at the α-carbon to both carbonyl groups and then converted into a ketone, or more specifically an α-substituted acetone. This is very similar to malonic ester synthesis.

A strong base deprotonates the dicarbonyl α-carbon.

Lithium diisopropylamide	Lithium diisopropylamide is the chemical compound with the formula $[(CH_3)_2CH]_2NLi$. Generally abbreviated LDA, it is a strong base used in organic chemistry for the deprotonation of weakly acidic compounds. The reagent has been widely accepted because it is soluble in non-polar organic solvents and it is non-pyrophoric.
Acetoacetic acid	Acetoacetic acid is the organic compound with the formula CHC(O)CHCOH. It is the simplest beta-keto acid group and like other members of this class is unstable. Acetoacetic acid is a weak acid (like most alkyl carboxylic acids) with a pK_a of 3.77. It can be prepared by the hydrolysis of the ethyl acetoacetate followed by acidification of the anion. In general, acetoacetic acid is generated at 0 °C and used in situ immediately.
Hydrogen bromide	Hydrogen bromide is the diatomic molecule HBr. HBr is a gas at standard conditions. Hydrobromic acid forms upon dissolving HBr in water.
Hydrogen cyanide	Hydrogen cyanide is a chemical compound with chemical formula HCN. It is a colorless, extremely poisonous liquid that boils slightly above room temperature at 26 °C (79 °F). Hydrogen cyanide is a linear molecule, with a triple bond between carbon and nitrogen. A minor tautomer of HCN is HNC, hydrogen isocyanide.
Hydrogen halide	Hydrogen halides (or hydrohalic acids) are inorganic compounds with the formula HX where X is one of the halogens: fluorine, chlorine, bromine, iodine, and astatine. Hydrogen halides are gases that dissolve in water to give acids. The hydrogen halides are diatomic molecules with no tendency to ionize in the gas phase.
Oxidation state	In chemistry, the oxidation state is an indicator of the degree of oxidation of an atom in a chemical compound. The formal oxidation state is the hypothetical charge that an atom would have if all bonds to atoms of different elements were 100% ionic. Oxidation states are typically represented by integers, which can be positive, negative, or zero.
Robinson annulation	The Robinson annulation is a chemical reaction used in organic chemistry for ring formation. It was discovered by Robert Robinson in 1935 as a method to create a six membered ring by forming three new carbon-carbon bonds. The method uses a ketone and a methyl vinyl ketone to form an α,β-unsaturated ketone in a cyclohexane ring by a Michael addition followed by an aldol condensation.
Periodic acid	Periodic acid is an oxoacid of iodine having chemical formula HIO_4 or H_5IO_6. In dilute aqueous solution, periodic acid exists as discrete hydronium (H_3O^+) and metaperiodate (IO_4^-) ions.

Chapter 22. THE CHEMISTRY OF ENOLATE IONS, ENOLS, AND a,b UNSATURATED CA

CHAPTER HIGHLIGHTS & NOTES: KEY TERMS, PEOPLE, PLACES, CONCEPTS

Grignard reaction	The Grignard reaction is an organometallic chemical reaction in which alkyl- or aryl-magnesium halides (Grignard reagents) add to a carbonyl group in an aldehyde or ketone. This reaction is an important tool for the formation of carbon-carbon bonds. The reaction of an organic halide with magnesium is not a Grignard reaction, but provides a Grignard reagent.
Nitro compound	Nitro compounds are organic compounds that contain one or more nitro functional groups ($-NO_2$). They are often highly explosive, especially when the compound contains more than one nitro group and is impure. The nitro group is one of the most common explosophores (functional group that makes a compound explosive) used globally.
Organolithium reagent	An organolithium reagent is an organometallic compound with a direct bond between a carbon and a lithium atom. As the electropositive nature of lithium puts most of the charge density of the bond on the carbon atom, effectively creating a carbanion, organolithium compounds are extremely powerful bases and nucleophiles. For use as bases, butyllithiums are often used and are commercially available.

CHAPTER QUIZ: KEY TERMS, PEOPLE, PLACES, CONCEPTS

1. _________ is an enzyme-catalyzed process in cells of living organisms by which substrates are converted to more complex products. The _________ process often consists of several enzymatic steps in which the product of one step is used as substrate in the following step. Examples for such multi-step biosynthetic pathways are those for the production of amino acids, fatty acids, and natural products.

   a. Chemosynthesis
   b. Biosynthesis
   c. Gluconeogenesis
   d. Glutaminolysis

2. The _________ is the effect exerted by a substituent on modifying electrostatic forces operating on a nearby reaction center. The main contributors to the _________ are the inductive effect, mesomeric effect and the through-space electronic field effect.

   An electron withdrawing group or EWG draws electrons away from a reaction center.

   a. Polar effect
   b. Taft equation
   c. Walsh diagram
   d. Ethylene carbonate

3. . In chemistry, a _________ is a mathematical function describing the wave-like behavior of an electron in a molecule.

This function can be used to calculate chemical and physical properties such as the probability of finding an electron in any specific region. The term 'orbital' was first used in English by Robert S. Mulliken as the English translation of Schrödinger's 'Eigenfunktion'.

a. Molecular orbital
b. Monte Carlo molecular modeling
c. Physical and Theoretical Chemistry Laboratory
d. Quantum chemistry

4. _________ is a naturally occurring chemical compound composed of two oxygen atoms covalently bonded to a single carbon atom. It is a gas at standard temperature and pressure and exists in Earth's atmosphere in this state, as a trace gas at a concentration of 0.039% by volume.

As part of the carbon cycle known as photosynthesis, plants, algae, and cyanobacteria absorb _________, light, and water to produce carbohydrate energy for themselves and oxygen as a waste product.

a. Carbon tetrachloride
b. Care 30
c. 1-Chloro-1,2,2,2-tetrafluoroethane
d. Carbon dioxide

5. _________, is the diethyl ester of malonic acid. It occurs naturally in grapes and strawberries as a colourless liquid with an apple-like odour, and is used in perfumes. It is also used to synthesize other compounds such as barbiturates, artificial flavourings, vitamin B_1, and vitamin B_6.

a. Dimethyl malonate
b. Diethyl malonate
c. Malonic acid
d. Connexon

ANSWER KEY

Chapter 22. THE CHEMISTRY OF ENOLATE IONS, ENOLS, AND a,b UNSATURATED CARBONYL COMPOUNDS

---

1. b

2. a

3. a

4. d

5. b

You can take the complete Chapter Practice Test

for Chapter 22. THE CHEMISTRY OF ENOLATE IONS, ENOLS, AND a,b UNSATURATED CARBONYL COMPOUNDS

on all key terms, persons, places, and concepts.

Online 99 Cents

http://www.epub86.14.20423.22.cram101.com/

Use www.Cram101.com for all your study needs

including Cram101's online interactive problem solving labs in

chemistry, statistics, mathematics, and more.

Chapter 23. THE CHEMISTRY OF AMINES

CHAPTER OUTLINE: KEY TERMS, PEOPLE, PLACES, CONCEPTS

- Amine
- Aniline
- Aziridine
- Heterocyclic compound
- Morphine
- Pinacol rearrangement
- Pyrrolidine
- Bond length
- Solvent effects
- Polar effect
- Molecular orbital
- Sodium amide
- Benzalkonium chloride
- Organolithium reagent
- Lithium amide
- Alkylation
- Ethylene oxide
- Ammonia
- Clemmensen reduction

Chapter 23. THE CHEMISTRY OF AMINES

CHAPTER OUTLINE: KEY TERMS, PEOPLE, PLACES, CONCEPTS

Reductive amination

Hofmann elimination

Ammonium hydroxide

Leaving group

Nitration

Nitrous acid

Sandmeyer reaction

Hypophosphorous acid

Methyl orange

Gabriel synthesis

Protecting group

Nitro compound

Reduction of nitro compounds

Aryl halide

Nitrobenzene

Reducing agent

Curtius rearrangement

Carbamic acid

Stille reaction

Chapter 23. THE CHEMISTRY OF AMINES

CHAPTER OUTLINE: KEY TERMS, PEOPLE, PLACES, CONCEPTS

_______________ Isocyanate

_______________ Rearrangement reaction

_______________ Claisen condensation

_______________ Hofmann rearrangement

_______________ Rosenmund reduction

_______________ Stereochemistry

_______________ Water splitting

_______________ Epinephrine

_______________ Hormone

_______________ Norepinephrine

Amine	Amines are organic compounds and functional groups that contain a basic nitrogen atom with a lone pair. Amines are derivatives of ammonia, wherein one or more hydrogen atoms have been replaced by a substituent such as an alkyl or aryl group. Important amines include amino acids, biogenic amines, trimethylamine, and aniline; see Category:Amines for a list of amines.
Aniline	Aniline, phenylamine or aminobenzene is an organic compound with the formula $C_6H_5NH_2$. Consisting of a phenyl group attached to an amino group, aniline is the prototypical aromatic amine. Being a precursor to many industrial chemicals, its main use is in the manufacture of precursors to polyurethane.
Aziridine	Aziridines are organic compounds containing the aziridine functional group, a three-membered heterocycle with one amine group and two methylene groups. The parent compound is aziridine with molecular formula C_2H_5N. The bond angles in aziridine are approximately 60°, considerably less than the normal hydrocarbon bond angle of 109.5°, which results in angle strain as in the comparable cyclopropane and ethylene oxide molecules.
Heterocyclic compound	A heterocyclic compound is a cyclic compound that has atoms of at least two different elements as members of its ring(s). The counterparts of heterocyclic compounds are homocyclic compounds, the rings of which are made of a single element. Although heterocyclic compounds may be inorganic, most contain at least one carbon atom, and one or more atoms of elements other than carbon within the ring structure, such as sulfur, oxygen, or nitrogen.
Morphine	Morphine (; MS Contin, MSIR, Avinza, Kadian, Oramorph, Roxanol, Kapanol) is a potent opiate analgesic drug that is used to relieve severe pain. It was first isolated in 1804 by Friedrich Sertürner, first distributed by him in 1817, and first commercially sold by Merck in 1827, which at the time was a single small chemists' shop. It was more widely used after the invention of the hypodermic needle in 1857. It took its name from the Greek god of dreams Morpheus .
Pinacol rearrangement	The pinacol rearrangement is a method for converting a 1,2-diol to a carbonyl compound in organic chemistry. This 1,2-rearrangement takes place under acidic conditions. The name of the reaction comes from the rearrangement of pinacol to pinacolone.
Pyrrolidine	Pyrrolidine, is an organic compound with the molecular formula C_4H_9N. It is a cyclic secondary amine with a five-membered heterocycle containing four carbon atoms and one nitrogen atom. It is a clear liquid with an unpleasant odor that is ammoniacal, fishy, shellfish-like.

Chapter 23. THE CHEMISTRY OF AMINES

CHAPTER HIGHLIGHTS & NOTES: KEY TERMS, PEOPLE, PLACES, CONCEPTS

Bond length	In molecular geometry, bond length is the average distance between nuclei of two bonded atoms in a molecule. Bond length is related to bond order, when more electrons participate in bond formation the bond will get shorter. Bond length is also inversely related to bond strength and the bond dissociation energy, as (all other things being equal) a stronger bond will be shorter.
Solvent effects	In chemistry, solvent effects is the group of effects that a solvent has on chemical reactivity. Solvents can have an effect on solubility, stability and reaction rates and choosing the appropriate solvent allows for thermodynamic and kinetic control over a chemical reaction. A solute dissolves in a solvent when it forms favorable interactions with the solvent.
Polar effect	The Polar effect is the effect exerted by a substituent on modifying electrostatic forces operating on a nearby reaction center. The main contributors to the polar effect are the inductive effect, mesomeric effect and the through-space electronic field effect. An electron withdrawing group or EWG draws electrons away from a reaction center.
Molecular orbital	In chemistry, a molecular orbital is a mathematical function describing the wave-like behavior of an electron in a molecule. This function can be used to calculate chemical and physical properties such as the probability of finding an electron in any specific region. The term 'orbital' was first used in English by Robert S. Mulliken as the English translation of Schrödinger's 'Eigenfunktion'.
Sodium amide	Sodium amide, commonly called sodamide, is the chemical compound with the formula $NaNH_2$. This solid, which is dangerously reactive toward water, is white when pure, but commercial samples are typically gray due to the presence of small quantities of metallic iron from the manufacturing process. Such impurities do not usually affect the utility of the reagent.
Benzalkonium chloride	Benzalkonium chloride, is a mixture of alkylbenzyldimethylammonium chlorides of various even-numbered alkyl chain lengths. This product is a nitrogenous cationic surface-acting agent belonging to the quaternary ammonium group. It has three main categories of use: as a biocide, a cationic surfactant and phase transfer agent in the chemical industry.
Organolithium reagent	An organolithium reagent is an organometallic compound with a direct bond between a carbon and a lithium atom. As the electropositive nature of lithium puts most of the charge density of the bond on the carbon atom, effectively creating a carbanion, organolithium compounds are extremely powerful bases and nucleophiles. For use as bases, butyllithiums are often used and are commercially available.

Lithium amide

Lithium amide is an inorganic compound with the chemical formula $Li^+NH_2^-$, i.e. it is composed of a lithium cation, and the conjugate base of ammonia. It is a white solid with a tetragonal crystal structure.

Lithium amides

The anionic conjugate bases of amines are known as amides.

Alkylation

Alkylation is the transfer of an alkyl group from one molecule to another. The alkyl group may be transferred as an alkyl carbocation, a free radical, a carbanion or a carbene . Alkylating agents are widely used in chemistry because the alkyl group is probably the most common group encountered in organic molecules.

Ethylene oxide

Ethylene oxide, is the organic compound with the formula C_2H_4O. It is a cyclic ether. This means that it is composed of two alkyl groups attached to an oxygen atom in a cyclic shape (circular).

Ammonia

Ammonia is a compound of nitrogen and hydrogen with the formula NH_3. It is a colourless gas with a characteristic pungent smell. Ammonia contributes significantly to the nutritional needs of terrestrial organisms by serving as a precursor to food and fertilizers.

Clemmensen reduction

Clemmensen reduction is a chemical reaction described as a reduction of ketones (or aldehydes) to alkanes using zinc amalgam and hydrochloric acid. This reaction is named after Erik Christian Clemmensen, a Danish chemist.

The Clemmensen reduction is particularly effective at reducing aryl-alkyl ketones.

Reductive amination

Reductive amination is a form of amination that involves the conversion of a carbonyl group to an amine via an intermediate imine. The carbonyl group is most commonly a ketone or an aldehyde.

In this organic reaction, the amine first reacts with the carbonyl group to form a hemiaminal species, which subsequently loses one molecule of water in a reversible manner by alkylimino-de-oxo-bisubstitution, to form the imine.

Hofmann elimination

Hofmann elimination is a process where an amine is reacted to create a tertiary amine and an alkene by treatment with excess methyl iodide followed by treatment with silver oxide, water, and heat.

After the first step, a quaternary ammonium iodide salt is created. After replacement of iodine by an hydroxyl anion, an elimination reaction takes place to the alkene.

Chapter 23. THE CHEMISTRY OF AMINES

CHAPTER HIGHLIGHTS & NOTES: KEY TERMS, PEOPLE, PLACES, CONCEPTS

Ammonium hydroxide	Ammonia solution, also known as ammonium hydroxide, ammonia water, ammonical liquor, ammonia liquor, aqua ammonia, aqueous ammonia, or simply ammonia, is a solution of ammonia in water. It can be denoted by the symbols $NH_3(aq)$. Although the name ammonium hydroxide suggests a base with composition $[NH_4^+][OH^-]$, it is actually impossible to isolate samples of NH_4OH, as these ions do not comprise a significant fraction of the total amount of ammonia except in extremely dilute solutions.
Leaving group	In chemistry, a leaving group is a molecular fragment that departs with a pair of electrons in heterolytic bond cleavage. Leaving groups can be anions or neutral molecules. Common anionic leaving groups are halides such as Cl^-, Br^-, and I^-, and sulfonate esters, such as para-toluenesulfonate ('tosylate', TsO^-).
Nitration	Nitration is a general chemical process for the introduction of a nitro group into a chemical compound. The dominant application of nitration is for the production of nitrobenzene, the precursor to methylene diphenyl diisocyanate. Nitrations are famously used for the production of explosives, for example the conversion of glycerin to nitroglycerin and the conversion of toluene to trinitrotoluene.
Nitrous acid	Nitrous acid is a weak and monobasic acid known only in solution and in the form of nitrite salts. Nitrous acid is used to make diazides from amines; this occurs by nucleophilic attack of the amine onto the nitrite, reprotonation by the surrounding solvent, and double-elimination of water. The diazide can then be liberated to give a carbene or carbenoid.
Sandmeyer reaction	The Sandmeyer reaction is a chemical reaction used to synthesize aryl halides from aryl diazonium salts. he Swiss chemist Traugott Sandmeyer. An aromatic (or heterocyclic) amine quickly reacts with a nitrite to form an aryl diazonium salt, which decomposes in the presence of copper(I) salts, such as copper(I) chloride, to form the desired aryl halide.
Hypophosphorous acid	Hypophosphorous acid is a phosphorus oxoacid and a powerful reducing agent with molecular formula H_3PO_2. Inorganic chemists refer to the free acid by this name (also as 'HPA'), or the acceptable name of phosphinic acid. It is a colorless low-melting compound, which is soluble in water, dioxane, and alcohols.
Methyl orange	Methyl orange is a pH indicator frequently used in titrations. It is often used in titrations because of its clear and distinct colour change.

Gabriel synthesis

The Gabriel synthesis is named for the German chemist Siegmund Gabriel. Traditionally, it is a chemical reaction that transforms primary alkyl halides into primary amines using potassium phthalimide.

The Gabriel reaction has since been generalized to include the alkylation of sulfonamides and imides, followed by deprotection, to obtain amines .

Protecting group

A protecting group is introduced into a molecule by chemical modification of a functional group in order to obtain chemoselectivity in a subsequent chemical reaction. It plays an important role in multistep organic synthesis.

In many preparations of delicate organic compounds, some specific parts of their molecules cannot survive the required reagents or chemical environments.

Nitro compound

Nitro compounds are organic compounds that contain one or more nitro functional groups ($-NO_2$). They are often highly explosive, especially when the compound contains more than one nitro group and is impure. The nitro group is one of the most common explosophores (functional group that makes a compound explosive) used globally.

Reduction of nitro compounds

The chemical reactions described as reduction of nitro compounds can be facilitated by many different reagents and reaction conditions. Historically, the nitro group was one of the first functional groups to be reduced, due to the ease of nitro-group reduction.

Nitro-groups behave differently whether a neighboring hydrogen is present or not.

Aryl halide

In organic chemistry, an aryl halide is an aromatic compound in which one or more hydrogen atoms directly bonded to an aromatic ring are replaced by a halide. The haloarene are distinguished from haloalkanes because they exhibit many differences in methods of preparation and properties. The most important members are the aryl chlorides, but the class of compounds is so broad that many derivatives enjoy niche applications.

Nitrobenzene

Nitrobenzene is an organic compound with the chemical formula $C_6H_5NO_2$. It is a water-insoluble pale yellow oil with an almond-like odor. It freezes to give greenish-yellow crystals.

Reducing agent

A reducing agent is the element or compound in a reduction-oxidation (redox) reaction that donates an electron to another species; however, since the reducer loses an electron we say it is 'oxidized'. This means that there must be an 'oxidizer'; because if any chemical is an electron donor (reducer), another must be an electron recipient (oxidizer). Thus reducers are 'oxidized' and oxidizers are 'reduced'.

Chapter 23. THE CHEMISTRY OF AMINES

CHAPTER HIGHLIGHTS & NOTES: KEY TERMS, PEOPLE, PLACES, CONCEPTS

Curtius rearrangement	The Curtius rearrangement as first defined by Theodor Curtius, is a chemical reaction that involves the rearrangement of an acyl azide to an isocyanate. Several reviews have been published. The isocyanate can be trapped by a variety of nucleophiles.
Carbamic acid	Carbamic acid is a compound that is unstable under normal circumstances. It is technically the simplest amino acid, though its instability (and the unique nature of the carboxyl-nitrogen bond) allows glycine to assume this title. Its importance is due more to its relevance in identifying the names of larger compounds.
Stille reaction	The Stille reaction is a chemical reaction coupling an organotin compound with an sp^2-hybridized organic halide catalyzed by palladium. The reaction is widely used in organic synthesis. X is typically a halide, such as Cl, Br, I. Additionally, X can be a pseudohalide such as a triflate, $CF_3SO_3^-$.
Isocyanate	Isocyanate is the functional group with the formula -N=C=O. Organic compounds that contains an isocyanate group are referred to as isocyanates. An isocyanate that has two isocyanate groups is known as a diisocyanate. Diisocyanates are manufactured for reactions with polyols in the production of polyurethanes.
Rearrangement reaction	A rearrangement reaction is a broad class of organic reactions where the carbon skeleton of a molecule is rearranged to give a structural isomer of the original molecule. Often a substituent moves from one atom to another atom in the same molecule. In the example below the substituent R moves from carbon atom 1 to carbon atom 2: Intermolecular rearrangements also take place.
Claisen condensation	The Claisen condensation is a carbon-carbon bond forming reaction that occurs between two esters or one ester and another carbonyl compound in the presence of a strong base, resulting in a β-keto ester or a β-diketone. It is named after Rainer Ludwig Claisen, who first published his work on the reaction in 1881 . At least one of the reagents must be enolizable (have an α-proton and be able to undergo deprotonation to form the enolate anion).
Hofmann rearrangement	The Hofmann rearrangement is the organic reaction of a primary amide to a primary amine with one fewer carbon atom.

This reaction is also sometimes called the Hofmann degradation or the Harmon Process, and should not be confused with the Hofmann elimination. Mechanism

The reaction of bromine with sodium hydroxide forms sodium hypobromite in situ, which transforms the primary amide into an intermediate isocyanate.

Rosenmund reduction

The Rosenmund reduction is a chemical reaction that reduces an acid halide to an aldehyde using hydrogen gas over palladium-on-carbon poisoned with barium sulfate. The reaction was named after Karl Wilhelm Rosenmund.

The catalyst must be poisoned because otherwise the catalyst is too active and will reduce the acid chloride to a primary alcohol.

Stereochemistry

Stereochemistry, a subdiscipline of chemistry, involves the study of the relative spatial arrangement of atoms within molecules. An important branch of stereochemistry is the study of chiral molecules.

Stereochemistry is also known as 3D chemistry because the prefix 'stereo-' means 'three-dimensionality'.

Water splitting

Water splitting is the general term for a chemical reaction in which water is separated into oxygen and hydrogen. Efficient and economical water splitting would be a key technology component of a hydrogen economy. Various techniques for water splitting have been issued in water splitting patents in the United States.

Epinephrine

Epinephrine is a hormone and a neurotransmitter. Epinephrine has many functions in the body, regulating heart rate, blood vessel and air passage diameters, and metabolic shifts; epinephrine release is a crucial component of the fight-or-flight response of the sympathetic nervous system. In chemical terms, epinephrine is one of a group of monoamines called the catecholamines.

Hormone

A hormone is a chemical released by a cell or a gland in one part of the body that sends out messages that affect cells in other parts of the organism. Only a small amount of hormone is required to alter cell metabolism. In essence, it is a chemical messenger that transports a signal from one cell to another.

Norepinephrine

Norepinephrine , or noradrenaline (BAN) , is a catecholamine with multiple roles including as a hormone and a neurotransmitter. Areas of the body that produce or are affected by norepinephrine are described as noradrenergic.

Chapter 23. THE CHEMISTRY OF AMINES

CHAPTER QUIZ: KEY TERMS, PEOPLE, PLACES, CONCEPTS

1. In molecular geometry, _________ is the average distance between nuclei of two bonded atoms in a molecule.

   _________ is related to bond order, when more electrons participate in bond formation the bond will get shorter. _________ is also inversely related to bond strength and the bond dissociation energy, as (all other things being equal) a stronger bond will be shorter.

   a. Cyclic compound
   b. Bond length
   c. LCP theory
   d. Linear molecular geometry

2. In chemistry, _________ is the group of effects that a solvent has on chemical reactivity. Solvents can have an effect on solubility, stability and reaction rates and choosing the appropriate solvent allows for thermodynamic and kinetic control over a chemical reaction.

   A solute dissolves in a solvent when it forms favorable interactions with the solvent.

   a. 1,2-Dioxetanedione
   b. Diatomic molecule
   c. LCP theory
   d. Solvent effects

3. _________s are organic compounds and functional groups that contain a basic nitrogen atom with a lone pair. _________s are derivatives of ammonia, wherein one or more hydrogen atoms have been replaced by a substituent such as an alkyl or aryl group. Important _________s include amino acids, biogenic _________s, trimethylamine, and aniline; see Category:_________s for a list of _________s.

   a. AS-19
   b. Amine
   c. Ammonia borane
   d. Aminoshikimic acid

4. In chemistry, a _________ is a mathematical function describing the wave-like behavior of an electron in a molecule. This function can be used to calculate chemical and physical properties such as the probability of finding an electron in any specific region. The term 'orbital' was first used in English by Robert S. Mulliken as the English translation of Schrödinger's 'Eigenfunktion'.

   a. Molecular symmetry
   b. Monte Carlo molecular modeling
   c. Physical and Theoretical Chemistry Laboratory
   d. Molecular orbital

5. . _________ (; MS Contin, MSIR, Avinza, Kadian, Oramorph, Roxanol, Kapanol) is a potent opiate analgesic drug that is used to relieve severe pain. It was first isolated in 1804 by Friedrich Sertürner, first distributed by him in 1817, and first commercially sold by Merck in 1827, which at the time was a single small chemists' shop.

It was more widely used after the invention of the hypodermic needle in 1857. It took its name from the Greek god of dreams Morpheus .

a. Morphine
b. Morphine-N-oxide
c. Morphinone
d. Mycophenolate mofetil

ANSWER KEY
Chapter 23. THE CHEMISTRY OF AMINES

---

1. b
2. d
3. b
4. d
5. a

Chapter 24. CARBOHYDRATES

CHAPTER OUTLINE: KEY TERMS, PEOPLE, PLACES, CONCEPTS

Sulfuric acid

Aldose

Disaccharide

Ketose

Monosaccharide

Oligosaccharide

Pentose

Polysaccharide

Trisaccharide

Eclipsed conformation

Fischer projection

Glucuronic acid

Glutamic acid

Absolute configuration

Epimer

Furan

Furanose

Pyranose

Anomer

Gluconic acid

Haworth projection

Squaric acid

Mutarotation

Claisen condensation

Steric effects

Glycoside

Hydrolysis

Acetic anhydride

Alkylating antineoplastic agent

Dimethyl sulfate

Methyl iodide

Sodium amide

Amino acid

Protecting group

Aldonic acid

Nitric acid

Aldaric acid

Periodic acid

Chapter 24. CARBOHYDRATES

CHAPTER OUTLINE: KEY TERMS, PEOPLE, PLACES, CONCEPTS

_______ Sodium borohydride

_______ Hydrogen bromide

_______ Hydrogen halide

_______ Tartaric acid

_______ Arabinose

_______ Glycosidic bond

_______ Levulinic acid

_______ Reducing sugar

_______ Lead acetate

_______ Sodium cyclamate

_______ Sodium nitrite

_______ Cell membrane

_______ Amylopectin

_______ Amylose

_______ Cellulose acetate

_______ Amino sugar

_______ Glycoprotein

Chapter 24. CARBOHYDRATES

CHAPTER HIGHLIGHTS & NOTES: KEY TERMS, PEOPLE, PLACES, CONCEPTS

Sulfuric acid

Sulfuric acid is a highly caustic strong mineral acid with the molecular formula H_2SO_4. It is a colorless to slightly yellow viscous liquid which is soluble in water at all concentrations. The historical name of this acid is oil of vitriol.

Aldose

An aldose is a monosaccharide (a simple sugar) that contains only one aldehyde (-CH=O) group per molecule. The chemical formula takes the form $C_n(H_2O)_n$. The simplest possible aldose is the diose glycolaldehyde, which only contains two carbon atoms.

Disaccharide

A disaccharide is the carbohydrate formed when two monosaccharides undergo a condensation reaction which involves the elimination of a small molecule, such as water, from the functional groups only. Like monosaccharides, disaccharides form an aqueous solution when dissolved in water. Three common examples are sucrose, lactose, and maltose.

Ketose

A ketose is a sugar containing one ketone group per molecule.

With three carbon atoms, dihydroxyacetone is the simplest of all ketoses and is the only one having no optical activity. Ketoses can isomerize into an aldose when the carbonyl group is located at the end of the molecule.

Monosaccharide

Monosaccharides are the most basic units of biologically important carbohydrates. They are the simplest form of sugar and are usually colorless, water-soluble, crystalline solids. Some monosaccharides have a sweet taste.

Oligosaccharide

An oligosaccharide is a saccharide polymer containing a small number (typically two to ten) of component sugars, also known as simple sugars (monosaccharides). Oligosaccharides can have many functions; for example, they are commonly found on the plasma membrane of animal cells where they can play a role in cell-cell recognition.

In general, they are found either O- or N-linked to compatible amino acid side-chains in proteins or to lipid moieties .

Pentose

A pentose is a monosaccharide with five carbon atoms. Pentoses are organized into two groups. Aldopentoses have an aldehyde functional group at position 1. Ketopentoses have a ketone functional group in position 2 or 3.

Polysaccharide

Polysaccharides are long carbohydrate molecules of repeated monomer units joined together by glycosidic bonds. They range in structure from linear to highly branched. Polysaccharides are often quite heterogeneous, containing slight modifications of the repeating unit.

Trisaccharide

Trisaccharides are oligosaccharides composed of three monosaccharides with two glycosidic bonds connecting them.

Similar to the disaccharides, each glycosidic bond can be formed between any hydroxyl group on the component monosaccharides. Even if all three component sugars are the same (e.g., glucose), different bond combinations (regiochemistry) and stereochemistry (alpha- or beta-) result in triaccharides that are diastereoisomers with different chemical and physical properties.

Eclipsed conformation

In chemistry an eclipsed conformation is a conformation in which two substituents X and Y on adjacent atoms A, B are in closest proximity, implying that the torsion angle X-A-B-Y is 0°. Such a conformation exists in any open chain single chemical bond connecting two sp^3 hybridised atoms, and is normally a conformational energy maximum. This maximum is often explained by steric hindrance, but its origins sometimes actually lie in hyperconjugation (as when the eclipsing interaction is of two hydrogen atoms).

Fischer projection

The Fischer projection, devised by Hermann Emil Fischer in 1891, is a two-dimensional representation of a three-dimensional organic molecule by projection. Fischer projections were originally proposed for the depiction of carbohydrates and used by chemists, particularly in organic chemistry and biochemistry. The use of Fischer projections in non-carbohydrates is discouraged, as such drawings are ambiguous when confused with other types of drawing.

Glucuronic acid

Glucuronic acid is a carboxylic acid. Its structure is similar to that of glucose. However, glucuronic acid's sixth carbon is oxidized to a carboxylic acid.

Glucuronic acid is common in carbohydrate chains of proteoglycans. It is part of mucous animal secretions (such as saliva), cell glycocalyx and intercellular matrix (for instance hyaluronan).

Glutamic acid

Glutamic acid is one of the 20-22 proteinogenic amino acids, and its codons are GAA and GAG. It is a non-essential amino acid. The carboxylate anions and salts of glutamic acid are known as glutamates. In neuroscience, glutamate is an important neurotransmitter that plays a key role in long-term potentiation and is important for learning and memory.

Absolute configuration

An absolute configuration in stereochemistry is the spatial arrangement of the atoms of a chiral molecular entity and its stereochemical description e.g. R or S.

Absolute configurations for a chiral molecule (in pure form) are most often obtained by X-ray crystallography. All enantiomerically pure chiral molecules crystallise in one of the 65 Sohncke Groups (Chiral Space Groups).

Alternative techniques are Optical rotatory dispersion, vibrational circular dichroism and the use of chiral shift reagents in proton NMR.

Chapter 24. CARBOHYDRATES

Epimer

In chemistry, epimers are diastereomers that differ in configuration of only one stereogenic center. Diastereomers are a class of stereoisomers that are non-superposable, non-mirror images of one another.

In chemical nomenclature, one of the epimeric pairs is given the prefix epi- for example in quinine and epi-quinine.

Furan

Furan is a heterocyclic organic compound, consisting of a five-membered aromatic ring with four carbon atoms and one oxygen. The class of compounds containing such rings are also referred to as furans.

Furan is a colorless, flammable, highly volatile liquid with a boiling point close to room temperature.

Furanose

A furanose is a collective term for carbohydrates that have a chemical structure that includes a five-membered ring system consisting of four carbon atoms and one oxygen atom. The name derives from its similarity to the oxygen heterocycle furan, but the furanose ring does not have double bonds.

The furanose ring is a cyclic hemiacetal of an aldopentose or a cyclic hemiketal of a ketohexose.

Pyranose

Pyranose is a collective term for carbohydrates that have a chemical structure that includes a six-membered ring consisting of five carbon atoms and one oxygen atom. The name derives from its similarity to the oxygen heterocycle pyran, but the pyranose ring does not have double bonds. A pyranose in which the anomeric OH at C(l) has been converted into an OR group is called a pyranoside.

Anomer

In carbohydrate chemistry, an anomer is a special type of epimer. It is one of two stereoisomers of a cyclic saccharide that differs only in its configuration at the hemiacetal or hemiketal carbon, also called the anomeric carbon. Anomerization is the process of conversion of one anomer to the other.

Gluconic acid

Gluconic acid is an organic compound with molecular formula $C_6H_{12}O_7$ and condensed structural formula $HOCH_2(CHOH)_4COOH$. It is one of the 16 stereoisomers of 2,3,4,5,6-pentahydroxyhexanoic acid.

In aqueous solution at neutral pH, gluconic acid forms the gluconate ion. The salts of gluconic acid are known as 'gluconates'.

Haworth projection

A Haworth projection is a common way of representing the cyclic structure of monosaccharides with a simple three-dimensional perspective.

A Haworth projection has the following characteristics :•Carbon is the implicit type of atom. In the example on the right, the atoms numbered from 1 to 6 are all carbon atoms.

Squaric acid

Squaric acid, because its four carbon atoms approximately form a square, is an organic compound with chemical formula $C_4H_2O_4$.

The conjugate base of squaric acid is the hydrogensquarate anion $C_4HO_4^-$; and the conjugate base of the hydrogensquarate anion is the divalent squarate anion $C_4O_4^{2-}$. This is one of the oxocarbon anions, which consist only of carbon and oxygen.

Mutarotation

Mutarotation is the change in the optical rotation that occurs by epimerization (that is the change in the equilibrium between two epimers, when the corresponding stereocenters interconvert). Cyclic sugars show mutarotation as α and β anomeric forms interconvert. The optical rotation of the solution depends on the optical rotation of each anomer and their ratio in the solution.

Claisen condensation

The Claisen condensation is a carbon-carbon bond forming reaction that occurs between two esters or one ester and another carbonyl compound in the presence of a strong base, resulting in a β-keto ester or a β-diketone. It is named after Rainer Ludwig Claisen, who first published his work on the reaction in 1881 .

At least one of the reagents must be enolizable (have an α-proton and be able to undergo deprotonation to form the enolate anion).

Steric effects

Steric effects arise from the fact that each atom within a molecule occupies a certain amount of space. If atoms are brought too close together, there is an associated cost in energy due to overlapping electron clouds , and this may affect the molecule's preferred shape (conformation) and reactivity. Steric hindrance

Steric hindrance occurs when the large size of groups within a molecule prevents chemical reactions that are observed in related molecules with smaller groups.

Glycoside

In chemistry, a glycoside is a molecule in which a sugar is bound to a non-carbohydrate moiety, usually a small organic molecule. Glycosides play numerous important roles in living organisms. Many plants store chemicals in the form of inactive glycosides.

Hydrolysis

Hydrolysis usually means the rupture of chemical bonds by the action of water. Generally, hydrolysis is a step in the degradation of a substance. In terms of the word's derivation, hydrolysis comes from Greek roots hydro 'water' + lysis 'separation'.

Acetic anhydride

Acetic anhydride, is the chemical compound with the formula $(CH_3CO)_2O$.

Commonly abbreviated Ac_2O, it is the simplest isolatable acid anhydride and is a widely used reagent in organic synthesis. It is a colorless liquid that smells strongly of acetic acid, formed by its reaction with the moisture in the air.

Formic anhydride is an even simpler acid anhydride, but it spontaneously decomposes, especially once removed from solution.

Alkylating antineoplastic agent

An alkylating antineoplastic agent is an alkylating agent used in cancer treatment that attaches an alkyl group (C_nH_{2n+1}) to DNA.

The alkyl group is attached to the guanine base of DNA, at the number 7 nitrogen atom of the purine ring.

Since cancer cells, in general, proliferate faster and with less error-correcting than healthy cells, cancer cells are more sensitive to DNA damage -- such as being alkylated. Alkylating agents are used to treat several cancers.

Dimethyl sulfate

Dimethyl sulfate is a chemical compound with formula $(CH_3O)_2SO_2$. As the diester of methanol and sulfuric acid, its formula is often written as $(CH_3)_2SO_4$ or even Me_2SO_4, where CH_3 or Me is methyl. Me_2SO_4 is mainly used as a methylating agent in organic synthesis.

Methyl iodide

Methyl iodide, and commonly abbreviated 'MeI', is the chemical compound with the formula CH_3I. It is a dense, colorless, volatile liquid. In terms of chemical structure, it is related to methane by replacement of one hydrogen atom by an atom of iodine. It is naturally emitted by rice plantations in small amounts.

Sodium amide

Sodium amide, commonly called sodamide, is the chemical compound with the formula $NaNH_2$. This solid, which is dangerously reactive toward water, is white when pure, but commercial samples are typically gray due to the presence of small quantities of metallic iron from the manufacturing process. Such impurities do not usually affect the utility of the reagent.

Amino acid

Amino acids are molecules containing an amine group, a carboxylic acid group, and a side-chain that is specific to each amino acid. The key elements of an amino acid are carbon, hydrogen, oxygen, and nitrogen. They are particularly important in biochemistry, where the term usually refers to alpha-amino acids.

Protecting group

A protecting group is introduced into a molecule by chemical modification of a functional group in order to obtain chemoselectivity in a subsequent chemical reaction. It plays an important role in multistep organic synthesis.

Aldonic acid	An aldonic acid is any of a family of sugar acids obtained by oxidation of the aldehyde functional group of an aldose to form a carboxylic acid functional group. Thus, their general chemical formula is $HOOC\text{-}(CHOH)_n\text{-}CH_2OH$. Oxidation of the terminal hydroxyl group instead of the terminal aldehyde yields a uronic acid, while oxidation of both terminal ends yields an aldaric acid. Aldonic acids are typically prepared by oxidation of the sugar with bromine.
Nitric acid	Nitric acid also known as aqua fortis and spirit of niter, is a highly corrosive and toxic strong mineral acid which is normally colorless but tends to acquire a yellow cast due to the accumulation of oxides of nitrogen if long-stored. Ordinary nitric acid has a concentration of 68%. When the solution contains more than 86% HNO_3, it is referred to as fuming nitric acid.
Aldaric acid	Aldaric acids are a group of sugar acids, where the terminal hydroxyl groups of the sugars have been replaced by terminal carboxylic acids, and are characterised by the formula HOOC-(CHOH)n-COOH. Aldaric acids are usually synthesized by the oxidation of aldoses with nitric acid. In this reaction it is the open-chain (polyhydroxyaldehyde) form of the sugar that reacts. An aldaric acid is an aldose in which both the hydroxyl function of the terminal carbon and the aldehyde function of the first carbon have been fully oxidized to carboxylic acid functions.
Periodic acid	Periodic acid is an oxoacid of iodine having chemical formula HIO_4 or H_5IO_6. In dilute aqueous solution, periodic acid exists as discrete hydronium (H_3O^+) and metaperiodate (IO_4^-) ions. When more concentrated, orthoperiodic acid, H_5IO_6, is formed; this dissociates into hydronium and orthoperiodate (IO_6^{5-}) ions.
Sodium borohydride	Sodium borohydride, is an inorganic compound with the formula $NaBH_4$. This white solid, usually encountered as a powder, is a versatile reducing agent that finds wide application in chemistry, both in the laboratory and on a technical scale. Large amounts are used for bleaching wood pulp.
Hydrogen bromide	Hydrogen bromide is the diatomic molecule HBr. HBr is a gas at standard conditions. Hydrobromic acid forms upon dissolving HBr in water.
Hydrogen halide	Hydrogen halides (or hydrohalic acids) are inorganic compounds with the formula HX where X is one of the halogens: fluorine, chlorine, bromine, iodine, and astatine. Hydrogen halides are gases that dissolve in water to give acids.

Chapter 24. CARBOHYDRATES

CHAPTER HIGHLIGHTS & NOTES: KEY TERMS, PEOPLE, PLACES, CONCEPTS

Tartaric acid

Tartaric acid is a white crystalline diprotic organic acid. It occurs naturally in many plants, particularly grapes, bananas, and tamarinds; is commonly combined with baking soda to function as a leavening agent in recipes, and is one of the main acids found in wine. It is added to other foods to give a sour taste, and is used as an antioxidant.

Arabinose

Arabinose is an aldopentose - a monosaccharide containing five carbon atoms, and including an aldehyde (CHO) functional group.

For biosynthetic reasons, most saccharides are almost always more abundant in nature as the 'D'-form, or structurally analogous to D-glyceraldehyde. However, L-arabinose is in fact more common than D-arabinose in nature and is found in nature as a component of biopolymers such as hemicellulose and pectin.

Glycosidic bond

In chemistry, a glycosidic bond is a type of covalent bond that joins a carbohydrate (sugar) molecule to another group, which may or may not be another carbohydrate.

A glycosidic bond is formed between the hemiacetal group of a saccharide and the hydroxyl group of some organic compound such as an alcohol. If the group attached to the carbohydrate residue is not another saccharide it is referred to as an aglycone.

Levulinic acid

Levulinic acid, is an organic compound with the formula $CH_3C(O)CH_2CH_2CO_2H$. It is a keto acid. This white crystalline is soluble in water, ethanol, and diethyl ether.

Related to its original synthesis, levulinic acid is prepared in the laboratory by heating sucrose with concentrated hydrochloric acid.

Reducing sugar

A reducing sugar is any sugar that either has an aldehyde group or is capable of forming one in solution through isomerism. The cyclic hemiacetal forms of aldoses can open to reveal an aldehyde and certain ketoses can undergo tautomerization to become aldoses. However, acetals, including those found polysaccharide linkages, cannot easily become a free aldehyde.

Lead acetate

Lead(IV) acetate or lead tetraacetate is a chemical compound with chemical formula $Pb(C_2H_3O_2)_4$ and is a lead salt of acetic acid. It is commercially available often stabilized with acetic acid.

It can be prepared by reaction of red lead with acetic acid The other main lead acetate is lead(II) acetate.

Sodium cyclamate

Sodium cyclamate is an artificial sweetener. It is 30-50 times sweeter than sugar (depending on concentration; it is not a linear relationship), making it the least potent of the commercially used artificial sweeteners.

Sodium nitrite

Sodium nitrite, with chemical formula $NaNO_2$, is used as a color fixative and preservative in meats and fish. When pure, it is a white to slight yellowish crystalline powder. It is very soluble in water and is hygroscopic.

Cell membrane

The cell membrane is a biological membrane that separates the interior of all cells from the outside environment. The cell membrane is selectively permeable to ions and organic molecules and controls the movement of substances in and out of cells. It basically protects the cell from outside forces.

Amylopectin

Amylopectin is a soluble polysaccharide and highly branched polymer of glucose found in plants. It is one of the two components of starch, the other being amylose.

Glucose units are linked in a linear way with $\alpha(1 \rightarrow 4)$ glycosidic bonds.

Amylose

Amylose is a linear polymer made up of D-glucose units.

This polysaccharide is one of the two components of starch, making up approximately 20-30% of the structure. The other component is amylopectin, which makes up 70-80% of the structure.

Cellulose acetate

Cellulose acetate first prepared in 1865, is the acetate ester of cellulose. Cellulose acetate is used as a film base in photography, as a component in some adhesives, and as a frame material for eyeglasses; it is also used as a synthetic fiber and in the manufacture of cigarette filters and playing cards.

Paul Schützenberger discovered that cellulose could react with acetic anhydride to form cellulose acetate in 1865. The use of chloroform to make it soluble was expensive, but in 1904 George Miles, an American chemist, discovered that hydrolyzed cellulose acetate is soluble in more solvents like acetone.

Amino sugar

In chemistry, an amino sugar contains an amine group in place of a hydroxyl group. Derivatives of amine containing sugars, such as N-acetylglucosamine and sialic acid, while not formally containing an amine, are also considered amino sugars.

Aminoglycosides are a class of antimicrobial compounds that inhibit bacterial protein synthesis.

Glycoprotein

Glycoproteins are proteins that contain oligosaccharide chains (glycans) covalently attached to polypeptide side-chains. The carbohydrate is attached to the protein in a cotranslational or posttranslational modification. This process is known as glycosylation.

Chapter 24. CARBOHYDRATES

CHAPTER QUIZ: KEY TERMS, PEOPLE, PLACES, CONCEPTS

1. An _________ is a monosaccharide (a simple sugar) that contains only one aldehyde (-CH=O) group per molecule. The chemical formula takes the form $C_n(H_2O)_n$. The simplest possible _________ is the diose glycolaldehyde, which only contains two carbon atoms.

   a. Aldose
   b. Telluric acid
   c. Tellurous acid
   d. Thallous malonate

2. _________ is a highly caustic strong mineral acid with the molecular formula H_2SO_4. It is a colorless to slightly yellow viscous liquid which is soluble in water at all concentrations. The historical name of this acid is oil of vitriol.

   a. Sulfurous acid
   b. Sulfuric acid
   c. Tellurous acid
   d. Thallous malonate

3. _________ is a chemical compound with formula $(CH_3O)_2SO_2$. As the diester of methanol and sulfuric acid, its formula is often written as $(CH_3)_2SO_4$ or even Me_2SO_4, where CH_3 or Me is methyl. Me_2SO_4 is mainly used as a methylating agent in organic synthesis.

   a. Dimethyl sulfate
   b. Methyl bisulfate
   c. Potassium lauryl sulfate
   d. Pregnenolone sulfate

4. The _________, devised by Hermann Emil Fischer in 1891, is a two-dimensional representation of a three-dimensional organic molecule by projection. _________s were originally proposed for the depiction of carbohydrates and used by chemists, particularly in organic chemistry and biochemistry. The use of _________s in non-carbohydrates is discouraged, as such drawings are ambiguous when confused with other types of drawing.

   a. Folding
   b. Fuzzy complex
   c. Haworth projection
   d. Fischer projection

5. . _________ is an oxoacid of iodine having chemical formula HIO_4 or H_5IO_6.

   In dilute aqueous solution, _________ exists as discrete hydronium (H_3O^+) and metaperiodate (IO_4^-) ions. When more concentrated, orthoperiodic acid, H_5IO_6, is formed; this dissociates into hydronium and orthoperiodate (IO_6^{5-}) ions.

   a. Peroxydisulfuric acid
   b. Periodic acid
   c. Phosphoric acid

ANSWER KEY
Chapter 24. CARBOHYDRATES

1. a
2. b
3. a
4. d
5. b

Chapter 25. THE CHEMISTRY OF THE AROMATIC HETEROCYCLES

CHAPTER OUTLINE: KEY TERMS, PEOPLE, PLACES, CONCEPTS

Heteroatom

Heterocyclic compound

Aromaticity

Electrophilic addition

Grignard reagents

Addition reaction

Nitric acid

Nitro compound

Polar effect

Clemmensen reduction

Carboxylic acid

Substitution reaction

Nicotinic acids

Nitration

Chichibabin reaction

Organolithium reagent

Leaving group

Pyridine

Reducing agent

Chapter 25. THE CHEMISTRY OF THE AROMATIC HETEROCYCLES

CHAPTER OUTLINE: KEY TERMS, PEOPLE, PLACES, CONCEPTS

_______________ Salicylic acid

_______________ Meta-Chloroperoxybenzoic acid

_______________ Methyl iodide

_______________ Acetic anhydride

_______________ Pi bond

_______________ Potassium ferricyanide

_______________ Amino acid

_______________ Phenyllithium

_______________ Keto acid

_______________ Guanine

_______________ Protecting group

_______________ Nucleic acid

_______________ Ritonavir

_______________ Double bond

_______________ Base pair

_______________ Mass spectrometry

_______________ Human genome

_______________ Messenger RNA

_______________ Sequencing

Chapter 25. THE CHEMISTRY OF THE AROMATIC HETEROCYCLES

CHAPTER OUTLINE: KEY TERMS, PEOPLE, PLACES, CONCEPTS

_______________ Alkylating antineoplastic agent

_______________ Dimethyl sulfate

_______________ Methyl methanesulfonate

CHAPTER HIGHLIGHTS & NOTES: KEY TERMS, PEOPLE, PLACES, CONCEPTS

Heteroatom

In organic chemistry, a heteroatom is any atom that is not carbon or hydrogen. Usually, the term is used to indicate that non-carbon atoms have replaced carbon in the backbone of the molecular structure. Typical heteroatoms are nitrogen, oxygen, sulfur, phosphorus, chlorine, bromine, and iodine.

Heterocyclic compound

A heterocyclic compound is a cyclic compound that has atoms of at least two different elements as members of its ring(s). The counterparts of heterocyclic compounds are homocyclic compounds, the rings of which are made of a single element.

Although heterocyclic compounds may be inorganic, most contain at least one carbon atom, and one or more atoms of elements other than carbon within the ring structure, such as sulfur, oxygen, or nitrogen.

Aromaticity

In organic chemistry, aromaticity is a chemical property in which a conjugated ring of unsaturated bonds, lone pairs, or empty orbitals exhibit a stabilization stronger than would be expected by the stabilization of conjugation alone There is no general relationship between aromaticity as a chemical property and the olfactory properties of such compounds.

Aromaticity can also be considered a manifestation of cyclic delocalization and of resonance.

Electrophilic addition

In organic chemistry, an electrophilic addition reaction is an addition reaction where, in a chemical compound, a π bond is broken and two new σ bonds are formed. The substrate of an electrophilic addition reaction must have a double bond or triple bond.

Chapter 25. THE CHEMISTRY OF THE AROMATIC HETEROCYCLES

CHAPTER HIGHLIGHTS & NOTES: KEY TERMS, PEOPLE, PLACES, CONCEPTS

Grignard reagents	The Grignard reaction is an organometallic chemical reaction in which alkyl- or aryl-magnesium halides (Grignard reagents) add to a carbonyl group in an aldehyde or ketone. This reaction is an important tool for the formation of carbon-carbon bonds. The reaction of an organic halide with magnesium is not a Grignard reaction, but provides a Grignard reagent.
Addition reaction	An addition reaction, in organic chemistry, is in its simplest terms an organic reaction where two or more molecules combine to form a larger one. Addition reactions are limited to chemical compounds that have multiple bonds, such as molecules with carbon-carbon double bonds (alkenes), or with triple bonds (alkynes). Molecules containing carbon--hetero double bonds like carbonyl (C=O) groups, or imine (C=N) groups, can undergo addition as they too have double bond character.
Nitric acid	Nitric acid also known as aqua fortis and spirit of niter, is a highly corrosive and toxic strong mineral acid which is normally colorless but tends to acquire a yellow cast due to the accumulation of oxides of nitrogen if long-stored. Ordinary nitric acid has a concentration of 68%. When the solution contains more than 86% HNO_3, it is referred to as fuming nitric acid.
Nitro compound	Nitro compounds are organic compounds that contain one or more nitro functional groups ($-NO_2$). They are often highly explosive, especially when the compound contains more than one nitro group and is impure. The nitro group is one of the most common explosophores (functional group that makes a compound explosive) used globally.
Polar effect	The Polar effect is the effect exerted by a substituent on modifying electrostatic forces operating on a nearby reaction center. The main contributors to the polar effect are the inductive effect, mesomeric effect and the through-space electronic field effect. An electron withdrawing group or EWG draws electrons away from a reaction center.
Clemmensen reduction	Clemmensen reduction is a chemical reaction described as a reduction of ketones (or aldehydes) to alkanes using zinc amalgam and hydrochloric acid. This reaction is named after Erik Christian Clemmensen, a Danish chemist. The Clemmensen reduction is particularly effective at reducing aryl-alkyl ketones.
Carboxylic acid	Carboxylic acids ( ) are organic acids characterized by the presence of at least one carboxyl group. The general formula of a carboxylic acid is R-COOH, where R is some monovalent functional group. A carboxyl group (or carboxy) is a functional group consisting of a carbonyl (RR'C=O) and a hydroxyl (R-O-H), which has the formula -C(=O)OH, usually written as -COOH or $-CO_2H$.

Substitution reaction	In a substitution reaction, a functional group in a particular chemical compound is replaced by another group. In organic chemistry, the electrophilic and nucleophilic substitution reactions are of prime importance. Organic substitution reactions are classified in several main organic reaction types depending on whether the reagent that brings about the substitution is considered an electrophile or a nucleophile, whether a reactive intermediate involved in the reaction is a carbocation, a carbanion or a free radical or whether the substrate is aliphatic or aromatic.
Nicotinic acids	Nicotinic acids are derivatives of pyridine which have a carboxy group. Although the term niacin is sometimes used interchangeably with 'nicotinic acid', it is more precise to only apply it to the 1-3 (meta) substituted form. Examples include:•arecoline•nicotinamide•nicorandil•nikethamide•nimodipine.
Nitration	Nitration is a general chemical process for the introduction of a nitro group into a chemical compound. The dominant application of nitration is for the production of nitrobenzene, the precursor to methylene diphenyl diisocyanate. Nitrations are famously used for the production of explosives, for example the conversion of glycerin to nitroglycerin and the conversion of toluene to trinitrotoluene.
Chichibabin reaction	The Chichibabin reaction (pronounced ' (che')-che-ba-ben) is a method for producing 2-aminopyridine derivatives by the reaction of pyridine with sodium amide. It was reported by Aleksei Chichibabin in 1914. The following is the overall form of the general reaction: The direct amination of pyridine with sodium amide takes place in liquid ammonia. Following the addition elimination mechanism first a nucleophilic NH_2^- is added while a hydride (H^-) is leaving.
Organolithium reagent	An organolithium reagent is an organometallic compound with a direct bond between a carbon and a lithium atom. As the electropositive nature of lithium puts most of the charge density of the bond on the carbon atom, effectively creating a carbanion, organolithium compounds are extremely powerful bases and nucleophiles. For use as bases, butyllithiums are often used and are commercially available.
Leaving group	In chemistry, a leaving group is a molecular fragment that departs with a pair of electrons in heterolytic bond cleavage. Leaving groups can be anions or neutral molecules. Common anionic leaving groups are halides such as Cl^-, Br^-, and I^-, and sulfonate esters, such as para-toluenesulfonate ('tosylate', TsO^-).
Pyridine	Pyridine is a basic heterocyclic organic compound with the chemical formula C_5H_5N.

It is structurally related to benzene, with one C-H group replaced by a nitrogen atom. The pyridine ring occurs in many important compounds, including azines and the vitamins niacin and pyridoxal.

Pyridine was discovered in 1849 by the Scottish chemist Thomas Anderson as one of the constituents of bone oil.

Reducing agent

A reducing agent is the element or compound in a reduction-oxidation (redox) reaction that donates an electron to another species; however, since the reducer loses an electron we say it is 'oxidized'. This means that there must be an 'oxidizer'; because if any chemical is an electron donor (reducer), another must be an electron recipient (oxidizer). Thus reducers are 'oxidized' and oxidizers are 'reduced'.

Salicylic acid

Salicylic acid is a monohydroxybenzoic acid, a type of phenolic acid and a beta hydroxy acid. This colorless crystalline organic acid is widely used in organic synthesis and functions as a plant hormone. It is derived from the metabolism of salicin.

Meta-Chloroperoxybenzoic acid

Meta-Chloroperoxybenzoic acid is a peroxycarboxylic acid used widely as an oxidant in organic synthesis. mCPBA is often preferred to other peroxy acids because of its relative ease of handling. The main areas of use are the conversion of ketones to esters (Baeyer-Villiger oxidation), epoxidation of alkenes (Prilezhaev reaction), conversion of silyl enol ethers to silyl α-hydroxy ketones (Rubottom oxidation), oxidation of sulfides to sulfoxides and sulfones, and oxidation of amines to produce amine oxides.

Methyl iodide

Methyl iodide, and commonly abbreviated 'MeI', is the chemical compound with the formula CH_3I. It is a dense, colorless, volatile liquid. In terms of chemical structure, it is related to methane by replacement of one hydrogen atom by an atom of iodine. It is naturally emitted by rice plantations in small amounts.

Acetic anhydride

Acetic anhydride, is the chemical compound with the formula $(CH_3CO)_2O$. Commonly abbreviated Ac_2O, it is the simplest isolatable acid anhydride and is a widely used reagent in organic synthesis. It is a colorless liquid that smells strongly of acetic acid, formed by its reaction with the moisture in the air.

Formic anhydride is an even simpler acid anhydride, but it spontaneously decomposes, especially once removed from solution.

Pi bond

In chemistry, pi bonds are covalent chemical bonds where two lobes of one involved electron orbital overlap two lobes of the other involved electron orbital. Only one of the orbital's nodal planes passes through both of the involved nuclei.

Pi bonds are usually weaker than sigma bonds. From the perspective of quantum mechanics, this bond's weakness is explained by significantly less overlap between the component p-orbitals due to their parallel orientation.

Potassium ferricyanide

Potassium ferricyanide is the chemical compound with the formula $K_3[Fe(CN)_6]$. This bright red salt contains the octahedrally coordinated $[Fe(CN)_6]^{3-}$ ion. It is soluble in water and its solution shows some green-yellow fluorescence.

Amino acid

Amino acids are molecules containing an amine group, a carboxylic acid group, and a side-chain that is specific to each amino acid. The key elements of an amino acid are carbon, hydrogen, oxygen, and nitrogen. They are particularly important in biochemistry, where the term usually refers to alpha-amino acids.

Phenyllithium

Phenyllithium is an organometallic agent with the empirical formula C_6H_5Li. It is most commonly used as a metalating agent in organic syntheses and a substitute for Grignard reagents for introducing phenyl groups in organic syntheses. Crystalline phenyllithium is colorless; however, solutions of phenyllithium are various shades of brown or red depending on the solvent used and the impurities present in the solute.

Keto acid

Keto acids (or oxoacids) are organic compounds that contain a carboxylic acid group and a ketone group. The alpha-keto acids are especially important in biology as they are involved in the Krebs citric acid cycle and in glycolysis. In several cases, the keto group is hydrated.

Guanine

Guanine is one of the four main nucleobases found in the nucleic acids DNA and RNA, the others being adenine, cytosine, and thymine (uracil in RNA). In DNA, guanine is paired with cytosine. With the formula $C_5H_5N_5O$, guanine is a derivative of purine, consisting of a fused pyrimidine-imidazole ring system with conjugated double bonds.

Protecting group

A protecting group is introduced into a molecule by chemical modification of a functional group in order to obtain chemoselectivity in a subsequent chemical reaction. It plays an important role in multistep organic synthesis.

In many preparations of delicate organic compounds, some specific parts of their molecules cannot survive the required reagents or chemical environments.

Nucleic acid

Nucleic acids are biological molecules essential for known forms of life on this planet; they include DNA (deoxyribonucleic acid) and RNA (ribonucleic acid). Together with proteins, nucleic acids are the most important biological macromolecules; each is found in abundance in all living things, where they function in encoding, transmitting and expressing genetic information.

Nucleic acids were discovered by Friedrich Miescher in 1869. Experimental studies of nucleic acids constitute a major part of modern biological and medical research, and form a foundation for genome and forensic science, as well as the biotechnology and pharmaceutical industries.

Ritonavir

Ritonavir, with trade name Norvir (Abbott Laboratories), is an antiretroviral drug from the protease inhibitor class used to treat HIV infection and AIDS.

Ritonavir is frequently prescribed with HAART, not for its antiviral action, but as it inhibits the same host enzyme that metabolizes other protease inhibitors. This inhibition leads to higher plasma concentrations of these latter drugs, allowing the clinician to lower their dose and frequency and improving their clinical efficacy. History

Ritonavir is manufactured as Norvir by Abbott Laboratories.

Double bond

A double bond in chemistry is a chemical bond between two chemical elements involving four bonding electrons instead of the usual two. The most common double bond, that between two carbon atoms, can be found in alkenes. Many types of double bonds between two different elements exist, for example in a carbonyl group with a carbon atom and an oxygen atom.

Base pair

In molecular biology and genetics, the linking between two nitrogenous bases on opposite complementary DNA or certain types of RNA strands that are connected via hydrogen bonds is called a base pair. In the canonical Watson-Crick DNA base pairing, adenine (A) forms a base pair with thymine (T) and guanine (G) forms a base pair with cytosine (C). In RNA, thymine is replaced by uracil (U).

Mass spectrometry

Mass spectrometry is an analytical technique that measures the mass-to-charge ratio of charged particles. It is used for determining masses of particles, for determining the elemental composition of a sample or molecule, and for elucidating the chemical structures of molecules, such as peptides and other chemical compounds. MS works by ionizing chemical compounds to generate charged molecules or molecule fragments and measuring their mass-to-charge ratios.

Human genome

The human (Homo sapiens) genome is stored on 23 chromosome pairs and in the small mitochondrial DNA. Twenty-two of the 23 chromosomes belong to autosomal chromosome pairs, while the remaining pair is sex determinative. The haploid human genome occupies a total of just over three billion DNA base pairs. The Human Genome Project (HGP) produced a reference sequence of the euchromatic human genome and which is used worldwide in the biomedical sciences.

Messenger RNA

Messenger RNA is a molecule of RNA that encodes a chemical 'blueprint' for a protein product.

mRNA is transcribed from a DNA template, and carries coding information to the sites of protein synthesis, the ribosomes. In the ribosomes, the mRNA is translated into a polymer of amino acids: a protein.

Sequencing

In genetics and biochemistry, sequencing means to determine the primary structure (sometimes falsely called primary sequence) of an unbranched biopolymer. Sequencing results in a symbolic linear depiction known as a sequence which succinctly summarizes much of the atomic-level structure of the sequenced molecule.

DNA sequencing is the process of determining the nucleotide order of a given DNA fragment.

Alkylating antineoplastic agent

An alkylating antineoplastic agent is an alkylating agent used in cancer treatment that attaches an alkyl group (C_nH_{2n+1}) to DNA.

The alkyl group is attached to the guanine base of DNA, at the number 7 nitrogen atom of the purine ring.

Since cancer cells, in general, proliferate faster and with less error-correcting than healthy cells, cancer cells are more sensitive to DNA damage -- such as being alkylated. Alkylating agents are used to treat several cancers.

Dimethyl sulfate

Dimethyl sulfate is a chemical compound with formula $(CH_3O)_2SO_2$. As the diester of methanol and sulfuric acid, its formula is often written as $(CH_3)_2SO_4$ or even Me_2SO_4, where CH_3 or Me is methyl. Me_2SO_4 is mainly used as a methylating agent in organic synthesis.

Methyl methanesulfonate

Methyl methanesulfonate is an alkylating agent and a carcinogen. It is also a suspected reproductive toxicant, and may also be a skin/sense organ toxicant. It is used in cancer treatment.

CHAPTER QUIZ: KEY TERMS, PEOPLE, PLACES, CONCEPTS

1. _________ is one of the four main nucleobases found in the nucleic acids DNA and RNA, the others being adenine, cytosine, and thymine (uracil in RNA). In DNA, _________ is paired with cytosine. With the formula $C_5H_5N_5O$, _________ is a derivative of purine, consisting of a fused pyrimidine-imidazole ring system with conjugated double bonds.

   a. Hoelite
   b. Kratochvilite
   c. Lamalginite
   d. Guanine

2. _________ is a basic heterocyclic organic compound with the chemical formula C_5H_5N. It is structurally related to benzene, with one C-H group replaced by a nitrogen atom. The _________ ring occurs in many important compounds, including azines and the vitamins niacin and pyridoxal.

   _________ was discovered in 1849 by the Scottish chemist Thomas Anderson as one of the constituents of bone oil.

   a. Pyrimidine
   b. Pyridine
   c. Thiazole
   d. NIH shift

3. In organic chemistry, a _________ is any atom that is not carbon or hydrogen. Usually, the term is used to indicate that non-carbon atoms have replaced carbon in the backbone of the molecular structure. Typical _________s are nitrogen, oxygen, sulfur, phosphorus, chlorine, bromine, and iodine.

   a. Mauveine
   b. Heteroatom
   c. Methylene
   d. Migratory aptitude

4. In molecular biology and genetics, the linking between two nitrogenous bases on opposite complementary DNA or certain types of RNA strands that are connected via hydrogen bonds is called a _________. In the canonical Watson-Crick DNA base pairing, adenine (A) forms a _________ with thymine (T) and guanine (G) forms a _________ with cytosine (C). In RNA, thymine is replaced by uracil (U).

   a. Conserved sequence
   b. Denaturation
   c. Base pair
   d. Genomic signature

5. . _________ are derivatives of pyridine which have a carboxy group.

   Although the term niacin is sometimes used interchangeably with 'nicotinic acid', it is more precise to only apply it to the 1-3 (meta) substituted form.

   Examples include:•arecoline•nicotinamide•nicorandil•nikethamide•nimodipine.

a. Nicotinic acids
b. TaqMan
c. Telomerization
d. Thermal decomposition

ANSWER KEY
Chapter 25. THE CHEMISTRY OF THE AROMATIC HETEROCYCLES

---

1. d

2. b

3. b

4. c

5. a

Chapter 26. AMINO ACIDS, PEPTIDES, AND PROTEINS

CHAPTER OUTLINE: KEY TERMS, PEOPLE, PLACES, CONCEPTS

Amino acid

Peptide

Zwitterion

Protein

Oligopeptide

Absolute configuration

Stereochemistry

Molecular orbital

Isoelectric point

Ion-exchange resin

Sulfonic acid

Mass spectrometry

Carboxylic acid

Hydrogen bromide

Hydrogen halide

Hydrogen cyanide

Acetic anhydride

Solid-phase synthesis

Protecting group

Chapter 26. AMINO ACIDS, PEPTIDES, AND PROTEINS

CHAPTER OUTLINE: KEY TERMS, PEOPLE, PLACES, CONCEPTS

- ______ Peptide synthesis
- ______ Pinacol rearrangement
- ______ Alkylating antineoplastic agent
- ______ Trifluoroacetic acid
- ______ Hydrogen fluoride
- ______ Nicotinic acids
- ______ Ninhydrin
- ______ Protease
- ______ Exopeptidase
- ______ Disulfide bond
- ______ Iodoacetic acid
- ______ Sequencing
- ______ Edman degradation
- ______ Phenyl isothiocyanate
- ______ Posttranslational modification
- ______ Intron
- ______ Kinase
- ______ Phosphorylation
- ______ Protein phosphorylation

Chapter 26. AMINO ACIDS, PEPTIDES, AND PROTEINS

CHAPTER OUTLINE: KEY TERMS, PEOPLE, PLACES, CONCEPTS

Structural formula

Random coil

Sigmatropic reaction

Active site

Enzyme

Aspartic acid

Enzyme catalysis

CHAPTER HIGHLIGHTS & NOTES: KEY TERMS, PEOPLE, PLACES, CONCEPTS

Amino acid

Amino acids are molecules containing an amine group, a carboxylic acid group, and a side-chain that is specific to each amino acid. The key elements of an amino acid are carbon, hydrogen, oxygen, and nitrogen. They are particularly important in biochemistry, where the term usually refers to alpha-amino acids.

Peptide

Peptides are short polymers of amino acid monomers linked by peptide bonds. They are distinguished from proteins on the basis of size, typically containing fewer than 50 monomer units. The shortest peptides are dipeptides, consisting of two amino acids joined by a single peptide bond.

Zwitterion

In chemistry, a zwitterion is a molecule with a positive and a negative electrical charge (n.b. not dipoles) at different locations within that molecule. Zwitterions are sometimes also called inner salts.

Examples

Amino acids are the best known examples of zwitterions.

Chapter 26. AMINO ACIDS, PEPTIDES, AND PROTEINS

Protein	Proteins are biochemical compounds consisting of one or more polypeptides typically folded into a globular or fibrous form in a biologically functional way. A polypeptide is a single linear polymer chain of amino acids bonded together by peptide bonds between the carboxyl and amino groups of adjacent amino acid residues. The sequence of amino acids in a protein is defined by the sequence of a gene, which is encoded in the genetic code.
Oligopeptide	An oligopeptide consists of between 2 and 20 amino acids and includes dipeptides, tripeptides, tetrapeptides, pentapeptides, etc. Examples of oligopeptides include:•Amanitins - Cyclic peptides taken from carpophores of several different mushroom species. They are potent inhibitors of RNA polymerases in most eukaryotic species, the prevent the production of mRNA and protein synthesis.
Absolute configuration	An absolute configuration in stereochemistry is the spatial arrangement of the atoms of a chiral molecular entity and its stereochemical description e.g. R or S. Absolute configurations for a chiral molecule (in pure form) are most often obtained by X-ray crystallography. All enantiomerically pure chiral molecules crystallise in one of the 65 Sohncke Groups (Chiral Space Groups). Alternative techniques are Optical rotatory dispersion, vibrational circular dichroism and the use of chiral shift reagents in proton NMR. When the absolute configuration is obtained the assignment of R or S is based on the Cahn-Ingold-Prelog priority rules.
Stereochemistry	Stereochemistry, a subdiscipline of chemistry, involves the study of the relative spatial arrangement of atoms within molecules. An important branch of stereochemistry is the study of chiral molecules. Stereochemistry is also known as 3D chemistry because the prefix 'stereo-' means 'three-dimensionality'.
Molecular orbital	In chemistry, a molecular orbital is a mathematical function describing the wave-like behavior of an electron in a molecule. This function can be used to calculate chemical and physical properties such as the probability of finding an electron in any specific region. The term 'orbital' was first used in English by Robert S. Mulliken as the English translation of Schrödinger's 'Eigenfunktion'.
Isoelectric point	The isoelectric point sometimes abbreviated to IEP, is the pH at which a particular molecule or surface carries no net electrical charge.

Amphoteric molecules called zwitterions contain both positive and negative charges depending on the functional groups present in the molecule. The net charge on the molecule is affected by pH of their surrounding environment and can become more positively or negatively charged due to the loss or gain of protons (H^+).

Ion-exchange resin

An ion-exchange resin is an insoluble matrix (or support structure) normally in the form of small (1-2 mm diameter) beads, usually white or yellowish, fabricated from an organic polymer substrate. The material has highly developed structure of pores on the surface of which are sites with easily trapped and released ions. The trapping of ions takes place only with simultaneous releasing of other ions; thus the process is called ion-exchange.

Sulfonic acid

A sulfonic acid refers to a member of the class of organosulfur compounds with the general formula $RS(=O)_2$-OH, where R is an organic alkyl or aryl group and the $S(=O)_2$-OH group a sulfonyl hydroxide. A sulfonic acid can be thought of as sulfuric acid with one hydroxyl group replaced by an organic substituent. The parent compound (with the organic substituent replaced by hydrogen) is the hypothetical compound sulfurous acid.

Mass spectrometry

Mass spectrometry is an analytical technique that measures the mass-to-charge ratio of charged particles. It is used for determining masses of particles, for determining the elemental composition of a sample or molecule, and for elucidating the chemical structures of molecules, such as peptides and other chemical compounds. MS works by ionizing chemical compounds to generate charged molecules or molecule fragments and measuring their mass-to-charge ratios.

Carboxylic acid

Carboxylic acids ( ) are organic acids characterized by the presence of at least one carboxyl group. The general formula of a carboxylic acid is R-COOH, where R is some monovalent functional group. A carboxyl group (or carboxy) is a functional group consisting of a carbonyl (RR'C=O) and a hydroxyl (R-O-H), which has the formula -C(=O)OH, usually written as -COOH or $-CO_2H$.

Carboxylic acids are Brønsted-Lowry acids because they are proton (H^+) donors.

Hydrogen bromide

Hydrogen bromide is the diatomic molecule HBr. HBr is a gas at standard conditions. Hydrobromic acid forms upon dissolving HBr in water.

Hydrogen halide

Hydrogen halides (or hydrohalic acids) are inorganic compounds with the formula HX where X is one of the halogens: fluorine, chlorine, bromine, iodine, and astatine. Hydrogen halides are gases that dissolve in water to give acids.

Chapter 26. AMINO ACIDS, PEPTIDES, AND PROTEINS

CHAPTER HIGHLIGHTS & NOTES: KEY TERMS, PEOPLE, PLACES, CONCEPTS

Hydrogen cyanide	Hydrogen cyanide is a chemical compound with chemical formula HCN. It is a colorless, extremely poisonous liquid that boils slightly above room temperature at 26 °C (79 °F). Hydrogen cyanide is a linear molecule, with a triple bond between carbon and nitrogen. A minor tautomer of HCN is HNC, hydrogen isocyanide.
Acetic anhydride	Acetic anhydride, is the chemical compound with the formula $(CH_3CO)_2O$. Commonly abbreviated Ac_2O, it is the simplest isolatable acid anhydride and is a widely used reagent in organic synthesis. It is a colorless liquid that smells strongly of acetic acid, formed by its reaction with the moisture in the air. Formic anhydride is an even simpler acid anhydride, but it spontaneously decomposes, especially once removed from solution.
Solid-phase synthesis	In chemistry, solid-phase synthesis is a method in which molecules are bound on a bead and synthesized step-by-step in a reactant solution; compared with normal synthesis in a liquid state, it is easier to remove excess reactant or byproduct from the product. In this method, building blocks are protected at all reactive functional groups. The two functional groups that are able to participate in the desired reaction between building blocks in the solution and on the bead can be controlled by the order of deprotection.
Protecting group	A protecting group is introduced into a molecule by chemical modification of a functional group in order to obtain chemoselectivity in a subsequent chemical reaction. It plays an important role in multistep organic synthesis. In many preparations of delicate organic compounds, some specific parts of their molecules cannot survive the required reagents or chemical environments.
Peptide synthesis	In organic chemistry, peptide synthesis is the production of peptides, which are organic compounds in which multiple amino acids are linked via amide bonds which are also known as peptide bonds. The biological process of producing long peptides (proteins) is known as protein biosynthesis. Peptides are synthesized by coupling the carboxyl group or C-terminus of one amino acid to the amino group or N-terminus of another.
Pinacol rearrangement	The pinacol rearrangement is a method for converting a 1,2-diol to a carbonyl compound in organic chemistry. This 1,2-rearrangement takes place under acidic conditions. The name of the reaction comes from the rearrangement of pinacol to pinacolone.
Alkylating antineoplastic agent	An alkylating antineoplastic agent is an alkylating agent used in cancer treatment that attaches an alkyl group (C_nH_{2n+1}) to DNA.

The alkyl group is attached to the guanine base of DNA, at the number 7 nitrogen atom of the purine ring.

Since cancer cells, in general, proliferate faster and with less error-correcting than healthy cells, cancer cells are more sensitive to DNA damage -- such as being alkylated. Alkylating agents are used to treat several cancers.

Trifluoroacetic acid

Trifluoroacetic acid is the simplest stable perfluorinated carboxylic acid chemical compound, with the formula CF_3CO_2H. It is a strong carboxylic acid due to the influence of the electronegative trifluoromethyl group. TFA is almost 100,000-fold more acidic than acetic acid. TFA is widely used in organic chemistry.

Hydrogen fluoride

Hydrogen fluoride is a chemical compound with the formula HF. This colorless gas is the principal industrial source of fluorine, often in the aqueous form as hydrofluoric acid, and thus is the precursor to many important compounds including pharmaceuticals and polymers (e.g. Teflon). HF is widely used in the petrochemical industry and is a component of many superacids. Hydrogen fluoride boils just below room temperature whereas the other hydrogen halides condense at much lower temperatures.

Nicotinic acids

Nicotinic acids are derivatives of pyridine which have a carboxy group.

Although the term niacin is sometimes used interchangeably with 'nicotinic acid', it is more precise to only apply it to the 1-3 (meta) substituted form.

Examples include:•arecoline•nicotinamide•nicorandil•nikethamide•nimodipine.

Ninhydrin

Ninhydrin is a chemical used to detect ammonia or primary and secondary amines. When reacting with these free amines, a deep blue or purple color known as Ruhemann's purple is produced. Ninhydrin is most commonly used to detect fingerprints, as the terminal amines of lysine residues in peptides and proteins sloughed off in fingerprints react with ninhydrin.

Protease

A protease is any enzyme that conducts proteolysis, that is, begins protein catabolism by hydrolysis of the peptide bonds that link amino acids together in the polypeptide chain forming the protein. Standard

Proteases are currently classified into six broad groups:•Serine proteases•Threonine proteases•Cysteine proteases•Aspartate proteases•Metalloproteases•Glutamic acid proteases

The threonine and glutamic-acid proteases were not described until 1995 and 2004, respectively.

Chapter 26. AMINO ACIDS, PEPTIDES, AND PROTEINS

CHAPTER HIGHLIGHTS & NOTES: KEY TERMS, PEOPLE, PLACES, CONCEPTS

Exopeptidase	An exopeptidase is an enzyme produced in the pancreas that catalyses the removal of an amino acid from the end of a polypeptide chain. Exopeptidase cleaves the end of a polypeptide chain. Aminopeptidase, an enzyme in the brush border of the small intestine, will cleave a single amino acid from the aminoterminal.
Disulfide bond	In chemistry, a disulfide bond is a covalent bond, usually derived by the coupling of two thiol groups. The linkage is also called an SS-bond or disulfide bridge. The overall connectivity is therefore R-S-S-R. The terminology is widely used in biochemistry.
Iodoacetic acid	Iodoacetic acid is a derivative of acetic acid. It is a toxic compound, because, like many alkyl halides, it is an alkylating agent. It reacts with cysteine residues in proteins.
Sequencing	In genetics and biochemistry, sequencing means to determine the primary structure (sometimes falsely called primary sequence) of an unbranched biopolymer. Sequencing results in a symbolic linear depiction known as a sequence which succinctly summarizes much of the atomic-level structure of the sequenced molecule. DNA sequencing is the process of determining the nucleotide order of a given DNA fragment.
Edman degradation	Edman degradation, developed by Pehr Edman, is a method of sequencing amino acids in a peptide. In this method, the amino-terminal residue is labeled and cleaved from the peptide without disrupting the peptide bonds between other amino acid residues. Phenylisothiocyanate is reacted with an uncharged terminal amino group, under mildly alkaline conditions, to form a cyclical phenylthiocarbamoyl derivative.
Phenyl isothiocyanate	Phenyl isothiocyanate is a reagent used in reversed phase HPLC. PITC is less sensitive than o-phthaldehyde (OPA) and cannot be fully automated. PITC can be used for analysing secondary amines, unlike OPA. It is also known as Edman's reagent and is used in Edman degradation. Commercially available, this compound may be synthesized by reacting aniline with carbon disulfide and concentrated ammonia to give the ammonium dithiocarbamate salt.
Posttranslational modification	Posttranslational modification is the chemical modification of a protein after its translation. It is one of the later steps in protein biosynthesis, and thus gene expression, for many proteins. A protein (also called a polypeptide) is a chain of amino acids.

Intron

An intron is any nucleotide sequence within a gene that is removed by RNA splicing while the final mature RNA product of a gene is being generated. The term intron refers to both the DNA sequence within a gene, and the corresponding sequence in RNA transcripts. Sequences that are joined together in the final mature RNA after RNA splicing are exons.

Kinase

In chemistry and biochemistry, a kinase, alternatively known as a phosphotransferase, is a type of enzyme that transfers phosphate groups from high-energy donor molecules, such as ATP, to specific substrates. The process is referred to as phosphorylation, not to be confused with phosphorolysis, which is carried out by phosphorylases. Phosphorylation is the transfer of a phosphate group to a molecule, not the reverse, i.e., phosphorolysis, the transfer of a molecular moiety to a phosphate group.

Phosphorylation

Phosphorylation is the addition of a phosphate (PO_4^{3-}) group to a protein or other organic molecule. Phosphorylation turns many protein enzymes on and off, thereby altering their function and activity.

Protein phosphorylation in particular plays a significant role in a wide range of cellular processes.

Protein phosphorylation

Protein phosphorylation is a post-translational modification of proteins in which a serine, a threonine or a tyrosine residue is phosphorylated by a protein kinase by the addition of a covalently bound phosphate group. Regulation of proteins by phosphorylation is one of the most common modes of regulation of protein function, and is often termed 'phosphoregulation'. In almost all cases of phosphoregulation, the protein switches between a phosphorylated and an unphosphorylated form, and one of these two is an active form, while the other one is inactive, respectively.

Structural formula

The structural formula of a chemical compound is a graphical representation of the molecular structure, showing how the atoms are arranged. The chemical bonding within the molecule is also shown, either explicitly or implicitly. There are several common representations used in publications.

Random coil

A random coil is a polymer conformation where the monomer subunits are oriented randomly while still being bonded to adjacent units. It is not one specific shape, but a statistical distribution of shapes for all the chains in a population of macromolecules. The conformation's name is derived from the idea that, in the absence of specific, stabilizing interactions, a polymer backbone will 'sample' all possible conformations randomly.

Sigmatropic reaction

A sigmatropic reaction in organic chemistry is a Pericyclic reaction wherein the net result is one σ-bond is changed to another σ-bond in an uncatalyzed intramolecular process.

The name sigmatropic is the result of a compounding of the long-established sigma designation from single carbon-carbon bonds and the Greek word tropos, meaning turn. In this type of rearrangement reaction, a substituent moves from one part of a π-bonded system to another part in an intramolecular reaction with simultaneous rearrangement of the π system.

Active site

In biology the active site is part of an enzyme where substrates bind and undergo a chemical reaction. The majority of enzymes are proteins but RNA enzymes called ribozymes also exist. The active site of an enzyme is usually found in a cleft or pocket that is lined by amino acid residues (or nucleotides in ribozymes) that participate in recognition of the substrate.

Enzyme

Enzymes ( ) are biological molecules that catalyze (i.e., increase the rates of) chemical reactions. In enzymatic reactions, the molecules at the beginning of the process, called substrates, are converted into different molecules, called products. Almost all chemical reactions in a biological cell need enzymes in order to occur at rates sufficient for life.

Aspartic acid

Aspartic acid is an α-amino acid with the chemical formula $HOOCCH(NH_2)CH_2COOH$. The carboxylate anion, salt, or ester of aspartic acid is known as aspartate. The L-isomer of aspartate is one of the 20 proteinogenic amino acids, i.e., the building blocks of proteins. Its codons are GAU and GAC.

Aspartic acid is, together with glutamic acid, classified as an acidic amino acid with a pKa of 3.9. Aspartate is pervasive in biosynthesis.

Enzyme catalysis

Enzyme catalysis is the catalysis of chemical reactions by specialized proteins known as enzymes. Catalysis of biochemical reactions in the cell is vital due to the very low reaction rates of the uncatalysed reactions.

The mechanism of enzyme catalysis is similar in principle to other types of chemical catalysis.

CHAPTER QUIZ: KEY TERMS, PEOPLE, PLACES, CONCEPTS

1. A _________ is a polymer conformation where the monomer subunits are oriented randomly while still being bonded to adjacent units. It is not one specific shape, but a statistical distribution of shapes for all the chains in a population of macromolecules. The conformation's name is derived from the idea that, in the absence of specific, stabilizing interactions, a polymer backbone will 'sample' all possible conformations randomly.

a. Reaction coordinate
b. Reaction quotient
c. Random coil
d. Reid Vapor Pressure

2. _________s are molecules containing an amine group, a carboxylic acid group, and a side-chain that is specific to each _________. The key elements of an _________ are carbon, hydrogen, oxygen, and nitrogen. They are particularly important in biochemistry, where the term usually refers to alpha-_________s.

a. Ammonia
b. Ammonium nitrate
c. Amino acid
d. Endothelium-derived relaxing factor

3. _________ is the addition of a phosphate (PO_4^{3-}) group to a protein or other organic molecule. _________ turns many protein enzymes on and off, thereby altering their function and activity.

Protein _________ in particular plays a significant role in a wide range of cellular processes.

a. Polyglutamylation
b. Polyglycylation
c. PolyQ
d. Phosphorylation

4. _________ is an analytical technique that measures the mass-to-charge ratio of charged particles. It is used for determining masses of particles, for determining the elemental composition of a sample or molecule, and for elucidating the chemical structures of molecules, such as peptides and other chemical compounds. MS works by ionizing chemical compounds to generate charged molecules or molecule fragments and measuring their mass-to-charge ratios.

a. Mass spectrometry
b. Nucleotidase
c. Polyol pathway
d. Pro-oxidant

5. . _________s are short polymers of amino acid monomers linked by _________ bonds. They are distinguished from proteins on the basis of size, typically containing fewer than 50 monomer units. The shortest _________s are dipeptides, consisting of two amino acids joined by a single _________ bond.

a. Peptide Spectral Library
b. Beefy meaty peptide

c. Peptide
d. BQ-123

ANSWER KEY
Chapter 26. AMINO ACIDS, PEPTIDES, AND PROTEINS

1. c
2. c
3. d
4. a
5. c

Chapter 27. PERICYCLIC REACTIONS

CHAPTER OUTLINE: KEY TERMS, PEOPLE, PLACES, CONCEPTS

Electrocyclic reaction

Perchloric acid

Pericyclic reaction

Sigmatropic reaction

Molecular orbital

Polar effect

Ground state

Microscopic reversibility

Protecting group

Stereochemistry

Cope rearrangement

Grignard reaction

Claisen condensation

Claisen rearrangement

Fluxional molecule

Curtius rearrangement

Keto acid

Aldol condensation

Aldol reaction

Chapter 27. PERICYCLIC REACTIONS

CHAPTER OUTLINE: KEY TERMS, PEOPLE, PLACES, CONCEPTS

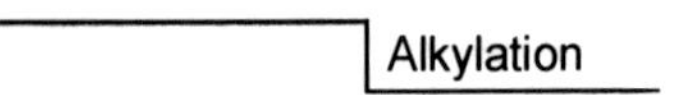

Alkylation

CHAPTER HIGHLIGHTS & NOTES: KEY TERMS, PEOPLE, PLACES, CONCEPTS

Electrocyclic reaction

In organic chemistry, an electrocyclic reaction is a type of pericyclic rearrangement where the net result is one pi bond being converted into one sigma bond or vice-versa. These reactions are usually categorized by the following criteria:•Reactions can be either photochemical or thermal.•Reactions can be either ring-opening or ring-closing (electrocyclization).•Depending on the type of reaction (photochemical or thermal) and the number of pi electrons, the reaction can happen through either a conrotatory and disrotatory mechanism.•The type of rotation determines whether the cis or trans isomer of the product will be formed.Classical Examples

The Nazarov cyclization reaction is a named electrocyclic reaction converting divinylketones to cyclopentenones.

A classic example is the thermal ring-opening reaction of 3,4-dimethylcyclobutene.

Perchloric acid

Perchloric acid is the inorganic compound with the formula $HClO_4$. Usually found as an aqueous solution, this colorless compound is a strong acid stronger then sulfuric and nitric acids. It is a powerful oxidizer, but its aqueous solutions up to appr. 70% are remarkably inert, only showing strong acid features and no oxidizing properties.

Pericyclic reaction

In organic chemistry, a pericyclic reaction is a type of organic reaction wherein the transition state of the molecule has a cyclic geometry, and the reaction progresses in a concerted fashion. Pericyclic reactions are usually rearrangement reactions. The major classes of pericyclic reactions are:

In general, these are considered to be equilibrium processes, although it is possible to push the reaction in one direction by designing a reaction by which the product is at a significantly lower energy level; this is due to a unimolecular interpretation of Le Chatelier's principle.

Sigmatropic reaction

A sigmatropic reaction in organic chemistry is a Pericyclic reaction wherein the net result is one σ-bond is changed to another σ-bond in an uncatalyzed intramolecular process. The name sigmatropic is the result of a compounding of the long-established sigma designation from single carbon-carbon bonds and the Greek word tropos, meaning turn.

Molecular orbital

In chemistry, a molecular orbital is a mathematical function describing the wave-like behavior of an electron in a molecule. This function can be used to calculate chemical and physical properties such as the probability of finding an electron in any specific region. The term 'orbital' was first used in English by Robert S. Mulliken as the English translation of Schrödinger's 'Eigenfunktion'.

Polar effect

The Polar effect is the effect exerted by a substituent on modifying electrostatic forces operating on a nearby reaction center. The main contributors to the polar effect are the inductive effect, mesomeric effect and the through-space electronic field effect.

An electron withdrawing group or EWG draws electrons away from a reaction center.

Ground state

The ground state of a quantum mechanical system is its lowest-energy state; the energy of the ground state is known as the zero-point energy of the system. An excited state is any state with energy greater than the ground state. The ground state of a quantum field theory is usually called the vacuum state or the vacuum.

Microscopic reversibility

The principle of Microscopic reversibility in physics and chemistry is twofold:•First, it states that the microscopic detailed dynamics of particles and fields is time-reversible because the microscopic equations of motion are symmetric with respect to inversion in time (T-symmetry);•Second, it relates to the statistical description of the kinetics of macroscopic or mesoscopic systems as an ensemble of elementary processes: collisions, elementary transitions or reactions. For these processes, the consequence of the microscopic T-symmetry is: '

Corresponding to every individual process there is a reverse process, and in a state of equilibrium the average rate of every process is equal to the average rate of its reverse process. 'History of Microscopic reversibility

The idea of microscopic reversibility was born together with physical kinetics.

Protecting group

A protecting group is introduced into a molecule by chemical modification of a functional group in order to obtain chemoselectivity in a subsequent chemical reaction. It plays an important role in multistep organic synthesis.

In many preparations of delicate organic compounds, some specific parts of their molecules cannot survive the required reagents or chemical environments.

Stereochemistry

Stereochemistry, a subdiscipline of chemistry, involves the study of the relative spatial arrangement of atoms within molecules. An important branch of stereochemistry is the study of chiral molecules.

Chapter 27. PERICYCLIC REACTIONS

CHAPTER HIGHLIGHTS & NOTES: KEY TERMS, PEOPLE, PLACES, CONCEPTS

Cope rearrangement	The Cope rearrangement is an extensively studied organic reaction involving the [3,3]-sigmatropic rearrangement of 1,5-dienes. It was developed by Arthur C. Cope. For example 3-methyl-1,5-hexadiene heated to 300°C yields 1,5-heptadiene.
Grignard reaction	The Grignard reaction is an organometallic chemical reaction in which alkyl- or aryl-magnesium halides (Grignard reagents) add to a carbonyl group in an aldehyde or ketone. This reaction is an important tool for the formation of carbon-carbon bonds. The reaction of an organic halide with magnesium is not a Grignard reaction, but provides a Grignard reagent.
Claisen condensation	The Claisen condensation is a carbon-carbon bond forming reaction that occurs between two esters or one ester and another carbonyl compound in the presence of a strong base, resulting in a β-keto ester or a β-diketone. It is named after Rainer Ludwig Claisen, who first published his work on the reaction in 1881 . At least one of the reagents must be enolizable (have an α-proton and be able to undergo deprotonation to form the enolate anion).
Claisen rearrangement	The Claisen rearrangement is a powerful carbon-carbon bond-forming chemical reaction discovered by Rainer Ludwig Claisen. The heating of an allyl vinyl ether will initiate a [3,3]-sigmatropic rearrangement to give a γ,δ-unsaturated carbonyl. Discovered in 1912, the Claisen rearrangement is the first recorded example of a [3,3]-sigmatropic rearrangement.
Fluxional molecule	Fluxional molecules are molecules that undergo dynamics such that some or all of their atoms interchange between symmetry-equivalent positions. Because virtually all molecules are fluxional in some respects, e.g. bond rotations in most organic compounds, the term fluxional depends on the context and the method used to assess the dynamics. Often, a molecule is considered fluxional if its spectroscopic signature exhibits line-broadening (beyond that dictated by the Heisenberg Uncertainty Principle) due to chemical exchange.
Curtius rearrangement	The Curtius rearrangement as first defined by Theodor Curtius, is a chemical reaction that involves the rearrangement of an acyl azide to an isocyanate. Several reviews have been published. The isocyanate can be trapped by a variety of nucleophiles.
Keto acid	Keto acids (or oxoacids) are organic compounds that contain a carboxylic acid group and a ketone group. The alpha-keto acids are especially important in biology as they are involved in the Krebs citric acid cycle and in glycolysis. In several cases, the keto group is hydrated.

CHAPTER HIGHLIGHTS & NOTES: KEY TERMS, PEOPLE, PLACES, CONCEPTS

Aldol condensation

An aldol condensation is an organic reaction in which an enol or an enolate ion reacts with a carbonyl compound to form a β-hydroxyaldehyde or β-hydroxyketone, followed by a dehydration to give a conjugated enone.

Aldol condensations are important in organic synthesis, providing a good way to form carbon-carbon bonds. The Robinson annulation reaction sequence features an aldol condensation; the Wieland-Miescher ketone product is an important starting material for many organic syntheses.

Aldol reaction

The aldol reaction is a powerful means of forming carbon-carbon bonds in organic chemistry. Discovered independently by Charles-Adolphe Wurtz and Alexander Borodin in 1872, the reaction combines two carbonyl compounds (the original experiments used aldehydes) to form a new β-hydroxy carbonyl compound. These products are known as aldols, from the aldehyde + alcohol, a structural motif seen in many of the products.

Alkylation

Alkylation is the transfer of an alkyl group from one molecule to another. The alkyl group may be transferred as an alkyl carbocation, a free radical, a carbanion or a carbene . Alkylating agents are widely used in chemistry because the alkyl group is probably the most common group encountered in organic molecules.

CHAPTER QUIZ: KEY TERMS, PEOPLE, PLACES, CONCEPTS

1. The _________ is the effect exerted by a substituent on modifying electrostatic forces operating on a nearby reaction center. The main contributors to the _________ are the inductive effect, mesomeric effect and the through-space electronic field effect.

   An electron withdrawing group or EWG draws electrons away from a reaction center.

   a. Ring strain
   b. Taft equation
   c. Polar effect
   d. Quantum chemistry

2. . In organic chemistry, an _________ is a type of pericyclic rearrangement where the net result is one pi bond being converted into one sigma bond or vice-versa. These reactions are usually categorized by the following criteria:•Reactions can be either photochemical or thermal.•Reactions can be either ring-opening or ring-closing (electrocyclization).•Depending on the type of reaction (photochemical or thermal) and the number of pi electrons, the reaction can happen through either a conrotatory and disrotatory mechanism.•The type of rotation determines whether the cis or trans isomer of the product will be formed.Classical Examples

   The Nazarov cyclization reaction is a named _________ converting divinylketones to cyclopentenones.

A classic example is the thermal ring-opening reaction of 3,4-dimethylcyclobutene.

a. Ene reaction
b. Overman rearrangement
c. Electrocyclic reaction
d. Ethyl maltol

3. _________, a subdiscipline of chemistry, involves the study of the relative spatial arrangement of atoms within molecules. An important branch of _________ is the study of chiral molecules.

_________ is also known as 3D chemistry because the prefix 'stereo-' means 'three-dimensionality'.

a. Bailar twist
b. Capped square antiprismatic molecular geometry
c. Chiral auxiliary
d. Stereochemistry

4. A _________ in organic chemistry is a Pericyclic reaction wherein the net result is one σ-bond is changed to another σ-bond in an uncatalyzed intramolecular process. The name sigmatropic is the result of a compounding of the long-established sigma designation from single carbon-carbon bonds and the Greek word tropos, meaning turn. In this type of rearrangement reaction, a substituent moves from one part of a π-bonded system to another part in an intramolecular reaction with simultaneous rearrangement of the π system.

a. Smiles rearrangement
b. Stevens rearrangement
c. Stieglitz rearrangement
d. Sigmatropic reaction

5. An _________ is an organic reaction in which an enol or an enolate ion reacts with a carbonyl compound to form a β-hydroxyaldehyde or β-hydroxyketone, followed by a dehydration to give a conjugated enone.

_________s are important in organic synthesis, providing a good way to form carbon-carbon bonds. The Robinson annulation reaction sequence features an _________; the Wieland-Miescher ketone product is an important starting material for many organic syntheses.

a. Ullmann condensation
b. Ullmann reaction
c. Fluocortin
d. Aldol condensation

ANSWER KEY
Chapter 27. PERICYCLIC REACTIONS

---

1. c

2. c

3. d

4. d

5. d

Other Cram101 e-Books and Tests

CPSIA information can be obtained at www.ICGtesting.com
Printed in the USA
LVOW12s1957230814

400608LV00002BA/50/P

9 781478 418603